THE JEET KUNE DO ARCHIVES

EDITED & COMPILED
JOSE M. FRAGUAS

EMPIRE BOOK/AWP LLC
Los Angeles, CA.

DISCLAIMER

Please note that the author and publisher of this book are NOT RESPONSIBLE in any manner whatsoever for any injury that may result from practicing the techniques and/or following the instructions given within. Since the physical activities described herein may be too strenuous in nature for some readers to engage in safely, it is essential that a physician be consulted prior to training.

First Edition published in 2025 by AWP LLC/Empire Books. Copyright (c) 2025 by Jose M. Fraguas and AWP LLC/Empire Books.

All rights reserved. No part of this publication may be reproduced or utilized in any form or by any means, electronic or mechanical, including photocopying, recording, or by any information storage and retrieval system, without prior written permission from AWP LLC/Empire Books.

Revised edition Library of Congress Catalog Number:
ISBN-13: 978-1-949753-86-8
25 24 23 22 21 20 19 18 17
Library of Congress Cataloging-in-Publication Data
The Jeet Kune Do Archives by Jose M. Fraguas -- ed. p. cm.
ISBN 978-1-949753-86-8 (pbk. : alk. paper) 1. Martial arts--philosophy. 3. Large type books. I. Title. GV1734.3. F715
20467361.815'3--dc25
20986731981
Printed in the United States of America.

CONTENTS

Preface
- My Way to Jeet Kune Do 5

Introduction 13
1. Liberate Yourself From Classical Karate 17
2. The History of Jeet Kune Do (1 – 4) 27
3. Dan Lee: The JKD/Tai Chi Connection 79
4. Dan Lee: The JKD Philosophy 93
5. Reflections on Jeet Kune Do 105
6. Wing Chun: The Nucleus of JKD 109
7. A JKD Reunion: Jerry Poteet & Dan Lee 115
8. The Evolution of the JKD Training 125
9. Bruce Lee's Chinatown Workout 133
10. Jeet Kune Do: Powerful & Deceptive 139
11. Making Bruce Lee's Notes Working For You 149

Columns
- Dan Inosanto 159
- Tim Tackett 205
- Ted Wong 237
- Cass Magda 251
- Paul Vunak 271

MY WAY TO JEET KUNE DO

by Jose M. Fraguas

Training in the old Filipino Kali Academy during the early 1980s offered a transformative experience for any martial artists seeking to immerse themselves in the revolutionary approach of Jeet Kune Do (JKD). As Bruce Lee's closest disciple, Dan Inosanto was entrusted with preserving and evolving the art of JKD after Lee's untimely passing in 1973. Alongside Richard Bustillo, Inosanto established the Kali Academy which became a sanctuary for martial artists eager to explore Bruce Lee's dynamic philosophy and training methods.

I moved to Los Angeles in 1980, where I was accepted as a student of Jeet Kune Do instructor Dan Inosanto, at the Academy in Torrance, California. It was a time when there was no confusion about the art. The terms "original JKD" or "JKD concepts" had not been coined yet and the turmoil and politics the art has experienced - in the last decades - didn't exist. JKD was the art and the philosophy of Bruce Lee and the technical foundation was there to be learned. Any kind of training in another system was a supplementary training for personal growth or for developing specific attributes, and it was not JKD.

At the time, Jeet Kune Do was never merely a martial art but a philosophy that emphasized simplicity, directness, and personal expression. It rejected rigid forms and embraced adaptability, practicality, and efficiency in combat. Lee's mantra of "using no way as way" and "having no limitation as limitation" encouraged students to transcend traditional styles and focus on what worked for them. The Kali Academy embodied these ethos, integrating elements of Wing Chun, Western boxing, fencing, and various other martial arts into its training.
The inclusion of Filipino Martial Arts was a defining characteristic of the Academy's curriculum. Dan Inosanto, being of Filipino descent, was deeply committed to preserving and promoting his heritage. Kali, Eskrima, and Arnis—arts centered around weapon-based combat—complemented the JKD framework and conceptual approach. This combination allowed students to train in both armed and unarmed combat, fostering

versatility and situational awareness.

I never saw any contradiction in preserving the Lee material handed down to Dan Inosanto, Dan Lee, Ted Wong, Jerry Poteet, and the other first generation students and applying the JKD philosophy to "accommodate" and "assimilate" useful elements of other arts discovered through an intense and demanding personal learning process. I believe that once you start to transcend from the idea of "fighting" as your main focal point and reason for your martial arts training, your understanding of the art suddenly expands and reaches another level. You do your best to prepare yourself to fight and defend your life if you have to—but fighting is not really an issue anymore. You've already been through the process of "finding what is useful for combat" and developed that JKD "inquiring mind" and "functional eye." By having that knowledge you don't become "caught" in that constant necessity of proving to your ego that you can beat the hell out of somebody else—which in the long run is just a psychological prison which prevents you from discovering a higher existence as a human being.

"When the ego is dissolved there is no need to impress your fellowman," said the wise man. It's not necessarily a matter of dissolving the ego, because the ego cannot be dissolved; rather it is about dealing with it according to the internalization of your own inner peace. Nevertheless, the understanding of the JKD art grows in the same manner that you grow as a person—through the process of being open- minded and receptive to everything around you. I've been very fortunate to have a job related to martial arts that does not depend on teaching martial arts to make a living. I perceived that the art was not meant for mass distribution, but that it was dependent on its precepts being passed down in a very personal way.

Studying and training as much as I could, I concurrently analyzed the philosophies of Taoism, Zen and Jiddu Krishnamurti to better understand the philosophy, conceptual structure, and roots of the JKD art. "If you understand the roots—you'll know the blossoms," the founder said. I have to gratefully acknowledge how valuable other JKD instructors have been in helping me to better understand my way to Jeet Kune Do. I feel truly grateful to all who contributed to my understanding of the art developed by Bruce Lee, and pointed me in the right direction to find the "truth" [efficiency in combat] as it applied to me.

In a very special way I was fortunate to be a small part of the historical Kali Academy, where Bruce Lee's presence hung in the air like autumn morning mist. If you didn't actually feel his being, you could always look at any wall which were adorned with his original pictures, sayings, and teachings. When Dan Inosanto was teaching and the classes were underway, you got the strange feeling that Bruce Lee was looking over the proceedings. Only 18 years old, and feeling that I was living in a dream, I could barely talk to my JKD si-hings. Despite my awkwardness, they were kind enough to help me in every aspect that I needed, never refusing to correct a physical technique, clarify a philosophical principle, or grant an embarrassed request to borrow a sleeping bag.

The Academy fostered an atmosphere of innovation and openness, a stark contrast to the rigid hierarchy typical of traditional martial arts schools at the time. It was always emphasized the importance of personal growth over competition. Students were encouraged to experiment, adapt techniques to their unique attributes, and explore martial arts beyond what it was being taught there.

Training sessions were intense and multifaceted. A typical class involved rigorous physical conditioning, technical drills, sparring, and philosophical discussions. The chief instructors, Dan Inosanto and Richard Bustillo believed that martial arts training are as much about mental acuity and emotional resilience as they are about physical skill. They encouraged students to think critically about techniques, question their effectiveness, and refine their movements continuously.

The impact of the Filipino Kali Academy extended far beyond its walls. It played pivotal role in popularizing both Jeet Kune Do and Kali globally and also contributed to the broader acceptance of cross-training in martial arts. In an era when many schools adhered strictly to a single style, the Kali Academy demonstrated the value of integrating diverse techniques and philosophies in a cohesive way having the JKD philosophy as its base and blueprint. This approach laid the groundwork for the modern Mixed Martial Arts (MMA) movement, which emphasizes adaptability and the blending of styles for efficiency in combat.

I'm deeply grateful to all my seniors - who kindly and patiently shared the JKD oral traditions with me by allowing me to be a listener in their JKD inner-circle conversations. As much as anything, this helped me to develop myself both as a martial artist and a JKD practitioner.

I feel sad for the discrepancies that I have seen grow among the members of the JKD family throughout the years. I'm a firm believer that even "being a free and creative martial artist" does not excuse you from maintaining some important traditions in order to keep your own roots and essential values and ethics. The student's behavior will directly affect his instructor's reputation. The student's wrong acts and attitude "will heap fiery coals upon his sifu's head." Everyone should know what his position in the JKD family is and should act toward his elders, seniors, and instructors in a very respectful way. Unfortunately, this is not the case nowadays. Bruce Lee firmly required the traditional address of "sifu" from his students—demanding it from Inosanto to Taky Kimura, and then from the students at the Chinatown kwoon to Dan Inosanto. Bruce Lee's modern approach to the technical aspects was not in opposition to his appreciation and respect for martial arts' deep traditional values.

Many of Bruce Lee's tea-

截拳道

1980   23018 Normandie Ave. Torrance. California   2025

chings dealt with individual philosophical development. A philosophy which is to have any value should be built upon a wide and firm foundation of knowledge which is not specifically "philosophical." Lee's philosophy was a battleground on which he fought a battle against himself; sometimes going one way and sometimes another. He covered the whole martial arts field before reaching conclusions diametrically opposed to those which he had followed in the earlier years of his martial arts career. The key to understanding Bruce Lee's philosophy is that it was essentially a by-product of his personal quest for knowledge. To treat it as though it were an end in itself is liable to render it meaningless. A sculptor is symbolically described as a man 'who gets rid of unnecessary chips of marble'; it is the same process known to every writer who whittles away unnecessary words from his manuscript, and to every mathematician and scientist who uses Occam's Razor to search for the most elegant proofs and theorems. It is the same method that Bruce Lee used for "shedding away the unessential for the JKD techniques." Due to

the limitations of language and linguistic expression when dealing with philosophical and spiritual issues, it is easier to understand why Lee's writings were so complex, subtle and intricate—particularly if his ideas are studied and analyzed out of context. It's paramount to understand Bruce Lee's way of "doing" philosophy and what his roots were. It's easy to quote somebody else in order to justify our preferences and personal inclinations. However, there are obvious dangers in using words without being completely sure what we really mean by them. But there is another less obvious danger in trying to provide exact definitions—the danger is that we may think we have succeeded.

The art of Jeet Kune Do was never meant to be a "straight line" but an infinite loop – a circle with no beginning and no end. As a JKD practitioners, our past and our future in the arts are not separate entities; they are a reflection of the "now' (living moment) filtered through the limitations of our own level of understanding at the moment. When we realize this, we can empower ourselves to step out of any JKD preconceptions and live only in the "present now" of our personal martial arts journey by honestly expressing ourselves.

The great mathematician Lindemann showed that it is impossible to square the circle. Perhaps, and not only using an acu⟲ and original

INTRODUCTION

by Jose M. Fraguas

Jeet Kune Do, the art and philosophy developed by Bruce Lee, was a groundbreaking movement that not only changed the world of martial arts but also redefined how we approach personal development and self-expression in the fighting arts. Lee's philosophy was not confined by tradition or rigid structure; it was dynamic, fluid, and ever-evolving, much like the man himself. This compilation is a tribute to the lasting legacy of JKD, bringing together key writings that offer insight into its history, philosophy, and evolution.
In an era of ever-changing ideas, fleeting trends, and the constant flow of information, it's easy to overlook the enduring power of the written word. This collection brings together a series of articles about the art of Jeet Kune Do written over a span of time, each piece representing a unique snapshot of thought, philosophy, and conversation from a previous period. These articles, though born from specific moments in time, carry with them ideas and reflections that resonate with us today in surpri-

sing and often profound ways. The objective of this work is to preserve what it was said originally in the past and rescue what [probably] has been lost along the way.

The decision to compile these writings is rooted in the belief that certain themes and insights, in the world of martial arts and life in general, hold universal truths that transcend time. And they are worth preserving. While the world around us continues to evolve, many of the ideas and philosophies discussed within these pages remain remarkably relevant but, unfortunately, it seems that have been forgotten by the new generations.

Some of the ideas and words may appear nostalgic, capturing a world now gone, but they continue to speak to the pressing issues of the art of Jeet Kune Do today, offering timeless perspectives and the answers to many current questions. What you hold in your hands is not merely a collection of writings—it's a conversation across time, a valuable bridge that connects the past of JKD with its present.

As you read through these pages, I invite you to explore how each article has aged, which ideas still spark curiosity, and which may inspire new thoughts for the current and future generations. Whether you're rediscovering familiar arguments about the JKD art or encountering fresh perspectives, this compilation aims to encourage reflection and dialogue, both with the past and with the present world around us.

The first part of this book features articles written during the 1970s, 1980s, and 1990s—decades in which Jeet Kune Do began to solidify its place in martial arts history. These articles reflect the pioneering work of Bruce Lee, the development of his philosophy, and the early days of JKD's dissemination through the martial arts community. Many of these writings were among the first to explore Lee's innovative approach to combat, shedding light on his core principles of efficiency, directness, and adaptability. They stand as a historical record of a transformative period in martial arts, capturing the essence of a revolutionary idea that was just beginning to make its mark.

The second part of this book shifts focus to a selection of columns by some of the most influential figures in the history of the art of Jeet Kune

Do. These men - amongst others - became key figures in preserving and passing on his art. Their contributions to JKD, through their own experiences and teachings, have shaped the direction of the art and helped it grow into a global phenomenon. The columns featured here are a legacy of written knowledge that serves as a bridge between the past and future, ensuring that the principles and insights of Jeet Kune Do remain accessible to generations of martial artists to come.

Through these collected works, we not only preserve the teachings of Bruce Lee but also the wisdom of those who carried his vision forward. The writings in this book are not simply relics of a bygone era—they are living documents that continue to inspire and inform. They offer invaluable insights into the philosophy and practice of JKD, and stand as a testament to the ongoing evolution of Lee's art.

As you read, you'll discover that Jeet Kune Do is far more than a martial art; it is a philosophy of constant learning, personal growth, and adaptability for daily life as well. Whether you are a seasoned practitioner or new to the art, this book serves as a guide to understanding the rich history of JKD, the foundational ideas that make it unique, and the ongoing efforts of its devoted practitioners to carry the torch into the future.

Walk on!

LIBERATE YOURSELF FROM CLASSICAL KARATE

by Bruce Lee

In September 1971, Bruce Lee authored perhaps the most important and controversial article for Black Belt magazine. Titled "Liberate Yourself from Classical Karate", the article introduced Lee's personal martial art and philosophy of Jeet Kune Do as a method for gaining freedom from the dictates of classical training.

I am the first to admit that any attempt to crystalize Jeet Kune Do into a written article is no easy task. Perhaps to avoid making a 'thing' out of a 'process', I have not until now personally written an article on JKD. Indeed, it is difficult to explain what Jeet Kune Do is, although it may be easier to explain what it is not.

Let me begin with a Zen story. The story might be familiar to some, but I repeat it for its appropriateness. Look upon this story as a means of limbering up one's senses, one's attitude and one's mind to make them pliable and receptive. You need that to understand this article, otherwise you might as well forget reading any further.

A learned man once went to a Zen teacher to inquire about Zen. As the Zen teacher explained, the learned man would frequently interrupt him with remarks like, "Oh, yes, we have that too…." and so on. Finally the Zen teacher stopped talking and began to serve tea to the learned man. He poured the cup full, and then kept pouring until the cup overflowed.
"Enough!" the learned man once more interrupted. "No more can go into the cup!"
"Indeed, I see," answered the Zen teacher. "If you do not first empty the cup, how can you taste my cup of tea?"

I hope my comrades in the martial arts will read the following paragraphs with open-mindedness leaving all the burdens of preconceived opinions and conclusions behind. This act, by the way, has in itself liberating power. After all, the usefulness of the cup is in its emptiness.
Make this article relate to yourself, because though it is on JKD, it is primarily concerned with the blossoming of a martial artist—not a "Chinese" martial artist, a "Japanese" martial artist, etc. A martial artist is a human being first. Just as nationalities have nothing to do with one's humanity, so they have nothing to do with martial arts. Leave your protective shell of isolation and relate 'directly' to what is being said. Return to your senses by ceasing all the intervening intellectual mumbo jumbo. Remember that life is a constant process of relating. Remember too, that I seek neither your approval nor to influence you towards my way of thinking. I will be more than satisfied if, as a result of this article, you begin to investigate everything for yourself and cease to uncritically accept prescribed formulas that dictate "this is this" and "that is that".

ON CHOICELESS OBSERVATION

Suppose several persons who are trained in different styles of combative arts witness an all out street fight. I am sure that we would hear different versions from each of these stylists. This is quite understandable for one cannot see a fight (or anything else) "as is" as long as he is blinded by his chosen point of view, i.e. style, and he will view the fight through the lens of his particular conditioning. Fighting, "as is," is simple and total. It is not limited to your perspective conditioning as a Chinese martial artist. True observation begins when one sheds set patterns and true freedom of expression occurs when one is beyond systems.
Before we examine Jeet Kune Do, let's consider exactly what a "classical" martial art style really is. To begin with, we must recognize the incontrovertible fact that regardless of their many colorful origins (by a wise, mysterious monk, by a special messenger in a dream, in a holy revelation, etc.) styles are created by men. A style should never be considered gospel truth, the laws and principles of which can never be violated.

截拳道

Man, the living, creating individual, is always more important than any established style.

It is conceivable that a long time ago a certain martial artist discovered some partial truth. During his lifetime, the man resisted the temptation to organize this partial truth, although this is a common tendency in a man's search for security and certainty in life. After his death, his students took "his" hypotheses, "his" postulates, "his" method and turned them into law. Impressive creeds were then invented, solemn reinforcing ceremonies prescribed, rigid philosophy and patterns formulated, and so on, until finally an institution was erected. So, what originated as one man's intuition of some sort of personal fluidity has been transformed into solidified, fixed knowledge, complete with organized classified responses presented in a logical order. In so doing, the well-meaning, loyal followers have not only made this knowledge a holy shrine, but also a tomb in which they have buried the founder's wisdom.

But distortion does not necessarily end here. In reaction to "the other truth," another martial artist, or possible a dissatisfied disciple, organizes an opposite approach – such as the "soft" style versus the "hard" style,

the "internal" school versus the "external" school, and all these separate nonsenses. Soon this opposite faction also becomes a large organization, with its own laws and patterns. A rivalry begins, with each style claiming to possess the "truth" to the exclusions of all others.

At best, styles are merely parts dissected from a unitary whole. All styles require adjustment, partiality, denials, condemnation and a lot of self-justification. The solutions they purport to provide are the very cause of the problem, because they limit and interfere with our natural growth and obstruct the way to genuine understanding. Divisive by nature, styles keep men 'apart' from each other rather than 'unite' them.

TRUTH CANNOT BE STRUCTURED OR DEFINED

One cannot express himself fully when imprisoned by a confining style. Combat "as is" is total, and it includes all the "is" as well as "is not," without favorite lines or angles. Lacking boundaries, combat is always fresh, alive and constantly changing. Your particular style, your personal inclinations and your physical makeup are all 'parts' of combat, but they do not constitute the 'whole' of combat. Should your responses become dependent upon any single part, you will react in terms of what "should be" rather than to the reality of the ever-changing "what is." Remember that while the whole is evidenced in all its parts, an isolated part, efficient or not, does not constitute the whole.

Prolonged repetitious drillings will certainly yield mechanical precision and security of that kind comes from any routine. However, it is exactly this kind of "selective" security or "crutch" which limits or blocks the total growth of a martial artist. In fact, quite a few practitioners develop such a liking for and dependence on their "crutch" that they can no longer walk without it. Thus, anyone special technique, however cleverly designed is actually a hindrance.

Let it be understood once and for all that I have NOT invented a new style, composite, or modification. I have in no way set Jeet Kune Do

within a distinct form governed by laws that distinguish it from "this" style or "that" method. On the contrary, I hope to free my comrades from bondage to styles, patterns and doctrines.

What, then, is Jeet Kune Do? Literally, "jeet" means to intercept or to stop; "kune" is the fist; and "do" is the way, the ultimate reality—the way of the intercepting fist. Do remember, however, that "Jeet Kune Do" is merely a convenient name. I am not interested with the term itself; I am interested in its effect of liberation when JKD is used as a mirror for self-examination.

Unlike a "classical" martial art, there is no series of rules or classification of technique that constitutes a distinct "Jeet Kune Do" method of fighting. JKD is not a form of special conditioning with its own rigid philosophy. It looks at combat not from a single angle, but from all possible angles. While JKD utilizes all the ways and means to serve its end (after all, efficiency is anything that scores), it is bound by none and is therefore free. In other words, JKD possesses everything, but is in itself possessed by nothing.

Therefore, to try and define JKD in terms of a distinct style—be it gung--fu, karate, street fighting, Bruce Lee's martial art, etc.—is to completely miss its meaning. It's teaching simply cannot be confined with a system. Since JKD is at once "this" and "not this", it neither opposes nor adheres to any style. To understand this fully, one must transcend from the duality of "for" and "against" into one organic unity which is without distinctions. Understanding of JKD is direct intuition of this unity.

There are no prearranged sets or "kata" in the teaching of JKD, nor are they necessary. Consider the subtle difference between "having no form" and having "no form"; the first is ignorance, the second is transcendence. Through instinctive body feeling, each of us 'knows' our own most efficient and dynamic manner of achieving effective leverage, balance in motion, economical use of energy, etc. Patterns, techniques or forms touch only the fringe of genuine understanding. The core of understanding lies in the individual mind, and until that is touched, everything is uncertain and superficial. Truth cannot be perceived until we come to fully understand ourselves and our potentials. After all, 'knowledge in the martial arts ultimately means self-knowledge.'

At this point you may ask, "How do I gain this knowledge?" That you will have to find out all by yourself. You must accept the fact that there is in help but self-help. For the same reason I cannot tell you how to "gain" freedom, since freedom exists within you. I cannot tell you what 'not' to do, I cannot tell you what you 'should' do, since that would be confining you to a particular approach. Formulas can only inhibit freedom, externally dictated prescriptions only squelch creativity and assure mediocrity. Bear in mind that the freedom that accrues from self-knowledge cannot be acquired through strict adherence to a formula; we do not suddenly "become" free, we simply "are" free.

Learning is - definitely - not mere imitation, nor is it the ability to accumulate and regurgitate fixed knowledge. Learning is a constant process of discovery, a process without end. In JKD we begin not by accumulation but by discovering the cause of our ignorance, a discovery that involves a shedding process.

Unfortunately, most students in the martial arts are conformists. Instead of learning to depend on themselves for expression, they blindly follow their instructors, no longer feeling alone, and finding

security in mass imitation. The product of this imitation is a dependent mind. Independent inquiry, which is essential to genuine understanding, is sacrificed. Look around the martial arts and witness the assortment of routine performers, trick artists, desensitized robots, glorifiers of the past and so on—- all followers or exponents of organized despair.

How often are we told by different "sensei" or "masters" that the martial arts are life itself? But how many of them truly understand what they are saying? Life is a constant movement—rhythmic as well as random; life is a constant change and not stagnation. Instead of choicelessly flowing with this process of change, many of these "masters", past and present, have built an illusion of fixed forms, rigidly subscribing to traditional concepts and techniques of the art, solidifying the ever-flowing, dissecting the totality.

The most pitiful sight is to see sincere students earnestly repeating those imitative drills, listening to their own screams and spiritual yells. In most cases, the means these "sensei" offer their students are so elaborate that the student must give tremendous attention to them, until gradually he loses sight of the end. The students end up performing their methodical routines as a mere conditioned response, rather than 'responding to' "what is." They no longer "listen" to circumstances; they "recite" their circumstances. These poor souls have unwittingly become trapped in the miasma of classical martial arts training.

A teacher, a really good sensei, is never a 'giver' of "truth"; he is a guide, a 'pointer' to the truth that the student must discover for himself. A good teacher, therefore, studies each student individually and encourages the student to explore himself, both internally and externally, until, ultimately, the student is integrated with his being. For example, a skillful teacher might spur his student's growth by confronting him with certain frustrations. A good teacher is a catalyst. Besides possessing a deep understanding, he must also have a responsive mind with great flexibility and sensitivity.

A FINGER POINTING TO THE MOON

There is no standard in total combat, and expression must be free. This liberating truth is a reality only in so far as it is 'experienced and lived' by the individual himself; it is a truth that transcends styles or disciplines. Remember, too, that Jeet Kune Do is merely a term, a label to be used as a boat to get one across; once across, it is to be discarded and not carried on one's back.

These few paragraphs are, at best, a "finger pointing to the moon." Please do not take the finger to be the moon or fix your gaze so intently on the finger as to miss all the beautiful sights of heaven. After all, the usefulness of the finger is in pointing away from itself to the light which illumines finger and all. ☉

THE HISTORY OF JEET KUNE DO - PART I

by Alan Sutton

"Bruce Lee showed me life and truth," states Dan Inosanto, the genius' premier disciple and the man he personally groomed to help point the way for those seriously interested in pursuing his recently conceived method of self-discovery, Jeet Kune Do.

Unlike many who came into contact with the person, who, more than any single individual, is responsible for the current world wide martial arts renaissance, Inosanto was not afraid to subjugate his ego to that of his mentor, thus avoiding their mistake, which frequently led to enmity and misunderstanding, instead of enlightenment. In his own words, "When most people met Bruce they either liked him or disliked him.

Bruce was so honest that sometimes he affected your ego. And if you can't take the truth, if you can't swallow your pride and if you have an ego problem, then you can't learn. Now I hit it off good with Bruce because I wanted to learn what he had to teach and I was willing to sacrifice at any length to study under him."

Born in Stockton, California, Inosanto opened his own dojo, the Filipino Kali Academy, in Torrance (CA) just this past May. His primary concern is to promote his cultural arts Escrima, Arnis, Sikaran and Kali while allowing the facility to be the center of the area's JKD flowerization. In addition to his mundane vocation as a physical education instructor at nearby Malaga Cove School in Palos Verdes, he teaches his first love, martial arts, three days a week, aided by former Bruce Lee pupils Jerry Poteet, Richard Bustillo and Dan Lee.

Outside the Academy, Inosanto informs us, only two other individuals are duly authorized to teach the formula, not art, of Bruce Lee. The first is Bruce's longtime friend and associate Taky Kimura of Seattle, Washington. "He (Kimura) teaches at Bruce's old Jun Fan Institute. . . and we still consider him, here in Los Angeles, as our senior or head instructor," says Inosanto. Headquartered at a friend's Kung-Fu school in Charlotte, North Carolina, Larry Hartsell is recognized as a legitimate instructor of what Inosanto refers to as the "kickboxing phase" of Jeet Kune Do. "He (Hartsell) is authorized to teach that stage," Inosanto confides, "and I gave him the authorization." He adds, "As far as I know, these are the only (other) two schools in Jeet Kune Do."

Aside from his immediate family, Dan Inosanto was as close to Bruce Lee as anyone. They experienced an immediate rapport based on mutual respect for each other's extraordinary martial capabilities, soon becoming fast friends. So much so, that in 1967, Dan named his first child, a girl, Diana Lee, after his now famous companion. The pair traveled together, trained together, gave demonstrations together, taught together, experimented together, socialized together, and yes, even made movies together at the same time cultivating one of the most heartwarming relationships in the torrid annals of martial arts. Unable to suppress his emotions any longer, Inosanto wept intermittently throughout the agonizing drive home from Seattle following Bruce Lee's funeral at which he paid his final respects as pallbearer.

To paraphrase songwriter Paul Simon (Simon & Garfunkel): "One man's Truth is another man's Falsehood." Bruce Lee said pretty much the same thing, recalls Dan Inosanto, " 'Dan,' he used to say, 'my truth will not be your truth.'"

What does all this have to do with martial arts? A decade ago, almost to the very day, Inosanto posed a similar query to himself after an initial face-to-face encounter with the enigmatic Mr. Lee. "For the first six months I was with Bruce Lee I felt that he was too philosophical. When I first met him, I wondered, 'Has this guy gone off the deep end?'

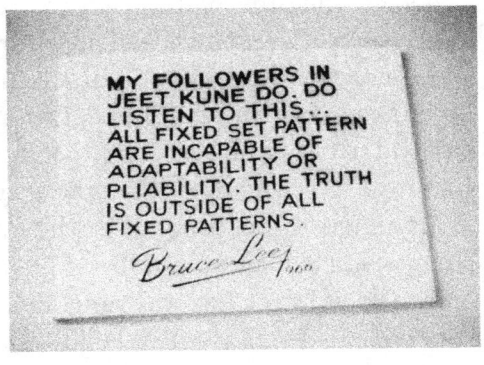

" It's easy to see why Inosanto suddenly found himself in such a quandary, to wit: "Let me read you something from *The Prophet* by Gibran it's on teaching." he said recently to an interviewer, adding, "Bruce gave me this book and he underlined it." Inosanto then launched into a recital of Lee's favorite passage. *"No man can reveal aught but that which already lies half asleep in the dawning of your knowledge. The teacher who walks in the shadow of the temple, among his followers, gives not of his wisdom but of his faith and his lovingness. If he is indeed wise he does not bid you enter the house of his wisdom, but rather leads you to the threshold of your own mind."* Skipping several lines from the original text, according to Lee's markings, Inosanto concluded his point, eloquently. *"For the vision*

of one man lends not its wings to another man." Indeed, not the sort of thing one would anticipate coming from the everyday martial artist. But then, Bruce Lee was not your average run-of-the-mill enthusiast nor, for that matter, is Dan Inosanto.

Before he ever heard of Bruce Lee, Dan Inosanto was already an accomplished martial artist in his own right, having sampled numerous arts, among them: Judo, Jiu-jitsu, Japanese Karate, Okinawan-te, Korean Karate, Escrima, Arnis, Kali and, of course, Kung-Fu. His exposure commenced at the age of ten, when a nominal Uncle Evangelista attempted to whet his appetite by introducing him to Okinawan Te and Jiu-jitsu during a memorable, but brief summer vacation. Uncle Evangelista had been a Commando in WWII, and, Inosanto appends, "Although I didn't know it at the time, he was also an Escrimador. He taught me informally at my house." Despite a gallant effort, Uncle was unable to sway Dan from such typical boyhood pursuits as football and track.

Looking back on his childhood, Inosanto reveals, "I was a loner. The average kid in Stockton is going to get into a little hassle now and then, but I kept my nose clean more than the average kid." This was in vivid contrast to his amigo-to-be, Bruce Lee, who once characterized his own youth in Hong Kong as that of a punk who went looking for trouble. Essentially opposites, if Bruce Lee was yang, then Dan Inosanto must be yin.

Football was Dan's sport in High School. He excelled tremendously and was the leading ground gainer in his junior and senior years. Later, at Whitworth College located in Spokane, Washington, he was a standout in track, winning his conference with a very respectful 9.5 sec. clocking in the 100 yard dash. . . . Not too shabby for a five-foot-five Filipino.

Nearly ten years after his maiden cruise in the infinite sea of martial artistry, 1957 to be precise, Inosanto embarked on a voyage that would last a lifetime ("I tried to quit for one month and it really drove me batty"). Judo, the most Circean art of all in America, that is finally caught his attention, this time for good. A life long sojourn in the martial arts began with judo lessons for two years.

"In the service I was really looking for Judo. I wanted a physical activity because I wasn't playing football and I wasn't running track anymore.

I really liked Judo; I thought it was a good conditioner." However, "They didn't have Judo: they had Karate."

The time was 1959, the place: Fort Campbell, Kentucky, home of the 101st Airborne Division. Harkening back to those beginning Karate classes under the direction of Henry Slomansky, Inosanto confesses, "I honesty didn't know what it was at first." But almost immediately, distant memories surfaced to the forefront of his mind's eye. "When I saw some of the kicking, I said, "Well I've seen that before from Uncle Vincent (Evangelista).""

Although Slomansky was primarily an exponent of Chito-ryu, Dan was bombarded by a potpourri of styles during his tour of duty since Fort Campbell was a stopping-off place for Navy and AirForce personnel as well. "It was kind of confusing, but I was exposed to Japanese and Korean and Okinawan influences." As far as Dan was concerned, this was a definite plus, establishing a pattern of

'cross-training' that has become his personal trademark.

While still in the paratroopers, Inosanto witnessed one style that he found particularly appealing. "At that time there was a guy from Hawaii, I can't remember his name. He was only a Brown Belt and he was knocking the hell out of second and third degree Black Belts. While he was sparring with all the different Black Belts, somebody said that he was from Hawaii and that it was Kenpo. I liked the way he moved around and I said, 'Gee, that's something I like because I'm small; that's the thing for me.'"

His hitch completed, Inosanto relocated in Southern California with the superb skills of the Kenpo stylist from Hawaii oven-fresh in his memory." When I came to Los Angeles I was looking all over and ended up at Ed Parker's because of the word Kenpo," he admits. As he casually strolled through Parker's doors back in 1961, martial arts still represented nothing more than an enjoyable pastime offering body conditioning and self-protection not yet elevated to the realm of 'truth'.

In the past twenty years Ed Parker has seen the best, trained with many of them, known of them all. . . Chow, Matsuoka, Ohshima, Ueshiba, Tohei, Choy, Oyama, Yamaguchi, Wong, the list could go on and on. The man universally acknowledged with having brought Karate out of the backrooms and cellars and into the public's eye, Ed Parker certainly knows a good martial artist when he seen one. Furthermore, Parker is not one who is prone to hyperbole. He had this to say regarding his former student and employee, Dan Inosanto: "Danny was very athletically inclined and a very good student. He was also very observant and absorbed as much as he could from anyone he came into contact with. 1 gave him little bits and pieces, then let him figure out the rest for himself.

Being an educated kid, everything soaked in. He was always seeking out other arts."

Parker himself, more often than not, has been maligned for his business practices, 'Too commercial' is the complaint most often voiced. Having studied or worked with Parker for a period exceeding seven years, Inosanto feels that such criticism is unjustified. "A lot of people may not like him because they say he's a businessman; but pound for pound, knowledge wise, I say he's one of the top, regardless of what people think of him. In fact, Ed is responsible for the movement in the United States more than any other man, next to Bruce Lee. And really, he was responsible for exposing Bruce Lee." Even more significant, Inosanto credits Parker with having pointed him in the direction of 'Truth', as we shall see shortly.

The moment Inosanto realized that his cultural and martial identities were starting to merge, he was well on his way down the long and winding road of truth. Discovering that his ancestors as well as the Chinese, Japanese, Koreans, Okinawans, etc. possessed a rich and colorful heritage all their own, removed the wool from over his 'third eye', thus providing the foundation that Bruce Lee would later expand upon. "I was beginning to see it (truth) with Ed," he explains, going on to say, "He asked me one day, 'Have you ever seen the art of Escrima?' And I said, 'stick fighting.' He said, 'No. There's more.' That's what kindled it."

Without further delay, the young twentieth century warrior sought vehemently for persons versed in the indigenous arts of the Philippines Escrima, Arnis and Kali, simultaneously maintaining his studies with Parker.

In his hometown of Stockton, Inosanto uncovered three Escrimamen: Max Sarmiento, Angel Cabales and John LaCoste. Through unremitting patience and diligent searching, he was able to train with a number of other experts who were little known outside the Filipino community, including Pasqual Ovalles, Pedro Apilado, Leo Giron, Braulio Pedroy and a gentleman by the name of Subingsubing.

"Kali," emphasizes Inosanto with a hint of pride in his voice, "is an ancient art of the Philippines. In my opinion, the leading exponent of Kali is in Hawaii. His name is Floro Villabrea. I studied under his foremost student, Ben Largusa.

"Now by their definition, Kali is the highest art of the Philippines, although in Escrima and Arnis there are phases of Kali. Most people mistake it for a stick art and they don't care to correct the public. But it's an empty-handed art, and also, in many ways, it might surpass Jeet Kune Do in the 'trapping hands' stage.

"The authority to teach," Inosanto continues, "is given by handing down a favorite weapon or pet movement there are no credentials. The 'empty hands' have to be some of the best I've ever seen.

"This art was in the Philippines before the coming of the Chinese during the Tang Dynasty. Magellan was killed with it. He was killed with a rattan stick, not a sword like the history books say."

"Before I met Bruce, I was seeking everywhere, striving to get this and that. Then when I met Bruce, my seeking stopped," says Inosanto, setting the scene for the classic confrontation which took place at the inaugural episode of Ed Parker's International Karate Championships in 1964.

"I was competing that year and I also had something to do with running the tournament. I was the elimination chairman; I kept up the charts, which they don't use anymore. I was helping Ed out and Bruce gave a demonstration (Parker had flown Lee down from Seattle where he was living at the time, expressly for the occasion), so I met him through that.

"He (Lee) gave a talk at the hotel room before all the Black Belts, and that night he had no place to go; so Taky and I tagged along and pretty soon we started running around together. Then I began to understand a little bit about what his theory (of martial arts) was.

"When I first met Bruce Lee, I couldn't sleep that night," Inosanto halts his narrative to say. The two had exchanged techniques, briefly, following the conclusion of the tournament and Inosanto was chagrined at the results. "I was really bothered because it was something that I'd never seen. It was like having learned an occupation for five years, and then having someone say, 'We no longer have any use for your occupation.' But in this case, I'd studied all these different arts I won't say that it was worthless but what he did was counter everything without really trying.

At that time I didn't understand about close range fighting. It was very frustrating.

"Then Bruce explained it by saying, "You only fight at a long distance and never get in close." After that, he told me that tournament fighting was mainly outside, not inside. When you get inside, he said, it's usually when the referee breaks it up.

"He was the big factor in me getting out of tournaments. At the time, I thought that the more tournaments I entered, the better 1 was going to get. Then Bruce said that tournaments were not the thing. Up until then I was going to enter every tournament in sight."

In addition to supreme technical mastery, Lee was also well-versed in the concepts behind the art. "The thing that impressed me most about Bruce was not his skill, but his knowledge," Inosanto declares. "Most people were impressed with his physical skill, but to me. . . it was his knowledge. The thing that was amazing about Bruce and we discussed it many times was that he could beat you with his brain.

"I've always maintained that he was the Leonardo DaVinci of the martial arts the Edison, the Einstein of the martial arts. I still feel that way, strongly, that he was ahead of his time. Someday, there might be a guy physically and speed-wise as good as Bruce Lee; but 1 don't feel that anyone will ever match the totality of the man, with his knowledge and his background."

The *Internationals* took place in July. and for the remainder of the summer, Inosanto and Lee were inseparable. "1 toured with him after the first Internationals (in order to promote a school that Bruce had opened in Oakland, California, with his good friend and namesake, James Lee). We traveled around and I was sort of like his dummy because Taky was in Seattle. We swung up through San Francisco, and then gave an exhibition in Los Angeles, where I dummied for him for four days. In the process, he taught me what at that time was his system (a devastatingly modified form of Wing chun. Jeet Kune Do had not yet been conceived).

"I didn't like the way he demonstrated," Inosanto admits. "Like when I trained with Ed Parker, we would do a little rehearsal so at least we would use techniques that we were familiar with. That gave you a sense

of security because you knew what was going to happen. But when I gave a demonstration with Bruce, he said, 'Just do what I tell you, and we'll make up the demonstration from there." He'd be talking, then all of a sudden he'd say, 'Move on me.' I'd say, 'With what?' And he'd say, "Just a punch or a kick. I'll take care of it; just punch or kick.' At first I didn't like it, then I got used to the way he did demonstrated. But at first, I didn't like it at all.
"Then he went back to Seattle and said he was coming back here (LA). He lived in Oakland for a while. . . then he went back to the Orient. We were corresponding at the time, and I kept hounding him to teach me. He said, 'If I decide to stay in the States, I will teach you. If I don't, go to James Lee." ◯

THE HISTORY OF JEET KUNE DO - PART II

by Alan Sutton

**628 College Street.
How an obscure hideaway on the outskirts of Los Angeles' Chinatown became the proving ground for Bruce Lee's martial-inspired philosophy.**

By 1966 Bruce Lee had officially opened his third and his last martial arts kwoon. He chose to set up shop on the bottom floor of an innocuous looking two-story edifice adjacent to Los Angeles' Old Chinatown. Like its predecessors in Seattle and Oakland, the indifferent, grey brick structure bore no identifying marks or sign whatsoever. To insure anonymity, he saw to it that the windows were painted over with red enamel. The casual passerby sauntering down College Street noticed nothing out of the ordinary about number 628. A majority of the traffic to and from consisted of befuddled baseball fans who had lost their way while headed for Dodger Stadium, a few blocks away. Absolutely no visitors were allowed inside the "Jun Fan Institute". He purposely limited enrollment to a select of martial arts "die hards" and a few high rollers he knew in the entertainment industry.

That was February. In May, satisfied that things were running smoothly, he transferred the teaching responsibilities over to Dan Inosanto the most unabashed "die hard" of them all.

"Most instructors don't have time for themselves that's why Bruce didn't want to teach in Chinatown." Inosanto explains, digging back more than eight years. "He started me off there, watching for the first three months, to be sure that I was headed in the right direction. But after three months, he would come in once a week or so and check it out. He said that he didn't want to teach because. 'I'd cheat my own body. I could be using this time to develop my own body.'"

No, Bruce Lee wasn't selfish just realistic. Although he was only 26, he had by then attained such an amazing level of proficiency that he was practically untouchable. There was simply no one around good enough to give him a meaningful workout. In lieu of a comparably matched opponent, he was forced to train alone against a veritable army of mechanical devices and traditional boxing apparatus which completely overran his uncar garage. He also kept abreast of all the up-to-the-minute breakthroughs in physical culture including isometrics, isotonics and nutritional hints. Aware that probably the best all-around collection of martial artists in the area could be found at the Jun Fan Institute, he dropped in regularly so as to maintain the keen edge of his already unrivaled skills. These visits also served a higher purpose: he was able to subject his most recent discoveries in the art of self-defense to the acid test free sparring.

At the time he opened in Los Angeles Lee was anticipating an acting career. The year before, he had returned to America following his father's funeral in Hong Kong. Accompanied by his wife Linda and their six-month old son, Brandon, he came back in order to follow-up on a part as Charlie Chan's famous sibling in an upcoming series to be called "Number One Son". Soon after his arrival he was informed that the series was definitely no go.

There was still another role in the offing: although, Inosanto interjects, "The Hornet series hadn't started yet. either, so he didn't have a job. Then he said, "Let's get a bunch of guys and workout." And I said, 'Can I get a bunch of my Kenpo buddies together?' That's how it started out. He was probably bored not doing anything. At first, it was mainly for fun.

"During that time we were training in Chinatown but not in a school right behind Wayne Chan's Pharmacy. It was a room that is now a movie theater. Then later on he decided that it would be kinda nice to bring in some money so we opened the school."

For a time, when work was scarce, the unemployed Thespian even considered a nationwide chain of Kung-Fu schools. "In March of '66 he was going to open up nationwide, starting with the Chinatown school in L.A. But he only had that thought for a month. He came back in April and said, 'Nope, that's not it. That's not the way to bring out the art.'" Inosanto remembers.

The scheme re-surfaced later again fleetingly as a means of exploiting his spiraling Kato fame. "More and more as the series progressed he was approached by people to open up a string of 'Kato's Gung-Fu Schools.' But he didn't do it. He said, I'm going to continue with this Kato thing, but I'm not going to open up nationwide." He told me, 'Don't do any advertising around the school.'" says Inosanto adding, "He didn't feel that he could truly represent the art that way."

Truthfully. Lee never intended to make a living by teaching Kung-Fu. His unwavering belief in the individual and that each deserved to be taught on a one-to-one basis would have meant that he was doomed to eternal poverty something he knew wasn't meant for him.

"Bruce hated big classes. It was a thing where he felt to maintain the quality it had to be one-on-one. And he was right. It's just like a boxing trainer: He can maybe train two or three at one time, but that's it. He has to know his fighter emotionally; he has to know his emotional hang-ups. 'Does he get scared before a fight? And if so, what can I do for him? How can I get him out of that state? Is he excitable? Is he calm? Is he lethargic?' In other words, you have to know the person inside and out," declares Inosanto, elaborating on why Lee ultimately rejected the "franchise concept."

Bruce Lee began studying Kung Fu as a teenager. At 22, he authored a most unique text on the subject which he titled CHINESE GUNG-FU: The Philosophical Art of Self-Defense reflecting his preoccupation with spiritual as well as physical development. And when the time came for him to pass his art along to others, he had no misgivings concerning his ability to do it better than anybody else. He was good and he knew it. Therefore, he gleefully thumbed his nose at tradition; cast the "book" out the window; and in the meantime he revolutionized the martial arts catapulting them into worldly prominence.

Understandably, the profile within the Chinatown school can best be described as "loose." Like most young people, Bruce Lee was fond of music; and he was not opposed to having the radio blaring or records spinning during class. The fact is, this super-real congregation of martial artists would warm-up (while also developing rhythm: a cornerstone in Lee's theory of martial arts) to the catchy theme from Hawaii Five-O. He was definitely an iconoclast. There almost seemed to be a Sawyeresque aura surrounding the kwoon. For instance, once class was underway all doors were securely locked ("He once told me, 'If knowledge is power, let's pass it on discriminately' "). After that, a tardy member who wished admittance had to give the "secret knock" before he could enter.

Nevertheless, the workouts themselves were far from fun and games. Revealing one of Lee's few compromises with the "classical way", Inosanto states, "I never called him Bruce. In and out of class, I would always refer to him as sifu." Jerry Poteet, who still bears his original Jun Fan Institute membership card number 102 and who currently teaches along with Inosanto at the Filipino Kali Academy, reveals why Lee put up with such "pagentry" as he called it. "He liked that because it showed that you meant business. He was the instructor, and you were going to go in there and get down to business. One time he got up in front of the class and said, "I know that socially a lot of us in here are friends; and outside the school,' he said, I'm Bruce. But in here you call me sifu. Because of the informality, there has to be some discipline. If this school was in China, there would be a few people in here now missing their front teeth.""

Yet, there was another side of Bruce Lee that most people never caught a glimpse of.

"I remember one episode in class where we had this kicking set not a kata, but a kicking exercise. We had a particularly clumsy guy doing it at the time; he looked really terrible and this guy was laughing. Bruce just looked over and said, "If you can do it better, come up here right now; or else, wipe that smile off your face and I want it silent from now on." That was pretty good because the guy was really clumsy, but he was trying the best he could; and the other guy was laughing. Bruce didn't like that. As talented as he was, he respected you for your ability. He hated what he called a B.S.'er; that he couldn't stand. But he always respected my students. He realized our capabilities and shortcoming," Inosanto praises. Poteet adds, "One time I was short of money and I felt badly because I could not pay. Then he wrote me a letter saying. "Come on in; forget all about it until you can.' He said, "You're sincere, that's what counts.""

As alluded to earlier, Bruce Lee's students fell into two distinct categories: those with martial arts experience and those without. Naturally, of the two, the former would profit more from his expert instruction. Inosanto, who witnessed Lee's methods more often than anyone, states that such was the case. "Some of the people from the film industry didn't last too long. You have to be dedicated or you can have the best teacher in the world and it doesn't make any difference. So those guys learned just enough self-defense to enjoy it. . . That's what I think." Poteet agrees. "I believe that the ones he taught at the highest level were the ones who had the background, who appreciated it because they had something to balance it against. There was sort of an in group, and he'd train us privately on Saturdays just this group at his house. The only stipulation was that you made classes during the week; and he'd charge you nothing for it."

"The emphasis," Inosanto goes on to say, "was on physical fitness. I think that's what weeded-out a lot of people. In other words, you had no business being in a martial art if you weren't physically fit. He used to say that if you didn't have the basic requirements like if you couldn't do at least 30 sit-ups and if you couldn't run a mile without stopping you had no business being in this class.

"Of course, he'd slack off in certain areas. For example, if you didn't have the flexibility, he'd say, "Okay. You work on it.' The thing that we liked about him was that everything was individual. Everyone had his own program. He took the time; for everyone. That's why he didn't like big classes."

Lee was a stickler for conditioning because of an unforgettable incident which occurred in Oakland, California a number of years earlier. There was a challenge, Lee accepted and the outcome, as it was originally reported, could be characterized as a "draw" at best. Although his mediocre showing was due in a large measure to his thick-headed adherence to his particular style at the time, Wing Chun, which was ill-suited to his opponent's Choy Li Fut techniques, Lee confessed to Inosanto afterwards: "I was tired, Dan. I was so tired I could not even punch him." Shortly thereafter, Lee scrapped the traditional Wing Chun style he had been addicted to in favor of his own pulverizingly modified system.

In attempting to get his point across, Lee was not above resorting to such Machiavellian ploys as "reverse" psychology.

"Our training was both physical and psychological. He taught us how to be mentally prepared for combat. That was his big thing the mental attitude. We formed a high opinion of ourselves; that's what he wanted. And then he would tear us down so we wouldn't get too cocky. It was a constant flow of yin and yang, " Inosanto muses.

"I'm very passive." he smiles, "at least I was until I ran into Bruce. I wasn't aggressive; I'd seldom speak up in a crowd. He changed my personality.

"To cite a case, we were practicing the side kick: He said, 'Dan, throw a side kick.' I threw a side kick and he said, 'No! No! You're just posing; throw me another, like you mean it.' So I kicked again this time he was holding a bag. He said, 'No, Dan, kick it hard. Think of something you hate.' I kicked it without thinking of something I hate. Then he nonchalantly walked over, and WHAP right across my face: he slapped me! For a second I forgot he was Bruce Lee and I came toward him. He laughed, 'Okay, now kick the bag; that's what I want.' And I kicked it; and he was right."

截拳道

Most classical Kung Fu systems insist that the beginning student spend anywhere from the first six-months to a year poised in the rudimentary stances or "horses." This is required in order to build strength, instill patience and check one's sincerity. Beyond this, their practical application is a topic of much debate.

Bruce Lee termed such ancient rituals "exercises in futility." He took nothing for granted. Whereas the majority of practitioners sheepishly imbibe their instructor's words as if they were ambrosia spilled from heaven; he scrutinized whatever he was asked to do and then announced, "How come?" Predictably, the reply was, "That's how it's been done for the past 1,000 years." Not good enough.

Still smarting from the drudgery which he himself endured for many years, Lee was determined to make things more utilitarian as well as stimulating for his followers. Showcasing his typically wry sense of humor, Lee once quipped, "If you were to teach basketball like they teach Gung-Fu, they wouldn't have a basketball in their hands for one year."

"You see," Inosanto begins, "people look at a man and say, 'Gee. .. look at his form; he's a good martial artist.' But Bruce didn't measure that way. The only thing that counted with Bruce was: Is it workable? Can it be used? Bruce was the kind of person who questions everything. That's why he grew because he questioned." Picking up the ball, Poteet concludes, "He admired that quality in other people. And when you started pushing him to answer, that's when he excelled. He loved it when you asked questions because it made him think; it made him do problem solving. That's why he called JKD problem solving."

Another basic tenet of Jeet Kune Do (although the name was not coined until 1967, "Intimations of JKD" were beginning to surface toward the end of the previous year) was self-knowledge, which Lee equated with creativity and ultimately, enlightenment. In short, he encouraged his students to question so that they would discover new ways of training, learning and, hopefully, living.

Interestingly, Lee arrived at the above axiom partly as a result of attending acting classes which came with the long awaited Kato role in the autumn of '66.

According to Inosanto, "He said, 'If you want to improve at this. Dan, you have to be creative. You have to constantly break tradition.' I think he got this from the Stanislavski Philosophy Method of Acting. "Look at this guy (Stanislavski)," Bruce said, "if he would have been a martial artist, he would have been fantastic. Here's a guy who says something that I believe in: that you constantly break tradition to improve it." In other words, it's a continual process of revision.

"He also gave me The Book of Changes, I-Ching. In the book, he underlined a whole chapter on creativity. It goes something like: If you don't get it from yourself, where can you get it?"

Lee never limited himself to martial arts handbooks, drawing from every available source at his disposal. Erudite, would be a fitting epithet, as anyone who has read his books (along with the already noted text, he co-authored a Wing Chun book with close friend, James Lee, in order to raise money for expensive cobalt treatments which the latter was undergoing at the time; and a five-volume masterpiece fully illustrated by his own hand the Tao of Jeet Kune Do, that to this day remains unpublished) or thought-provoking articles will attest.

"The school opened in '66 but the term Jeet Kune Do was not developed until '67," Inosanto continues. "By this. I mean the term Jeet Kune Do the principle behind it. I know it was 1967 when he came up with the term, but he was already JKD by the end of '66, November or December.

"All the students could tell that something was going on inside of him. He forsook his modified form of Wing Chun which we felt was really good. I still think that it was very good because it had a lot of truth in it. But you could see that he was progressing.

"He went on this thing with the body. "Don't look for secret moves,' he used to tell me. 'Don't look for secret movements. If you're always hunting for secret techniques, you're going to miss it. He said, "It's you, Dan; it's your body that's the key.'

"A lot of people think that JKD is something metaphysical; but it's not. It's really quite simple. Basically, I think this is what it is: JKD is Bruce Lee's philosophy, based on things be observed to be true."

Today, 628 College Street houses a sewing factory. The windows are no longer obliterated by red paint; and the interior is clearly visible with nary a trace remaining of its former tenants. Gone is the imitation tombstone that once greeted students with the famous inscription:

"In memory of a once fluid man, crammed and distorted by the classical mess." ☯

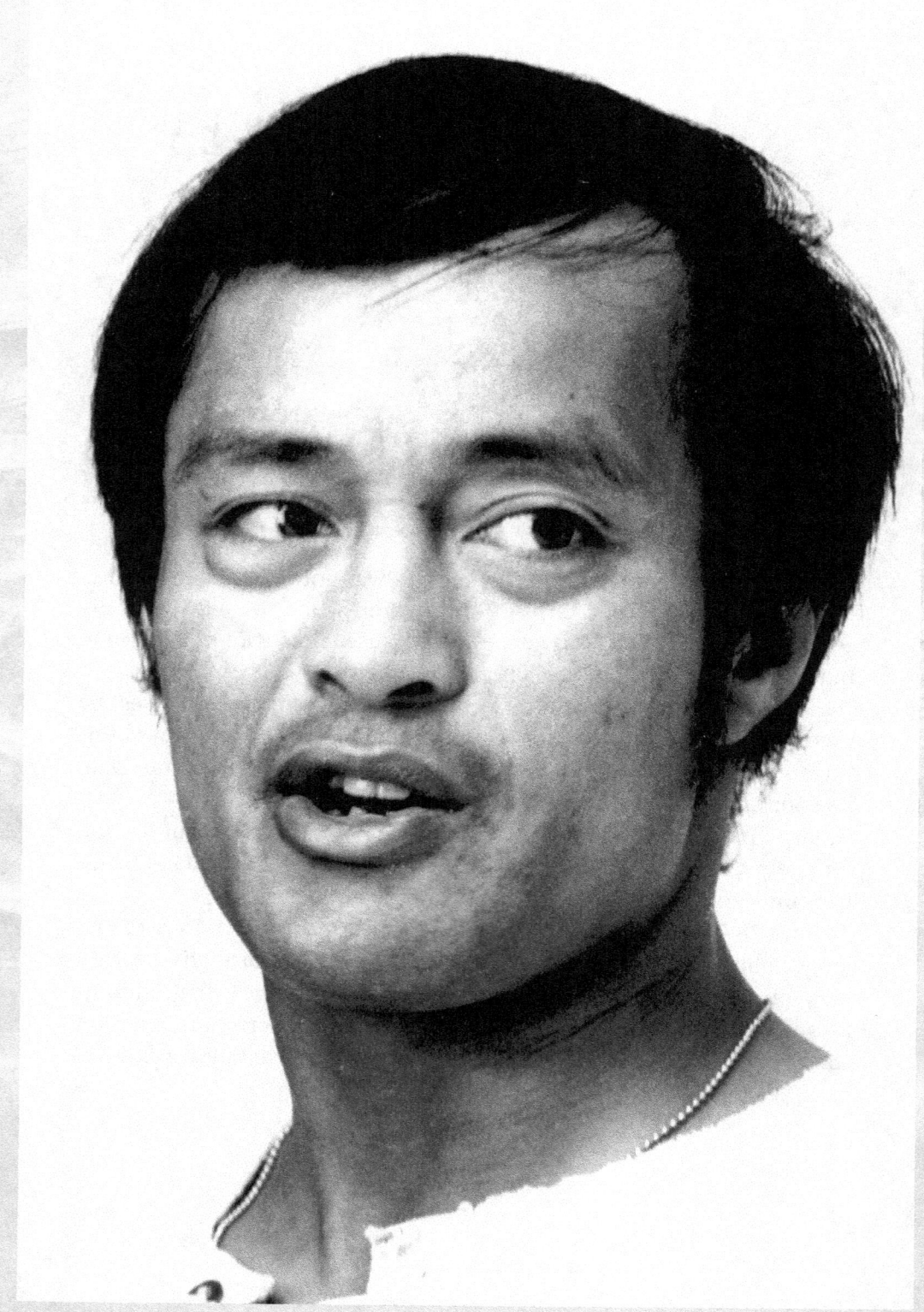

THE HISTORY OF JEET KUNE DO - PART III

by Alan Sutton

**THE TRUTH IN COMBAT IS DIFFERENT FOR
EACH INDIVIDUAL IN THIS STYLE
1. RESEARCH YOUR OWN EXPERIENCE
2. ABSORB WHAT IS USEFUL
3. REJECT WHAT IS USELESS
4. ADD WHAT IS SPECIFICALLY YOUR OWN**

AFFICIONADOS will no doubt remember a brief, lighthearted scene from "The Way of the Dragon" (shown in the U.S. as "Return of the Dragon") in which one of Tang Lung's (Lee) foils attempts to unnerve one of the heavies with an elaborate rigamarole somewhat akin to a kata. Unimpressed, the heavily-mustached bully lets this would-be terror have it right on the kisser. So much for the power of intimidation. Besides the obvious comic relief, this footage is significant for two reasons. One, in it Lee (who in addition to starring in, scripted, directed and co-produced the film) cleverly depicts a basic premise of Jeet Kune Do: simplicity, as opposed to extraneous therefore useless motion. Secondly as a footnote its relatively mild didacticism explains in part the motivation behind his pursuing a motion picture career with such preternatural obstinance as was characteristically Bruce Lee.

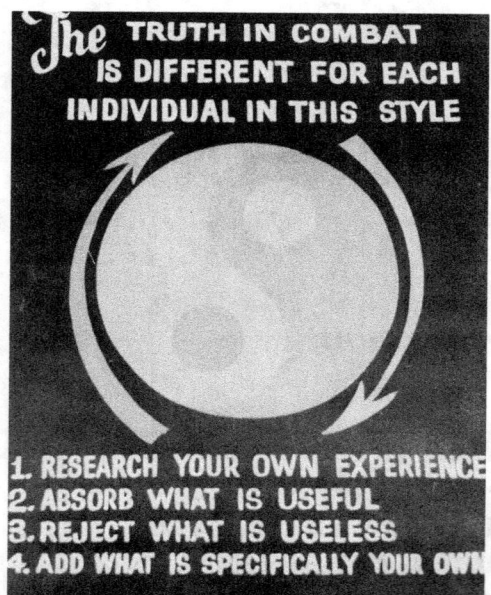

Dan Inosanto received an all-expense paid trip to Hong Kong in 1972. At Lee's insistence, he was making his personal film debut as an enemy Escrima wizard in an upcoming feature prophetically titled "The Game of Death". Today, he discloses just exactly what Lee hoped to get across to his audience. "In Hong Kong, this is what he told me .... for what it's worth: He said that through the movies he could give the public what he wanted. He could express what he felt was martial arts, which he felt was part of life. He said, "Through the movies, I can do this. If I open a school I cannot." And each of the pictures was supposed to bring out a lesson.

"For instance I don't even remember which picture ("The Chinese Connection") but you see a guy grab him. Most styles would have taken three moves to get free. So in the movie, when the guy grabs him, Bruce just punches back and answers with simplicity. He also shows where the Judo grab is limited."

Thanks to the space age magic of motion pictures, Lee was able to have his cake and eat it too. "Jesus, where else can you get a job doing side-kicks, hook-kicks and spin-kicks," he once joked to Inosanto. Levity notwithstanding, his often misunderstood film career could not have broken at a more opportune moment.

The Green Hornet series was short-lived, surviving only a single season. With it went the much coveted and oft discussed Kato role, Lee's first real break. The interim had produced only a trickle of walk-ons and several well done yet undistinguishing technical advisory assignments. Parts calling for Orientals were few and far between; and the only thing that seemed to be on the upswing was the size of his family. It was now 1969, and the Lee's had a second child, a girl, which they named Shannon. To make ends meet, he could have gone on teaching Kung Fu or went looking for a regular nine-to-five; but his artistic sensibilities pre-empted either of these alternatives. Then just in the nick of time, like a G-rated movie, word came that re-runs of The Green Hornet had martial arts fans by the millions in Hong Kong clamoring for more especially when they found that Kato was a homegrown product.

Knowing that Hong Kong production methods were primitive to say the least, Lee frantically began devouring every piece of literature he could get his hands on dealing with film making. This was his once-in-a-lifetime opportunity, and he wasn't going to leave anything to chance. He boned up on direction, lighting, camera techniques, editing and production just in case before leaving California in search of greener pastures. The ever-increasing demands all this put on the quantity most dear to him: time, coupled with insurmountable overcrowding problems, forced him to disband the now famous Chinatown school at the end of the year. (Following the close of the 628 College Street location, at Lee's suggestion Inosanto gathered up fifteen of his most dedicated pupils and started holding regular workouts at his home first in the garage, then in a homemade gym in the backyard until moving to his present headquarters in March, 1974.)

The beginning of the seventies saw Lee spending more and more time commuting between Hollywood and its counterpart to the East, Hong Kong. Offers began pouring in from numerous sources, and he was continually in transit firming up commitments and scouting locations for future projects. By this time he only accepted private students, at his convenience. Always in demand, his fees skyrocketed accordingly, finally peaking at such never-before-heard of rates as $275 an hour; or, if traveling was required: $1,000 per week plus expenses. Nonetheless, he had a waiting list. Before embarking for good on his glamorous new profession abroad, he left to his head instructor and trusted confidant, Dan Inosanto, a "flexible" game plan for the perpetuation of Jeet Kune Do. "I had a lesson plan which he said was not to be rigid. He wanted me to incorporate my own innovations. Like he set up certain principles on speed, balance, weight distribution, etc. that are true regardless of the method or style but I had my choice as to what to cover each night," Inosanto recalls. Although he was unaware at the time, the future of Jeet Kune Do had just been placed squarely in his hands.

Action (not violence) was the name of the game in Lee's films, and the same held true for his art, Jeet Kune Do (hereafter referred to as JKD): The Way of the Intercepting Fist. Fast, powerful and above all deceptive, JKD is the only non-classical form of Kung Fu presently in existence. Non-classical, that is, only in terms of training: for Lee faithfully adhered to the timeless concepts embodied in Taoism, Zen, the I-Ching and Yin

and Yang which form the basic foundation of Chinese Boxing meanwhile chipping away at non-essentials and applying his own revolutionary theories on teaching and learning.

Like most creative geniuses, Lee was only concerned with "What Is", not what could or should be. JKD is. Period. Spontaneous and explosively unpredictable, like a contemporary jazz solo, this direct fighting art was designed to prepare the student for the uncertainties he was sure to encounter in actual combat. The analogy to the so-called "new jazz" or "free form jazz" obtains on yet another level. Proponents of this new and tradition shattering wave of musical expression: Ornette Coleman, John Coltrane and Pharoah Sanders, among others, were initially criticized for their apparent disregard for lyricism and structure. Later. when opponents finally caught on, their accolades flowed like cheap whiskey during Prohibition. Likewise. Lee was condemned as being merely a "streetfighter" and "brawler." Nonplused, he painstakingly outlined the difference between having no form and having the "no form." The former denotes incompetence; the latter, transcendence, he replied to his detractors. He also liked to stress that JKD was really intended as a means of "self-discovery" or "enlightenment." In the liner notes to his album Tauhid, Sanders describes the process of self-realization: "I don't see the horn anymore," [he says.] "I'm trying to see myself. .. all of what I try to do in music, comes back to my conviction that if you have the discipline, you can do whatever you want to. You yourself are the key to the universe." An ardent and vocal admirer of musicians, Lee would certainly concur.

The most visible distinctions between JKD and all other existing modes of self-defense are the stance, the emphasis on "broken" rhythm and the absence of classic blocking techniques. Lee preferred a southpaw stance with right hand lead because he believed in putting the best foot forward. The left heel is raised slightly to enhance mobility a must when one is confronted with a more powerful adversary. He paid particular attention to footwork bobbing and weaving, feinting so as to present an undetectable rhythm that would confuse the opponent, allowing a JKD practitioner to slip-in-between his cadence and deliver a telling blow.

Traditional blocking tactics were discarded since he considered them the least efficient means of counter. JKD was meant to be organic, alive, not passive; each move of itself and offensively inclined.

As a more dynamic substitute for blocking, Lee perfected what is now referred to as the "trapping hands" stage. Trapping becomes more effective than blocking because there is less wastage of motion, and the opponent's hand is fully immobilized instead of deflected. Also, it affords the JKD man the luxury of "isolating the linebacker," so to speak, creating a favorable one-on-one situation. Its lineage is traceable to his original style, Wing Chun, whose practitioners sustain the theory that attack is the best form of defense. They reject the conventional one-two sequence of block then counter-attack in favor of simultaneous blocking and punching, Pak Sau.

Chi Sau or "sticky hands" practice is a form of sparring not unique to Wing Chun, where two opponents face off forearms barely touching and try to uproot the other while maintaining their own sense of balance. This exercise, in which Lee was a master, is performed over and over in order to perfect hand techniques already learned, toughen the forearms and hands and develop sensitivity so that the practitioner reacts to an attacker's advance automatically, without thinking.

Incorporating Chi Sau and Pak Sau with Bong Sau (deflecting) and Lap Sau (warding-off, almost grabbing) tempered, of course, by his extensive knowledge of body mechanics and motion Lee came up with "trapping hands." Says Inosanto, "The trapping is definitely Wing Chun; but it's modified. ("Absorb what is useful; reject what is useless; add what is specifically your own", was Lee's motto.) He said, 'I don't care where it comes from. If it is useable, it belongs to no one; it's yours." That was Bruce. He'd see something, then take it one step further."

"At a certain range, at a certain time, one type of combat becomes superior," observes Inosanto.

It was Lee's habit to forever expound the advantages and disadvantages of the various combat styles none were overlooked. He counseled his disciples not to think in terms of East vs. West, Chinese vs. Japanese, Okinawan vs. Korean, Karate vs. Judo, etc., for the purpose of determining which is better; but, rather, to examine each method individually, find its pluses and minuses, then inquire of themselves: "When will this work for me?" In other words, "If I have a grenade and a knife, and you ask which is superior, I'd reply: 'It depends.' Suppose the guy is 50 yards away: I'll heave the grenade. But if we're in a phone booth, I'd be better off with a shorter weapon," Inosanto illumes.

Another, perhaps more startling, consequence of Lee's life-long research into all forms of combat from fisticuffs to Fencing was the discovery that despite the myriad styles there existed but a finite number of ways in which to initiate an attack. Five to be exact all others being variations. He catalogued them as follows: ABC, attack by combination; ABD, attack by drawing; HIA, hand immobilization attack (or foot immobilization attack, FIA); PIA, progressive indirect attack: and SDA, single direct attack (or single angular attack, SAA).

The majority of self-defense systems boast one, maybe two, and rare in instances: three variations of attack. Two of the most versatile (surprise!) are Western inventions: boxing and Fencing (from which Lee drew quite extensively in terms of rhythm and direction), Bruce included all five bearing his personal stamp in JKD.

It's a tribute to his synoptic genius that Lee was so unerringly precise in mapping out the true nature of combat. Granted, anyone who devotes an entire lifetime to meticulously dissecting each and every fighting

art known to man, might conceivably unravel such subtle nuances as progressive indirect attack. But there is more to it than that. By far, his greatest oblation to those who looked to him for guidance was that he disclosed his revelations withholding nothing to them through intimate personal experiences, with poetic grace and intensity that inspired their own creative talents. For example, the following excerpt from a letter to Inosanto back in the early sixties:

"I hope that my thinking on the art will help you in your training, or in choosing what is beneficial and what is futile. Then use your common sense to see what is the real thing and what is merely lessons in routine dancing. To me, Gung Fu is so extraordinary because it is nothing at all special. Gung Fu is simply the direct expression of one's feelings with the minimum lines and energy; every movement being so of itself, without the artificialities of which 99% of all Masters tend to complicate. Always remember that closer to the true way of Gung Fu, the less wastage of expression there is. The art is the expression of the self. The more complicated and restrictive the method is, the less the opportunity for the expression of one's original sense of freedom. .. After all, how many ways are there to come in on an opponent without deviating from the natural course?"

As usual, he confirms that simplicity is the key; complexity, the lock, to self discovery. Even something as obviously sophisticated as PIA, then, just boils down to this: distance (progressive) and timing (indirect).

Divulging these five modes of attack is one thing, but what about their application? Like when somebody attacks a JKD man does he immediately retaliate with an ABC? Or should he, in fact, rely on SAA? Or maybe PIA? Or FIA ?. .. Or STP, CIA, BBC?

None of the above.

Because in the real world one never gets to choose the time and place, Lee felt that there should be no concrete rules as to what, when or how. Stuff like: "I'm gonna hit that fatal spot two inches below his left armpit!" just doesn't work. Everybody knows that. So the smart thing to do, he said to his followers, is to let your opponent decide for you which technique to apply. A JKD man reacts instantly doing what the situation dictates, fitting in with not resisting his opponent's energy. There may be certain "keys" he can recognize, but ultimately, when assaulted, his answer is: Your technique is my technique.

"It is true that the mental aspect of Gung Fu is the desired end; however, in order to achieve this stage, technical skill has to come first." This quote, taken from the introduction to his first book: *Chinese Gung Fu The Philosophical Art of Self-Defense*, pretty much sums up Lee's ideas on learning. He believed that it was essentially a three-step process by which one passes from the purely mechanical or how-to-do stage, through the technical or when and where stage finally arriving at the emotional or performing level. Furthermore, he took exception with those who tried to "teach swimming on dry land" to revive one of his favorite analogies. He insisted that without delay, from the earliest beginnings, students should be taught to spar effectively, thus increasing their chances for survival on the street.

Before he can even touch his opponent, the JKD man knows that he must first overcome a more immediate foe: the distance between them. This procedure of traversing "no man's land," of transition and moving in for the kill, is known as "bridging the gap" in JKD terminology. Within a fraction of a second, the practitioner intuitively sizes-up his opponent -thereby establishing his "flight tendency" (a hypothetical aura defining the parameter of any technique he can muster) and adjusts his rhythm (coordination of feet and hands) accordingly prior to penetrating his defenses by catching him at his "unprepared state of mind" (the exact instant he is withdrawing a strike or block or thinking about delivering same). Throughout this critical period there is no time for wasted movements. One slip, and the advantage is lost: his opponent is upon him, and strength inevitably becomes the deciding factor.

It follows, logically, that a portion of the JKD practice schedule is devoted to "awareness" training. Forever creative, Lee got a kick out of devising various exercises more accurately, games that would cultivate the lightening-quick reflexes necessary for performing the no nonsense JKD techniques. One such drill closely resembles the familiar shot of a hitter glancing down at his third base coach just before stepping up to the plate. Two students face each other, about five yards apart. The object is for one to give the sign a twitch, scratch. blink, squirm, any movement, no matter how miniscule and the other to acknowledge it by clapping. This seemingly childish game in reality develops concentration and heightens one's speed of recognition. There are many similar drills that are amusing as well as instructive, to be found in the JKD program.

During the actual hand-to-hand encounter, one is seldom fortunate enough to be presented with a primary target right-off-the-bat. "Sometimes you have to attack a minor target," Inosanto relates, "in order to get to a major one. You have to inflict pain upon a minor target to reach a major." Invariably, the JKD student learns that a well-executed kick to the shins can be the password for a knockout punch.

Which brings up the question of the relative importance of kicking and punching.

截拳道

Some styles - notably Korean - rely on kicking to a great extent, perhaps 60-70% of the time. On the other hand. a die-hard Shotokan Karate man would rather punch-it-out. In Lee's opinion, Inosanto reveals, many instructors require their students to spend an inordinate number of hours practicing overly-stylized kicking techniques. He took a dim view of the raise-cock-deliver with-the-toes-pointing "this-way-or-that-way" school of thought. He also claimed them for not practicing against objects bags, focusing mitts, trees especially instead of thin air. "The only criteria, he said, is that they be delivered from a single position. He never felt that the foot had to be horizontal like a lot of schools say. To kick, you have to have strength. Strength comes from running. The second thing you need is flexibility. That comes from stretching. Other than that, he said, 'If you want to kick - kick!'"

From a combative standpoint, Inosanto summarizes the JKD philosophy. "It works out that the hands are probably superior. The feet are used mainly as a bothering technique, to close the gap. Again, it will vary with the individual, depending on his speed and flexibility. But on the whole, I think that most JKD men are hand men. If I had to put a percentage on it, I'd say as much as 70% hands, 30% feet. . . maybe even more. "I won't make any hard and fast statements, but, I feel that kicking is overplayed," he says. Then catching himself, "But the object is to be balanced. I believe that against an untrained man, it's better to kick because he's not used to it. Against a trained man, against a martial artist, I feel it's better to use hands." Your technique is my technique.

For Bruce Lee, acting and martial arts were one in the same. He never separated his way of life from his vocation. They were two sides of the same coin: Yin and Yang, work and play, feeding his family and nurturing his soul. The similarity arises in that a martial artist, like an actor, has to discard his own personality, likes and dislikes, prejudices and so on in order to concentrate on the task at hand. Whether it be creating a character or defeating an opponent, the mind must be cleared of all preconceived notions as to what should or should not be included. Ever wonder why in his films, Lee is always pictured as a humble, non-obtrusive individual; and then when the fighting begins, he resembles a screaming, ranting lunatic? ""Dan,' he used to say, you've got to become another person, A fighter must be a madman, crazy.' " Every picture tells a story. ☯

THE HISTORY OF JEET KUNE DO - PART IV

by Alan Sutton

Bruce Lee was undergoing a spectacular metamorphosis - physical, psychological and, naturally, financial during the last years of his life. In a little more than a decade, fate had transformed the cocky 18-year-old Chinese American, who grew up in Hong Kong, into an international superstar.

As the Seventies came into full swing he was one of the most widely accepted and worshipped matinee idols in the world. After the unqualified success of his first two films, "Fists of Fury" and "Chinese Connection", he formed his own production company with ex-boss, Raymond Chow. Besieged with offers from all sides, his salary per picture had soared from $10,000 to nearly $500,000. So genuine and all-pervasive was his appeal, that the omniscient "Playboy" magazine saw fit to include him in their year end cinema review, posthumously, in December of 1973. They called him a "major star," "indisputably male," and labeled his Kung Fu epics "successors to the spaghetti Westerns made famous by Clint Eastwood." Be that as it may, Lee was certainly beginning to feel the full effects of instant stardom when he moved his family to Hong Kong the previous year. Aside from the easily foreseeable invasion of privacy (whi-

ch, incidentally, he had learned to live with ever since "The Green Hornet" days), something else was gnawing at his insides; and it kept him from enjoying the fruits of his labor as much as he might have. According to informed sources, Bruce decried the fact that he didn't know who his friends were in Hong Kong because everyone wanted a favor. He said things were different there. He had nobody he could trust with the exception of his wife Linda and it made him very sad.

It seemed that

everywhere he turned somebody was asking for a handout, and being the epitome of self-sufficiency, he found such overtures eminently distasteful. It was a sore spot, and not only with Lee. Close friends, too, were distressed because they vividly recalled the "hard times" that characterized much of his married life - for years barely seeking out a living while his family and frustrations continued to multiply. Eventually, he came to accept it, along with the more desirable trappings of success. And insiders agree that he "mellowed" considerably in his thirties.

Physically, Lee would reach one incredible plateau after another, and it was hard to believe for those near him who could see the transition. "The Bruce Lee of '68 was far superior to the Bruce Lee of '67, and so on," notes his protege, Dan Inosanto. "If you would have asked me in '69 if he could have improved, I would have probably said 'No.' But he just kept getting better, faster and stronger. Then when I saw him in Hong Kong in '72, he had reached a stage where it was almost unbelievable." Dan Lee, another one of Bruce's senior students, says that this steady development and improvement was an inspiration to his followers. "Through all these years Bruce was a walking example of the value of basic exercise and fitness. This was the most important thing, because we could see him improving and maturing toward ultimate reality."

Lee's training methods were also in a constant state of flux. According to Inosanto and others, he felt that frequent revisions were a must if one was to keep up with the break-neck pace of an overly mechanized society. Some things stayed the same, yet there was continual modification.

Nowhere was the element of revision more apparent than in his art, Jeet Kune Do. Lee accepted - actually believed in the inevitability of change, and the evolution of JKD reflects this belief. Beginning in 1966 (although the seeds of change had been planted years before) he started adjusting the stances, footwork and angles of his original style, Wing Chun, realizing that it was too square - too "rigid," as he said - although he felt that Wing Chun was very good. The resultant art was called "Jun Fan Gung Fu" (a variation of Lee's Chinese name). The process seems to have run in two-year cycles, for 1968 marked the next improvement when, after much addition and subtraction to his modified Wing Chun system, he came up with Jeet Kune Do the first non-classical form of Kung Fu. Then in 1970, while sidelined and semi-invalid as a result of a self-inflicted back injury, he began to intellectualize out of necessity. And when he emerged, as Inosanto puts it. "He beats you with his brain. He doesn't even block anymore, which is remarkable; he controls your distance. You throw a kick, and there's nothing there."

The development of Jeet Kune Do didn't cease once Lee became a star. While he was living in the Orient, he showed one of the servants, a cook, how to kick, punch, hold the bag, etc., in order to have someone to train with. He still did his roadwork religiously and he would invariably get a strenuous workout on the set, as the inexperience and ineptitude of the Mandarin camera crews often necessitated take after take after take. In addition, having to choreograph the numerous fight scenes stimulated his creative juices, and the inspiration would naturally carry over into things that never found their way onto the silver screen. And then there were the times, when exploring for dramatic effect, he would re-evaluate a certain move or weapon long ago discarded as "ineffectual" and uncover something that could be used in the real world. "As early as '64 at the first Internationals, I introduced Bruce to Escrima. At that time he took a pretty dim view of it. Then when I was in Hong Kong, he told me what he liked and what he didn't like about Escrima. I think the emphasis on the empty hands and seeing in the movies that it had a lot of functional value, changed his mind. That's probably why he took more of a liking to it later on." Inosanto speculates.

As was his custom, Bruce then attempted to enhance the potential of something he considered useful. "What really flabbergasted me," Inosanto recalls, "was when he grabbed the sticks and said, "Okay, now I'll show you what I would do.' And I looked at it, and with no previous background or training, everything he did was what they call "Largo Mano". It's a system in itself. With no previous training whatsoever, he had adlibbed a style of Escrima that already existed! I said, 'Hey, that's Largo Mano." He said, "I don't know what you call it, but this is my method."

Although he would be the last to admit it, Lee also practiced meditation. Being a hipster, such "occult" practices just didn't fit his image, so he always poo-pooed concepts like "internal power," meditation and Chi, In the privacy of his own home, however, it was a different story. About three-quarters of the way down his daily list of Things You Must Do, he had scribbled in the words: Mental and Meditation Training.

Finally, on his frequent trips to the States, Lee never missed an opportunity to combine business with pleasure. In between meetings, conferences and promotional engagements, he without fail made time for Inosanto and one or two other "select" disciples. On such occasions he would usually begin by having them feel his "gut" or some other prominent feature of his extraordinary anatomy, making sure that they took note of his most recent development. Then he would check their progress, commending them on improvements and suggesting areas which still needed work. The sessions would conclude with a few invaluable rounds of free-sparring with the Master.

It was during one such visit that Inosanto saw his mentor, alive, for the last time. Following a near-fatal collapse - due to exhaustion and ove-

rwork - while in the midst of the final sound dub for "Enter the Dragon", Lee journeyed Stateside for a check-up by a team of American physicians in the early part of 1973. The incident had received much ballyhoo from the "yellow" Hong Kong press, and Lee's spirits were at their lowest ebb in years. But after a comprehensive battery of tests failed to pinpoint any specific ailment, he once again regained his composure. "The last time I saw him," Inosanto relates, "was two months before his death. We were taking care of his dog at the time, and he came over to my house. We had lunch together and he said, jokingly, "You almost lost your sifu. I passed out and my heart stopped." He was really jovial about it. Then he showed me how much he had progressed, physically - made me feel his gut - and we worked out a little in the gym in my backyard."

Lee then returned to Hong Kong to finalize the script for The Game of Death, and passed away shortly there after exact cause of death still open to conjecture.

Regardless of the ultimate disposition of Lee's controversial autopsy, one thing is for sure. The founder is dead and the future of Jeet Kune Do is

now in the hands of his disciples. When he died, he left behind a tightly knit organization of cooperating individuals and a wealth of written material that, despite his untimely passing, keep the art flourishing and, indeed, expanding in new and exciting directions.

The cornerstone of Lee's written legacy is the approximately five and a half volume Tao (Way) of Jeet Kune. Only one of the volumes has thus far been circulated among his former students. Initially, Inosanto tells us, the "Tao" was meant for his students; but later on, Bruce changed his mind and decided that the complete set should be reserved for his son Brandon. He began working on the project when he was laid up indefinitely after straining his back by overextending himself during weight training. The exercise was intended to be performed at a 35-40 pound maximum, and he had been doing reps at over 100 pounds when suddenly he felt something give in his back, followed by agonizing pain.

The framework of the "Tao" is strikingly similar to the ancient Chinese classic, The Art of War, by Shin Gee, There is no wastage of expression, dialogue is kept to a minimum, everything is concise and to the point. In it he establishes various "truths," according to principles which he sets up in a challenging, philosophical manner. If Lee had failed as an actor, he certainly could have made it as a writer, "If the 'Tao' is ever published and that would be up to Linda Lee 1 think that it will shed some insight on his personality," Inosanto predicts. "Many people still think of him as a movie star at least that's the impression I get from a lot of people, But regardless of what they think of him, he was a philosopher, an artist."

Another vital source of information concerning the art of Bruce Lee can be extracted from the privileged few who experienced his teaching first hand. Lee was very selective about who he taught, and judging from the reluctance of his disciples to capitalize on their training, his discretion seems to have paid off. Those who have elected to teach certain phases of JKD, do so with little fanfare, screening prospective students with the utmost diligence.

Almost all of Lee's past students had previous martial arts training before they were introduced to JKD. Similarly, they require that students attain considerable proficiency in a somewhat modified version of their former art as a prerequisite for JKD instruction. All out training in JKD then becomes sort of a "graduate" course an added bonus for deserving pupils.

All in all, though, literature and sporadic instruction no matter how competent are not enough to insure the continued evolution of Jeet Kune Do. There is, however, a more all-inclusive influence that has tended to provide the impetus for the further development of JKD in a manner befitting the memory of Bruce Lee. Two of the original four persons Lee authorized to teach his art (himself and close friend James Y. Lee of Oakland, California) have shed their mortal skins and returned to the everlasting Tao, and now a new breed is moving into the limelight. Some can trace their lineage directly to the founder; others have only read about him or seen him in the movies. Some, like Inosanto, have studied numerous arts for many years, but many have never thrown a side-kick, torqued a punch, been in a street fight or seen the inside of a kwoon. Nearly all are middle class raised, college prep types, versed in the more cerebral aspects of life. They look like they would be at home in an accounting office; they are indistinguishable from the multitude of starry-eyed Bruce Lee fans around the world. But without them, it is doubtful that the "Filipino Kali Academy" could have survived - let alone doubled in size - during the past nine months.

It is every serious martial artist's dream to one day have his own school. Dan Inosanto and Richard Bustillo were no exceptions. Both had studied under Lee for a considerable length of time, and they were working men, too, and looking for a way out of the drudgery inherent in the all familiar   get-up-go-to-work-come-home-watch-television-then-go-to--sleep routine which threatens to turn America into a nation of vidiots. They longed to see JKD continue to flourish, yet didn't want to see it perpetuated in any way that would demean the spirit and teachings of their beloved sifu. Then nearly a year after he was gone, they decided that, misgivings aside, they were the most qualified of anyone to publicly teach his art. They also decided not to call their retreat "The Bruce Lee Memorial School of Kung Fu" or "The Jeet Kune Do Institute of Self Defense" or to refer to it by some other such exhibitionist moniker; but instead. to seize the opportunity and kill two birds with one stone. Thus, the "Filipino Kali Academy" was born out of a desire to promote their cultural arts while at the same time providing a rallying point for those who sincerely wished to continue in Lee's footsteps.

"What we teach at the Filipino Kali Academy." states Inosanto, "is a combination of four things: Escrima, Arnis, Kali and Sikaran. We put them

all together, and most classes start off with a general course - sort of a modified form of Wing Chun. And then they progress. The last stage is the Kali stage the Filipino art - and Jeet Kune Do. We put them together because they complement each other so well. And we feel that these are the two highest stages in our art.

"Beginning students are told that they are not learning Jeet Kune Do; we don't advertise as Jeet Kune Do. And they aren't learning Jeet Kune Do until they reach a certain stage. We do that both with the Filipino art of Kali and Jeet Kune Do. In many ways, I even feel more possessive about the Kali. I like both arts; I consider them two halves of one whole. They complement each other, and to us, the Kali has opened our eyes in JKD and vice versa."

In the main, a name is just a name, a means of identification; names tell nothing about the relative efficacy of a particular martial art. The curriculum at the Academy can be described as Jeet Kune Do or Filipino Escrima it makes no difference because, as Inosanto reveals, "Bruce hated to name his arts." In any event, the Filipino arts are a natural vehicle for the maturation of JKD.

Bustillo points out some of the similarities between the Filipino arts and Lee's revolutionary style of Kung Fu. "They both use the lead hand, lead foot. In Jeet Kune Do the front hand is dominant over the rear hand. Whether it is the left or right, it is the live hand, the parrying hand or the sliding hand. In Escrima, it's the same way. In JKD you would say "trapping'; in Escrima you say "checking.' " In addition, there are probably just as many different styles and systems of Escrima as there are Kung Fu. It is not merely a "stick art" as many believe. Escrima encompasses the entire spectrum of weaponry and is a most devastating empty-handed art to boot. So devastating, in fact, that the .45 had to be invented during the Spanish American War, because the .38 proved worthless against the Moros of the Southern Philippines whom the Americans were attempting to colonize (in the name of Manifest Destiny) after having been granted the islands as reparation from Spain.

Mirroring the Chinese art of Kung Fu, the martial arts of the Philippines are irrevocably intertwined with all aspects of the culture at large. In

every sense of the words, they were regarded as religious and philosophical. An Escrimador had the ability to heal not unlike the peripatetic monks who traveled throughout early China, spreading the art of Kung Fu. They were treated with awe and deference by the common people, and were believed to have possessed "magical" powers. They practiced meditation and also cultivated a highly sophisticated internal system. Lastly, some aspects of the Filipino tradition as with the Chinese can be traced all the way back to ancient Indian sources. For example, the Filipino word for instructor, 'Guro', is strikingly similar to the Indian term, Guru.

Bruce Lee was Jeet Kune Do. The art was inseparable from the man. It was his religion, his philosophy, his ode to immortality. It was his life and it was his wife. It permeated every cell of his being, every corner of his soul. Ironically, it may well have been his demise.

"If you had to name one shortcoming of Bruce Lee, I'd say that it was lack of patience with himself and with other people," Inosanto recounts with a sigh. "To cite an example, one time he was on the set and the stick he was using kept slipping out of his hand because it's so humid there (Hong Kong). He got angry and threw two of them away. He'd get really upset if he couldn't get something right away; he was a perfectionist." What Inosanto neglects to add, however, are reports that Lee severed the sweat glands under his arms in order to alleviate the problem a drastic remedy to say the least. But that was Bruce forever impatient with himself and the world around him. "One time he told me that he couldn't stand anybody that was slow moving, slow thinking. If there was a flaw or shortcoming whatever you want to call it that was it: he had a really short fuse."

Lee came to the end of his fuse on July 20, 1973, at the age of 32. At that very moment, he was on the verge of becoming the biggest box-office attraction in the world. The picture he was working on at the time. "The Game of Death", would have surely catapulted him ahead of such established and unfailingly consistent theater-packers as Charles Bronson, Robert Redford, Burt Reynolds and yes, Linda Lovelace in spite of its "G" rating. Briefly, a hypothetical country's national treasure is purloined, threatening economic collapse. The culprits have stashed the treasure safely away in the top floor of a towering pagoda, located on a mysterious island, ringed with metal detectors. Lee is summoned, and along

with a small handful of allies, sets out for the island. Upon arriving, he discovers that in order to retrieve the treasure he and his companions must fight their way to the top of the pagoda, floor by floor each guarded by a progressively more powerful adversary. On the first floor, manned by a sizable contingent of Karatekas, they encounter little difficulty. The second floor is a different story. Lee loses most of his men before destroying three Kung Fu masters. The rest of Lee's men fall victim to the "Escrima Wizard" (played by Dan Inosanto) on the next floor, leaving him to face the final and most deadly foe (played by basketball NBA star Kareem Abdul Jabbar) in the "Temple of the Unknown". Tragically, the grim reaper called Lee's number before the film was half completed.

Yet, Bruce Lee lives. "It's my feeling that Bruce Lee will become a James Dean figure of the Seventies." wrote folksinger Phil Ochs in the music magazine Zoo World.

True, Lee was a savior in the eyes of millions of hero-starved individuals the world over who could no longer blindly place their faith in traditional demagogues - generals, politicians, sports figures - when faced with the startling revelations of the Watergate era. However, Inosanto opines, he should most be remembered for the legacy he bequeathed to martial artists everywhere, because he always thought of himself first as one of them. "His message is to question, to seek the truth not in terms of what is the accepted standard. Never be afraid to question; never be afraid to be creative; never be afraid to do your own thing. what you think is correct. Bruce used to say, "Life is combat." That's why everything we learned could be applied elsewhere.

"When Bruce died, I didn't know which way to go. But I feel that this is the best way to have some kind of a line. Funny, but he said, "When I die, these guys will probably do something that I won't like. They'll probably build monuments, have impressive creeds, hang pictures of me in the halls and bow to me.' So I often think about that as I go through our salutation where the last thing we do is salute Bruce's picture. But to me it's an honor, a sign of respect. To me it's important that there be a line, so that's what I'm working on now. I'm going to make sure that, if I go, there's always somebody. That is why we opened." ◯

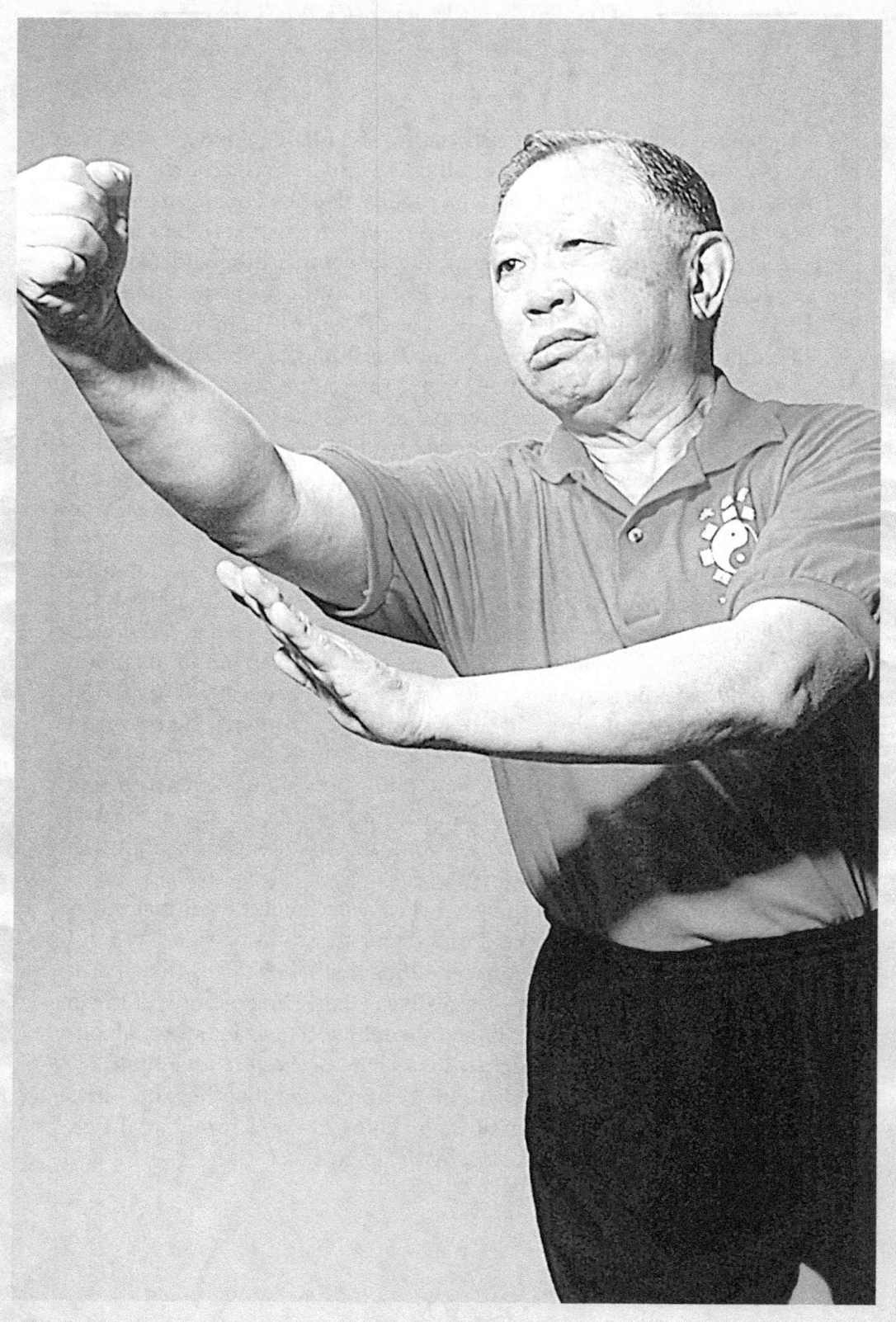

THE HARMONIOUS JEET KUNE DO-TAI-CHI SYNTHESIS

by Richard Imamura

A cross the expansive spectrum of the Kung-Fu way of life, no two arts appear more dissimilar than Jeet Kune Do and T'ai-chi ch'uan.

Thousands of years stand between the two, yet even that gap is dwarfed by the void separating the devastating and lightning-quick fighting art of Bruce Lee from the graceful, slow-motion exercises of the health-conscious Taoists. Fundamentally apart, if T'ai-chi ch'uan was Day, then Jeet Kune Do (or JKD for short) would have to be Night.
But Day and Night exist in harmony. With each morning, Night yields

to Day... only to return with the sunset to prevail over Day... and begin the cycle anew. Within the oneness of the Universe, Day and Night co--exist in a yin/yang harmony... and in much the same way, within the remarkable personage of Professor Daniel Lee, the violence of JKD merges harmoniously with the passive philosophies of T'ai-chi ch'uan.

An electrical engineer and college Chinese language and culture instructor, Prof. Lee was the first student admitted to the Los Angeles kwoon to study the newly-developed JKD under Bruce Lee and his assistant, Danny Inosanto, in 1967. He still values highly the "freedom of expression" he found through that association. Sure, the offense-oriented principles unleashed a most effective fighting system, but "it's a means of expressing myself without artificiality," he says. "It is an all-out fighting art, and I like it. To me, it's like watching a football game. You don't see the one who falls down, you see the one who faked him out of his pants and went on to score the touchdown. That's what I enjoy in JKD, sharpening my skills and techniques so I can cope with the changing situations present in combat. I never go out with the intention of hurting someone, and though the (free) sparring has a lot of body contact, our protective gear and awareness prevent injuries."

However, while he still works out once a week at the JKD kwoon (now operated by Inosanto), Prof. Lee devotes the majority of his time and interest to the gentler art of T'ai-chi ch'uan. "When I'm working out in JKD I'm very physical and intense," he notes, "but I don't want to remain in that mental state all the time. I want to be calm, quiet, relaxed and centered. I want to be gentle and at peace with myself. T'ai-chi helps me reach these goals.

"We all have our emotional ups and downs," he continues, "but practicing T'ai-chi stabilizes me and provides evenness. I guess what it boils down to is yin and yang - the JKD training me to be effective in combat, honing the fighting reflexes; and the T'ai-chi ch'uan promoting tranquility and harmony within myself, and oneness with the world around me. I'm a firm believer in non-violence, and yet I feel strongly that only a person who has undergone the discipline of training to master himself can truly be in charge of any situation that might arise... one who is truly

strong can afford to be gentle."
And gentleness is the way of T'ai-chi ch'uan. True T'ai-chi is hard to come by outside of China, but in the eight years that he has studied the art. Prof. Lee has had the good fortune to study under a number of masters. "I'm continually searching for good teachers I can learn from, masters who are willing to teach with openness." he explains. "I don't jump around. When I stick with a teacher. I stick for many years, and I associate with them for life."
Prof. Lee's first exposure to a genuine matter of T'al-chi ch'uan was in 1966, one year prior to the opening of the Los Angeles JKD kwoon. At that time, Master Tung Fu Ling visited Los Angeles to try and drum up interest in the then-unknown (outside of the Orient) art. One of the world's foremost masters of the classical Yang style, Master Tung "was very discouraged because very few people knew about T'ai-chi." Prof. Lee recalls. "He tried to open up a school, but there wasn't any interest in T'ai-chi then. When I started learning from him it was three times a week. I knew it would only be a short stay, so I dropped all other training in order to learn." Then, after one discouraging year. Master Tung returned to Hong Kong, (He has since relocated in Honolulu).

Finding himself without a teacher who could even come close to Master Tung - Tung Fu Ling being the son of the Grand Master Tung Yen Jet, probably the greatest T'ai-chi ch'uan practitioner of modern times - Prof Lee's T'ai-chi training was sustained only through correspondence with his mentor and his own daily practice. When the opportunity was opened for him to learn the JKD process under Bruce Lee himself, Prof. Lee responded immediately.

For two years, Prof. Lee's T'ai-chi ch'uan practice paralelled the four workouts a week in JKD, but in 1969, he was able to study again under a T'ai-chi ch'uan master with the arrival of Master Mary Chu.

"When Mrs. Chu came over here I was really excited." Prof. Lee noted "You see, back in China Mrs. Chu had studied for many years with Grand Master Tung - so she and Master Tung [Fu Ling] were on the same level. You see, in China, within the school system, family titles like brother and sister are used instead of ranks. So, since I had studied under Master Tung [Fu Ling] in 1966, when Mrs. Chu came over, she was considered as my aunt. She liked me very much right from the start, and took me in like a son." He studied with her for almost three years, firming up his movements and weapons skills in the Yang style, and becoming the senior student in her class.

In 1972, he was given permission by Mrs. Chu to conduct T'ai-chi ch'uan classes - something absolutely required if proper protocol and respect for a teacher is followed. "I treasure this privilege very much, for it offers me a new dimension in my learning," the professor adds. And although he no longer attends Mrs. Chu'a classes, he still feels the deepest respect and affection for her. "I will always consider Mrs. Chu my teacher," he emphasizes "I still go back to visit sometimes, and we keep in touch on the phone."

Ever on the lookout for new directions to explore, recent months have found Prof. Lee again studying under someone he considers "a great master," Y. C. Chiang. Accomplished in the lesser-known northern Kuang Ping style of T'ai-chi ch'uan and Kung-Fu, too, Master Chiang is again widening Prof. Lee's totality of experience... the new and unfamiliar element being the rigorous, almost contortionistic, stretching exercises so typical of the northern systems. "The northern systems use all high kicks, which is why they emphasize stretching," Prof. Lee explains. "Their flexibility is so good, they can develop faster kicks and recover faster."

However, beyond merely becoming more flexible in order to kick faster or higher, Prof. Lee sees a deeper benefit in the practice of T'ai-chi ch'uan. "All that we do here is really discipline of the mind and body," he says. "To accomplish anything in life. you've got Io discipline yourself, keep your mind on what you're doing, in order to be successful. If your mind's wandering off, occupied with different things here and there, you'll never get anything done.

"So T'ai-chi ch'uan is a means of discipline. It takes 35 minutes to do the whole set. Slowly and persistently... that's discipline!" With the slowing down comes even greater benefits. "It is actually achieving balance - mind, body and spirit." Prof. Lee points out. "People say, 'Take it easy,' but they don't spell out how to do it. Well, you can't take it easy if your body's too tense or if your mind's still in tension... T'ai-chi ch'uan puts your mind in neutral gear and relaxes your body."

The slow-motion movements, developed to emulate the give and take harmony of the yin and yang, recall the wisdom of the ancient sages. "You see, Lao Tzu, in the Tao Te Ching, said rigidity is the symbol of death, and suppleness and softness are the symbols of life," points out the professor. "The flexible bamboo bends with the wind, the rigid branch snaps. In the same way, the T'ai-chi ch'uan movements are to varied so as to put into play every part of the body, from the smallest joint to the largest muscle, with harmonious design and graceful patterns. The result is glowing health - suppleness in the joints, your blood circulation is stimulated, the nervous system it activated and the respiratory system is exercised. On top of all this, the body is so strong and healthy that sickness and disease is held off easier. In other words. T'ai-chi ch'uan refreshes your body so that every cell feels charged with new energy and vitality."

And T'ai-chi doesn't even stop at good health. Along with the exercise benefits, changes come over the practitioner, according to Prof. Lee. "One gains a feel for the correct use of the body's energies without waste. With this new sensitivity, one learns to apply it in his everyday life so that in any task, he spontaneously employs the right amount of energy for the task at hand, thus decreasing tension and fatigue." Relaxation of the mind and body frees one from many of the trivial day-to-day irritations that can sometimes accumulate and make life miserable. Instead, fresh energy and a relaxed mind open new avenues of interest.

"From my long practice of T'ai-chi ch'uan. I found my interest began to grow beyond the physical movement, and into the realm of cosmology and reflection of the yin/yang principles underlying universal activity," Prof. Lee adds. "I began my deep study into Chinese philosophy, I have since built up a library of Chinese philosophy – I-ching, Lao Tzu's Teo Te Ching, Zen discipline, Chinese literature devoted to hygienic and meditative techniques, and of course, books on T'ai-chi ch'uan and all branches of the Chinese martial arts." A teacher of Chinese language and culture at Pasadena City College for the past 12 years, Prof. Lee is able to integrate the purely physical aspects of the art with the undiluted wisdom and reflections contained in the original Chinese manuscripts.

"In the Chinese way of life," Prof. Lee points out, "mental, physical and spiritual development are all valued equally. T'ai-chi ch'uan has been regarded as a unique meditative art which satisfies the needs of man on these three levels of his existence. It is often referred to as the Chinese yoga - mind in action, meditation in motion. It is a meditative art for achieving the harmony of the mind and body.

"The harmonious development of man's body and mind are essential if one is to realize the profound possibilities of his life and enfoldment. With the harmony of body and mind, the ch'i [life energy] begins to flow. When the flow of ch'i through one's body is free and uninhibited, spiritual energy begins to develop, which ultimately leads one to the attainment of spiritual enlightenment. Through practice of T'ai-chi ch'uan, one develops a deep inner awareness, he is in touch with himself and with the universe. As one establishes harmony within himself, he becomes calm and balanced. He is no longer selfish or self-centered. Loving and sharing become his way of life and in his mind there is joy and peace. Myself. I feel I'm headed in the right direction, although I'm not anywhere near where I would ideally like to be," says Prof. Lee.

Born in Shanghai, China, in 1930, Prof, Lee was always a person with more than a normal amount of drive. Coupled with a sharp mind and a naturally athletic body, the young Lee often pursued goals beyond the

aspirations of his peers.

Recalling an incident from hit childhood neighborhood, Prof. Lee tells of two Russian brothers who attacked him and tried to steal his bicycle. Saving his bike with the aid of a bystander, Prof. Lee, nevertheless, took a pretty good beating. With a 12-year-old's vow to avenge the wrong, the young Lee proceeded to the nearest gym to learn Western boxing. "I figured I should beat them at their own game," he remembers. But after an afternoon of terrible beatings, "the coach must have had pity on me. He came up to me and asked, 'why do you want to learn so fast? Why don't you start off with the beginners?' It was then that I found out that this was the professional's class! The beginners class was the next day."

From that point, the young Lee pursued his goal with determination. After training hard enough to settle his score with the Russians, he found the physical sport of boxing held an appeal for him that went beyond revenge. Diligent training sharpened his skills and honed his combat instincts, and by 1948. he had become the amateur welter-weight champion of China.

Following the Communist revolution, Prof. Lee's family moved to Taiwan in 1949. This was followed three years later with his emigrating to the United States to further his education.

Studying at Utah State University and UCLA, Prof. Lee earned his advanced degrees in electrical engineering – a profession he has practiced to this day at the Jet Propulsion Lab of Caltech. He currently resides in Altadena. Calif., with his wife, May, and their four children Debbie, 15; Robert, 14, Diane, 9, and Donna, 8. At this point, none of his children have taken up either of his martial arts, "but I don't want to pressure them into taking it up," he explains. "I encourage them, and they've been exposed to it, but I'm not going Io force them."

Describing himself as a "family man," Prof. Lee makes a point of setting aside Sunday of each week for religion and "a family afternoon outing or home entertainment. I want to make sure that I have some time set aside from my busy schedule to communicate with my children, too. My family is wry important to me."

And it's plain to see that Prof Lee hopes that someday his children will take up the arts that have given him so much personally. "Bruce Lee had a great impact on my life," he states. "I worked out with him quite a bit and I consider myself wry fortunate... you know, it's just a handful of people who eventually encountered him."

Thinking back on the early days of the JKD kwoon in Los Angeles' Chinatown, Prof. Lee remembers that "this was the time [1967-8] when Bruce was uncommitted to the movies or television. He spent more time to train us, and be put such high standards for our training that he also gave everyone a special prescribed supplementary fitness program. He'd look at you and say, 'you've got to work on this area, that area, stretching, and so on.' He really meant business and he worked very hard - four times a week. That's dedication."

Inspired by Bruce Lee's example, those who studied under him stand in awe of his greatness. "He was probably the one person I respected the most," says Prof. Lee of his mentor. "Bruce Lee was a very straight-forward person - very straight-forward, very intense, but most of all, very honest. If he liked you, he liked you. He didn't hold back any punches, if he didn't like you, he said so... and that's the kind of person you like because you know he's going to say exactly the same thing behind you as he would to your face."

This same honesty that Bruce Lee lived also permeates the principles of his fighting art - Jeet Kune Do, "The Way of the Intercepting Fist". In the same way that Bruce Lee would never think of applying fixed formulas or ideas to his honest approach to life, the principles of JKD depend upon total freedom.

Developing from Bruce Lee's firm conviction that actual combat rarely, if ever, conformed to the dogmatic dos and don'ts of systematized styles, JKD's only bounds and limits exist in the individual abilities of the practitioners. It is an art where the only rule is that there are no rules. "Bruce Lee wanted to liberate us from a fixed pattern period," Prof. Lee recalls of his instructor. "He told us, 'I am no style, but I'm all styles... you don't know what I'm going to do, and I don't even know what I'm going to do. My movement is the result of your movement, my technique is the result of your technique.'"

The resulting art is one of simple (and remarkably efficient) techniques, honed to a razor's edge and guided by an intuitive combat awareness developed during all-out sparring. "You really go right in," says Prof. Lee, who feels that most other martial arts could do themselves good by incorporating more realistic conditions into the training. "You put all the body protectors on and go at it. That's the only way... When it's going to be all-out. Your frame of mind changes because you know if you make one mistake, he's coming right at you. And then you really begin to respect his punch as the real thing."

Emphasizing large doses of almost-real combat to teach calm and quick reaction under pressure. JKD is most effective in actual use. In the advanced practitioners, punches and other attacks become reflex actions, guided solely by senses heightened through countless hours of almost--real sparring... The instant an opening occurs, the attack is already on the way. Because of the simplicity of the techniques, the attack is extremely powerful and effective.

Yet. beyond the techniques and their infinite variations and applications, JKD is not a style, but a transcendence of style. By removing the bonds of set patterns and fixed responses, a freedom to flow with reality comes about. The closer you get to reality, the less you need complicated devices and techniques as crutches.

Recalling the words of his mentor, Prof. Lee explained the simplicity of JKD: "We didn't have many complicated techniques. Bruce Lee believed and said that 'in JKD, one does not accumulate, but rather, he eliminates the non-essential. It is not daily increase, but daily decrease. The height of cultivation always runs to simplicity; it is the halfway cultivation that runs to ornamentation. So it is not how much fixed knowledge one has accumulated, rather, it is what he understands and can apply alively that counts. 'Being' is far more valued than doing... That's all there is.... It is indeed difficult to convey simplicity."

Bruce Lee, in many ways, WAS Jeet Kune Do. His leadership and his innovation provided much of the soul and spirit of the free-form principles at the heart of the art, and he will be missed. Mere words could not convey the loss felt by Prof. Lee, both on the personal level of friendship and the art's loss of it's founder and leader. "We are indeed saddened beyond words by his sudden passing... But the philosophy and principles he left behind for us will be cherished forever. It was always Bruce's wish that his art never be commercialized or exploited. We shall honor that wish."

Prof. Lee now devotes the majority of his time to T'ai-chi ch'uan. Thoroughly convinced that the JKD method of free sparring to develop combat skills is indeed, very effective, Prof. Lee has of late been applying those same techniques to T'ai-chi. "I hope if I ever contribute to T'ai-chi," he says, "one way is, in a general sense, to help people to find these exercises as a means of relaxation, finding calmness, and the center within yourself. On the other hand, I would like to explore why T'ai-chi has been called the superior fighting art. I haven't met a master yet who practices this aspect of the art."

Indeed, many T'ai-chi instructors refuse to discuss the fighting aspects of their art - claiming either that the techniques are too dangerous, or just plain unimportant; while others make the claim that practice of the 'Solo Exercise', coupled with the 'Joint Hands Practice' (sport T'ai-chi), is all that is needed.

Prof. Lee disagrees. "If a so-called master pushes his beginning student around in Joint Hand Practice while the student only acts as a passive dummy, not trying to counter or even defend, then the so-called master has not convinced me that he knows anything about reality in combat. As Bruce Lee once said, 'he is like a man swimming on dry land!'"

However, says Prof. Lee, "T'ai-chi ch'uan is an effective fighting art. It's been proved through history. Master Yang Lu-Ch'an, nicknamed Yang Wu Ti or Yang the Unsurpassable. was once asked by the court to teach T'ai-chi. Because of that, Kung-Fu Masters challenged him from all over China and couldn't beat him. But Master Yang didn't learn how to fight just by doing T'ai-chi everyday. He gained his experience through his fighting. He used T'ai-chi both offensively and defensively, but that art is lost. All you see in Tai-chi demonstrations are merely prearranged and fixed attacks and responses. But fighting is dynamic, so if you want to be good, you have to use it in a more live situation, 'Joint Hands' is only the beginning."

So applying JKD training methods to the forms of the Solo Exercise, Prof. Lee is trying to rediscover some of the lost art. "Now when I try to work on some of my T'ai-chi self-defense techniques," says Prof. Lee, "I put on my JKD protective equipment and spar. Once I asked a friend of mine to attack me whatever way he wanted to, and I would try to defend myself. It was difficult to cover myself completely all the time, and I got clobbered many times.

"What was wrong," Prof. Lee explains, "was that my opponent knew that I was only going to try to block his attack, and he became fearless and kept charging towards me. Finally, I said to myself, 'hold it. I'm going to use offensive movement as well,' and I did. All of a sudden, the picture changed my opponent didn't come in wildly any longer, because he realized he would get hit as well. You see, I was no longer totally passive in my mind. I was now applying the yin/yang principle by using both offensive and defensive movement. With my mind open and my body relaxed, I was able to sense his movement, fitting in with his attack and using whatever technique I found appropriate. Eventually, I was able to handle his attacks with ease. I realized again what Bruce Lee had said was right - 'totality and freedom of expression toward the ultimate reality in combat is the key.'"

Fluid and quick, fighting ability demands all of the conditioning. flexibility and agility provided by the Solo Exercise, plus much more. "You've got to have that intuitive feeling of timing." Prof. Lee believes, "A sense of distance and knowledge of your own limitations you can learn, rhythm you can train for, but timing, you've got to work on it all the time."

Comparing his Tai-chi to JKD, Prof. Lee remarks. "T'ai-chi is circular movement, spiral movement, on and on, keep going in... I find a total harmony when I blend T'ai-chi and JKD principles in combat They all express the interchangeability of yin and yang. There is a place for straight line [JKD], and there is a place for circular line. Applying Tai-chi and JKD principles open up new dimensions and latitude in combat. I could use circular movement to neutralize the straight aggressive punch, thus nullifying its power, or I could use straight line punch to intercept a straight line punch, a hook or a roundhouse kick. To cling stubbornly to the straight line and reject the circular line, or vice versa, is to become forever bound by their limitations."

So even in combat. the yin/yang harmony holds appeal for Prof. Daniel Lee - engineer, philosopher and martial artist. Combining the offense of JKD and the health and yielding of T'ai-chi ch'uan, he has found a truly harmonious balance of opposites... and in the process, has expanded his knowledge and skills just a little bit more.

"To me, a person has to be dedicated to the art because he loves it... Through my daily practice of T'ai-chi and deep reflection on the philosophy, I hope to reach the understanding and appreciation of my own cultural heritage. I do not want to reside only at the conceptual level, but by experiencing the operating yin/yang principles in my own body and mind, be able to bring my understanding of these principles to bear upon my daily life as a whole, thus living every moment in total harmony with myself and with the unnerve. I hope to be a clear channel of blessing to the people that cross my path, through my teaching to instruct the correct use of one's energy without waste, to draw, to conserve and channel one's energy normally untapped. To promote to the public, body vitality, well-being and spiritual renewal. I haven't reached the final blooming yet in my learning... I don't think I ever will, but the journey

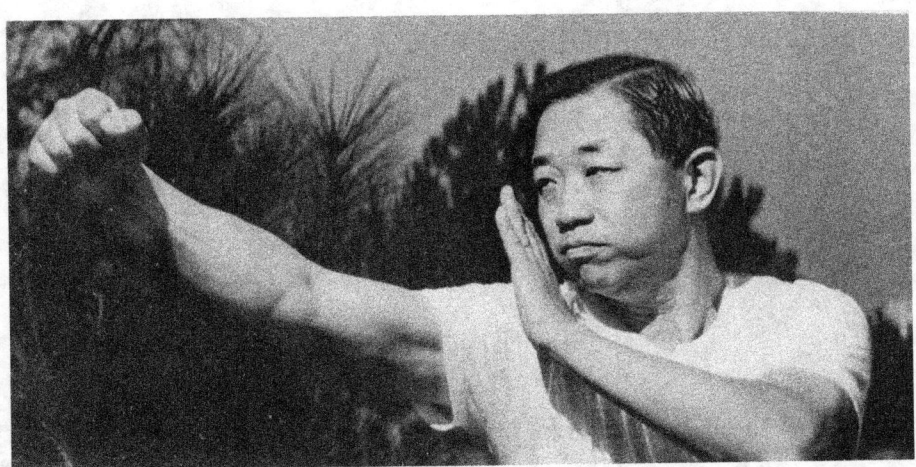

THE JEET KUNE DO ARCHIVES

JEET KUNE DO & TAI CHI CHUAN

by Steve Smoke

Dan Lee spent half his life in China, going through universities there and half his life in the United States doing his advanced schooling and working in a scientific vocation. In his daily activity, Lee represents both Eastern and Western ideals quite dramatically.

By day, he works for the Jet Propulsion Lab at the Telecommunications division where magnetic tape and mathematic calculations are always the order of the day. His current assignment involves him with the orbiting and landing functions of the Viking spacecraft. By night, Mr. Lee teaches Tai Chi Chuan, an aesthetic and consciousness-expanding art which represents what could be considered by some to be paradoxical to his daily routine. Yet the closest points on a circle are also the furthest from one another. And so it is with Lee as the two systems of thought blend to form a complete and satisfyingly patterned lifestyle.

"A logical and analytical mind is required to work with precision instruments," explains Lee. "All activities are conducted with order and proper sequence of execution. The success of a project often depends on much pre-planning and pre-programming as well as continual checking and re-checking. We are in the scientific forefront here because everything we learn on these missions can directly affect people all over this planet. It's very rewarding and exciting."

In those hours which follow such logical activities come pursuits of "detached calmness" through Tai Chi. Lee draws the parallel between the right and left hemispheres of the brain (the right being the creative, non-rational and the left being the logical and analytical) and the hemispheres of the world; the Eastern being the more subjective and the Western being oriented toward logic and analysis. His daily activities can also be divided into similar categories with his working hours directed by analytical thought and his afterwork hours by the more subjective nature of Tai Chi.

A good portion of Lee's thinking has been shaped by his study of the Tao Te Ching, probably the most translated book in the world besides the Bible. Lee sees much pertinence of the Tao to today's ecological, sociological and scientific problems. He observes that certain passages actually describe an electromagnetic field of force and the Quantum theory. "Some psychologists appear to be fond of it as well," says Lee, "because the text seems to be describing consciousness itself."

Tai Chi is a very healthy, understandable wholeistic approach to the body. Lee feels that the understanding of traditional Chinese philosophy, particularly the Tao, is essential to the understanding of Tai Chi in terms of doing the movement and finding the harmony inside oneself. Such philosophy is actually a guideline for those learning Tai Chi. In China, books written in the past century have usually been written by those who lived the Tai Chi way of life each day, practicing endless hours every day, for twenty years or more; this is a high viewpoint unable to be duplicated by many contemporary proponents today. "Such writing crystallized all the Tai Chi principles for the sincere student," says Lee. "Without such understanding, the goals attained become severely limited in comparison."

Lee has carefully studied the Tai Chi Chuan Classics and says, "These are as important as the Tao and must be studied by any serious Tai Chi student."

Lee feels that the bridge between East and West is not as large as some would imagine and it is continuing to become even smaller. As technology in the West increases, so too does its interest in the philosophies of the East. e.g., yoga, martial arts, meditation, etc. The same is true of the East which seeks, and actively pursues, Western modes of thinking and Western technology. It appears to be symptomatic of Western man, until recently, to be out of touch with his body and quite willing to relegate the importance of a healthy, active, vital body to those for whom such specifications would suit their particular purpose (e.g., the boxer, the gymnast, the construction worker), but not for the businessman, housewife or clerk. Such thinking has given way to more realistic thinking in the form of fads, with the initial thrust of such movements being based firmly on the actual fact that to believe that a healthy and active body is not essential to one's well-being is erroneous and inevitably predisposes one to illness.

Says Lee, "We live in two universes, the inner and the outer. The body goes through changes of rhythm as well as other cyclical changes just like the outer world goes through its seasonal changes. In Tai Chi, I want my students to feel what's happening. Sometimes we move so fast that the mind does not have time to comprehend what is happening so we slow down in order to feel, really feel, what is going on inside us when we go through our movements. All the subtle changes with the relationships of the joints and muscles, etc. Find that relationship; find the center. Therein a student will find a dynamic balance which will be flowing, moving and not static."

An important aspect of the 'Two-Universe' idea of the inner and outer worlds is illustrated in Lee's analogy in which he describes the difference between tension and pressure. Both are things the Western world has become painfully aware of as undesirable; especially tension. The difference

is that pressure comes from outside while tension exists from within. In his work at the Jet Propulsion Lab, Lee is constantly under pressure yet claims he is rarely tense. The relaxation inherent in his Tai Chi training and discipline carries over to cause such an effect.

Throughout the years. Lee has received many benefits from his Tai Chi practice. Among them is the cultivation of a meditative state of consciousness. "When my intellectual mind is quieting down and I allow the body to move with spontaneity, I feel peace and serenity pervade my whole being. I experience harmonious existence between the body and the mind. In my Tai Chi I find a way to put the Taoist philosophy into action. During my first year of training, I could relax neither my mind nor my body and I usually shed a trail of sweat wherever I practiced. As I learned the movements of Tai Chi, I truly learned to relax my body and calm my mind. As I went through the movements, I began to see how each part of the body was interrelated to the other. Through my practicing, I gradually began to move more effortlessly, naturally and breathe deeper and more naturally with the lower abdomen. This was a beautiful experience because I sensed the harmonious existence between the mind and the body."

This is very much the Taoist mode of exercise the Chinese call Hsiu Yang Sheng Hsin (to cultivate and nurture the body and mind). It implies the relationship of the body and mind. Therefore, one must employ techniques that will promote a unified development of the body and mind. Lee's favorite Lao Tzu saying is, "Knowing others is wisdom; knowing yourself is enlightenment. Mastering others requires force; mastering the self requires strength "

Tai Chi as taught and expressed by Lee is a mechanism by which one can sense the idea of the "here and now," or the idea that it isn't so much getting to a point, but experiencing how one gets there; the here and now being all there is. For wherever one is, be it New York, Los Angeles or China, when he is there, for him, it "here." And whenever one arrives at any point in the past or the future, upon arrival at that point it is always "now." Thus, to relegate living to the future or the past is to never live. The philosophy behind Tai Chi describes such insight and its movements facilitate a direct experience of such wisdom.

The most influential teacher in Dan Lee's life was Bruce Lee. Lee found in the latter a man whom he could trust and learn from; a man in whom the profound wisdom of the East was matched with the pragmatism of the West; a man in whom burned a brilliant passion for life and a never-ending thirst for knowledge. Below are some of Dan Lee's favorite quotes he has saved from his instruction with Bruce Lee.

Sharpen one's tools. A JKD man faces reality and not crystallization of form. His tool is a tool of formless form.

My followers in Jeet Kune Do, do listen to this: All fixed set patterns are incapable of adaptability or pliability. The truth is outside of all fixed patterns.

When one has reached maturity in this art, one will have the formless form. It is like the dissolving of a thawing ice into water that can shape itself to any structure. When one has no form, one can be all forms; when one has no style, one can fit in with any style.

While being trained in JKD, the student is to be active and dynamic in every way. But in actual combat, his mind must be calm and not at all disturbed. He must feel as if nothing critical is happening (the art of detachment).

In JKD. all techniques are to be forgotten and the unconscious is to be left alone to handle the situation, when the technique will assert its wonders automatically or spontaneously. To float in Totality, to have no technique is to have all techniques.

The JKD man should be on the alert to meet the interchangeability of the opposites. As soon as his mind "stops" with either of them, it loses its own fluidity. A JKD man should keep his mind always in the state of emptiness so that his freedom in action will never be obstructed. When there is no obstruction, the JKD man's movements are like flashes of lightning or like the mirror reflecting images.

When you perceive the truth in Jeet Kune Do, you are at an undifferentiated center of a circle that has no circumference.

Learn the principles, abide by the principles and dissolve the principles. In short, to enter a mold without being caged in it, and to obey the principles without being bound by them.

Utilize the art as a means in the study of the WAY (Tao).

Ultimately JKD is not a matter of technology, but of spiritual insight and training.

Lee looks at his martial arts training as being three-directional. First, from above he seeks instruction from masters. Secondly, on an even level, he seeks exchange with his peers sharing ideas. Lastly, he passes on knowledge below to others; especially perpetuating Bruce Lee s JKD philosophy.

Lee is currently teaching Tai Chi at UCLA extension. Claremont College, and at Cal Tech, as well as conducting his Pasadena-based private classes. "I always teach my classes personally; especially beginning classes. A new student is like a piece of white paper, totally blank. It is an honor and a responsibility to teach new students. I am strongly opposed to the practice of many commercial establishments which advertise that you will learn from a certain instructor when, in fact, you rarely even see him let alone have him as an instructor."

When Lee has new students simply relax their shoulders, they are often surprised at how difficult such an apparently easy thing is to do. Most new students are also shocked to realize how really awkward they are. But with such knowledge comes new insight and a legitimate starting point for improvement.

Being an engineer professionally, Lee leaches Tai Chi mostly out of his love for the art. He often refers to his teaching not as teaching, but as sharing for he speaks of continual personal growth for himself as well as his students. To Lee, form is but a mechanical movement, feeling that in order to truly learn a form, it is necessary to understand what is behind the movements. In the past it has sometimes been considered disrespectful or untraditional to ask questions of one's teacher and to simply mimic the movements handed down by the instructor. Lee feels that one key aspect of the Western mind is that it questions why a thing is done. "This is a healthy point of

view and one that I not only encourage, but insist upon both for myself and for my students," says Lee. "Bruce Lee once told me, 'Dan, always stress for understanding. Find the roots, then you can see the flower. Without knowing the relationship of the timing, space and function, the form can degenerate quickly. If it is not functional, it is merely ornamentation and the martial art aspect of Tai Chi is lost.'"

Technology is advancing, sports are advancing, records are breaking. Why? Are bodies stronger? Perhaps, but Lee feels that the real reason is that training methods have improved. Thus, he is constantly searching for the best, most applicable and most understandable methods to teach the art. Being an engineer in the West, as well as having been raised in the East. Lee now takes his basic understanding of the oriental arts and makes them vital and interesting to the Western mind. "How can a student apply what he learns to his daily life?" he asks himself. "If he can't, what he is learning is purely academic, partial and limited."

On training, Lee says that everything physical must follow physical laws. And Tai Chi is a physical activity, thus following the laws of leverage, gravity, etc. Essential to the training in, and learning of, Tai Chi is sensing body movement. An old axiom is that "if your arms moved independent of the body movement, it was no real gung-fu." Often when a new student observes a form, he sees apparencies and not what is actually taking place. For instance, many forms appear to imply a multitude of hand movements and the novice then concentrates on imitating those movements without realizing that there is a subtle body movement that must go before the implementing of the hand motions. "One way I try to illustrate this," says Lee, "is by explaining that the movement of 'brushing the knee' can be likened to a baseball pitcher throwing a ball. Then, by having a person who is generally familiar with the latter movement go through such a motion, he can understand the body movement involved in the Tai Chi form." Lee feels it is necessary to draw a Western parallel in order to not only bring home the point, but to illustrate pertinence to the student. His classes take place in what he calls a "non-judgmental, non-competitive environment."

The early awkwardness experienced by Tai Chi students is manifested by wobbliness while doing the exercises. "When one is centered," explains Lee, "his movements become smooth and graceful. But how do I explain such an abstract concept as this to my students?" Congruent with his illustrative teaching methods, Lee then produced two toy "tops" to demonstrate the principle of "centering." Putting an extra weight (a piece of metal) on the bottom of one top, and no restrictions on another, he set both of them spinning with the inevitable result of the weighted one tipping over while the unobstructed one spun, perfectly centered, strongly balanced for a considerable time. By way of further explanation Lee says, "If we are driving on the freeway and the car starts shaking, we know that something, usually the tires, are out of balance and require adjustment in order to run at optimum efficiency. The same is true of ourselves. Thus, balance and centering is most important."

Another key principle of Tai Chi is the idea of "yielding." For example, when an attacker comes at you, and he lands an effective blow to a rigid area, the recipient of the blow is usually knocked off balance. While, conversely, if the recipient is fluid and yielding, the blow will be as though striking thin air and often the mere momentum alone of an unlanded punch will be sufficient to throw an attacker off balance enough to make him hopelessly vulnerable. "Such examples," says Lee, "provide just enough of a learning tool so that the student sees these things for himself as a flash of insight."

Such concepts as "yielding" often strike the Western mind the wrong way. There is the idea that strength always wins out when Lee encounters such a viewpoint, he asks them to consider the tough cowboy in the rodeo riding the broncos and bulls.

If one observes successful riders, one will note that if one were to remain tough and rigid while trying to ride a bucking bull, one would be thrown immediately to the ground. Successful riders ride like they ate riding a wave; moving as it does, following its every movement; going with it, riding it out without resistance. "The important point is to be 'one' with the hostile force," says Lee, "and not to resist it. Go with it and don't use force; blend with it. It is like a pliable reed in the wind: it neither opposes nor gives way. That is the essence of Tai Chi."

Lee says that during one conversation with Bruce Lee, the former spoke of maturity at which point Bruce cut him short, saying, "Dan, never talk of 'maturity,' but rather of 'maturing' because a person is constantly maturing and blossoming. Never stop being a student. Life is always a learning, searching and finding experience. A teacher is not a giver of wisdom but simply a guide."

To many, Daniel Lee is just such a guide: inspiring and setting a glowing example and teaching Tai Chi out of his love to share his art. ○

REFLECTIONS OF THE ART OF JEET KUNE DO

by Dan Inosanto

While Bruce Lee was alive, there were only three individuals who were ever certified and authorized by him to teach the art of Jeet Kune Do.

The highest-ranked instructor ever certified by Bruce Lee was Taky Kimura, who attained the level of fifth rank and is my senior. The only other instructors certified by Bruce Lee were the late James Lee and myself. Both James Lee and I were awarded third rank. The most senior advanced student at this time was Ted Wong, a classmate of mine and a private, personal student of Bruce Lee, who attained the level of second rank in jeet kune do. Most other students at this time were ranked in 'Jun Fan Gung Fu', not jeet kune do. Ted Wong was one of the few people to have achieved rank in Jeet Kune Do founder Bruce.

You could receive a Jun Fan Gung Fu certificate by training in a small group session, class session or private session under Bruce Lee, Taky Kimura, James Lee or myself. But to receive the Tao of Chinese Gung Fu certificate or the Jeet Kune Do certificate, you had to be personally trained under Bruce Lee on a one-to-one basis. Only Bruce Lee could give this certificate in jeet kune do. That is why I have never given a Jeet Kune Do ranking certificate to anyone to this day. If everyone in the Jeet Kune Do clan would read his certificate, you will see it reads Jun Fan Gung Fu, Jun Fan martial arts or Jun Fan martial arts (Jeet Kune Do Concepts).

A Jeet Kune Do certificate means you trained with Bruce Lee on a one-to-one basis. He reserved the right for himself; only he could give a certificate in jeet kune do. Since Bruce died I cannot issue a certificate in jeet kune do, but I can issue a 'Jun Fan Gung Fu' certificate and pass on the concepts and principles that he gave me. In honor and memory of Bruce Lee I still have a Jeet Kune Do family and clan tree, which teaches the 'Jun Fan Gung Fu' and 'Jeet Kune Do Concepts.'

In other words, we are constantly researching and developing the goals of Jeet Kune Do Concepts, beginning with the basics of Jun Fan Gung Fu, and exploring other existing methods with which we personally and individually come into contact. Jeet Kune Do is not a style, but a way of thinking, training, researching, and experimenting. We are constantly exploring ourselves, internally and externally. I have been asked many times if I am teaching what Bruce Lee taught me, and the answer is 'yes and no.' Bruce Lee taught everyone differently. I observed him on what he taught, what he shared and how he shared that knowledge with that individual. He was unique as a teacher, especially when dealing one-to-one. Bruce Lee taught me how to train, research and experiment for myself. This was Jeet Kune Do Concepts. Some of these things can be passed on, but others are harder to disseminate because they may not fit a particular student.

To further explain, let's compare Bruce Lee's Jeet Kune Do to writing a history term paper. Let's say Bruce Lee was writing a term paper on

World War II and he used seven sources to compile his material. The paper was turned in and his teacher termed the work "brilliant." He receives an "A." The next year I take the same class, and I am going to do my term paper on the same subject. Let us say that Bruce Lee wants to help me write this term paper and he recommends the same seven books he used to get his "A." I use identical material but get a "B." The material was there but I could not receive the same grade Bruce got by using his method. Now let's say instead of using just the books Bruce recommended, I use 15 other books and 12 magazine articles on the war for my research. Then I talked to people who were in the second World War, and I included that in my research. I also included passages from books written by a Japanese author, a German author, an Italian author, a Korean author, an English author, a French author, and views from a soldier, a housewife and a sailor. Whether or not I received an "A" from my teacher depends on my ability to express myself. But regardless of the grade, I would have gained much more insight, knowledge and understanding than if I had stayed with the seven books which comprised the method used by my friend Bruce.

And this is the method I like to think I am using with the Jeet Kune Do Concepts.

To follow Bruce Lee's way would be wrong; but to use his formula for research, development and growth is a more valid way to go. ☯

WING CHUN KUNG FU THE NUCLEUS

by Dan Inosanto

Reprinted from Jeet Kune Do: The Art and Philosophy of Bruce Lee.

In setting up his art Bruce Lee seems to have acknowledged the fact that there is nothing so permanent as change. Down through the years some things stayed the same, but there was continual modification.

For example. when I first met Bruce back in 1964, he had by then considerably altered his original style, Wing Chun.
Upon returning to the States from Hong Kong at the age of 18 (Lee was born in San Francisco), he began almost immediately to adjust the angles, stances and footwork of Wing Chun because it

was too "rigid." as he put it. The end product of all his experimentation, which he called Jun Fan(a variation of his Chinese name). was the art that was taught at the schools he opened in Seattle and Oakland in the early Sixties. And though he considered this new art to be more fluid and direct than its predecessor. Bruce always expressed a very high opinion of Wing Chun. Indeed, even after he had taken it a step further to create Jeet Kune Do, he would still say: I would like to stress the fact that though my present style is more totally alive and efficient. I owe my achievement to my previous training in the Wing Chun style, a great style."

Wing Chun (meaning "beautiful springtime") was reportedly founded by a woman. Yim Wing Chun, some 400 years ago. The style was based on the techniques of Shaolin nun Ng Mui of the southern temple in Fukien province.

But Yim Wing Chun felt that Ng Mui's style was too complex and placed too much reliance on power techniques and strong horse stances. She was looking for, instead, the simplest, least complicated, most efficient means of defending herself; and not finding it among the existing styles, she created her own.

Yim Wing Chun taught the art to her husband -an actor by profession who was also versed in the martial arts and it was passed down through the centuries to Leong Bok Sul. Wong Wah Bo. Leong Yee Tai, Leong Jon, Chan Wah Soon, Yip Man (Lee's instructor), Leong Sheong and Wong Soon Sum.

Despite its roots deep within the legendary Shaolin Temples of Old China, Wing Chun comes to the twentieth century as one of the most modern styles of the ancient art of Kung Fu.

Based on the theory that the shortest distance between two points is a straight line, Wing Chun lacks the elongated, flowing motions that are a part of most other forms of Kung-Fu. The centerline, an imaginary line that runs down the center of the body. forms the basis of Wing Chun movements -the axis around which the blocks and strikes revolve. Wing Chun practitioners are taught when in combat to have their centerline directly opposite the opponent's chin.

The immovable elbow theory, the four corners and lin sil die dar (simultaneous block and attack), contribute to the overall economy of movement which is characteristic of Wing Chun. The first of these concepts--which holds that the hand and forearm can move in any direction, but the elbow must remain in position about three inches in front of the body -defines the boundary lines for proper utilization of Wing Chun techniques.

The boundaries of the four corners are identical to those of the immovable elbow: the eyebrows at the top, the groin area at the bottom and the region just past the shoulders on either side. Also, the body is divided into four areas, or gates as they are called. And within each gate there is a forward area and a rear area.

Lin sil die dar, though quite simple in theory, is harder to implement in practice. As the natural tendency is to either retreat or try to block an attack. this concept can only be mastered after much training and discipline.

The simplicity of Wing Chun is reflected in the total number of (kuens) in the style-three! In one way or another. all Wing Chun techniques are contained within the sil lum tao ("little idea"), the chum kil ("searching for the bridge") or the bil jee ("shooting fingers").

Wing Chun training starts with sil lum tao, the basic foundation of all that will follow, and progresses through chum kil and bil jee, in that order. Along the way, the student is also taught the chi sao ("sticky hands") exercise. This exercise. based on the dynamic balance of opposing forces (yin and yang). heightens the student's sensitivity in his hands and arms to the point where he can detect the intentions of his opponent by feel.

Finally, after the three forms and chi sao have been mastered, the student applies what he has learned in the 108 movements of the mook jong (wooden dummy). A training method unique in all the martial arts, the 108 movements simulate every conceivable situation and stand as the pinnacle of Wing Chun training-all previous knowledge contained and applied therein.

Although Bruce's father had introduced him to the graceful flowing movements of Tai-chi when he was just a youngster growing up in Hong Kong, he did not begin training in earnest until he was about 13. As the story goes, he decided to take up Wing Chun out of a feeling of insecurity that arose once he had established a reputation as a gang leader and street fighter. "I kept wondering." he once confided to many of his close friends, "what would happen to me if my gang was not around when I met a rival gang."

So in the fifties Bruce became a student of the famed master Yip Man. then patriarch of the Wing Chun school in Hong Kong-and he would go to any length to further his instruction. One of his favorite ploys, for example, was to arrive at the training hall long before any of the other students. And then as they began to show up for class, they would be greeted by Bruce who would assure himself of a private lesson by shaking his head and telling them, "The old man's not in. No class today." He also had friends in other styles, which gave him an opportunity to broaden his horizons as the energetic Chinese youths practiced tirelessly after school and even during recess.

During his senior year in high school, Bruce developed a fascination for boxing and decided to enter an amateur contest. An uncommonly fierce competitor, his being crowned the high-school champion of Hong Kong is only surprising in light of the fact that he had never before put on a glove!

Yet the real purpose of the countless hours he spent sharpening his techniques with Yip Man's senior students and friends in other styles. as well as the experience he got in the unfamiliar confines of the ring, was purely structural: according to Bruce, the ideal proving grounds for combat remained the ever-dangerous backstreets and alleyways of Hong Kong.

Taking into account the myriad styles of Kung-Fu that were - and still are - taught openly in Hong Kong, why did Bruce select Wing Chun? From all indications I have gathered over the years, there were three things he liked especially about Wing Chun: (1) its economical structure; (2) its directness: and (3) its emphasis on energy or sensitivity training (chi sao).

In any event, I think it is safe to say that Wing Chun does in fact form the nucleus of Jeet Kune Do. For only with a basic foundation that is already stripped down practically to the essentials could he have made such rapid and amazing strides in the development of his own art. ◯

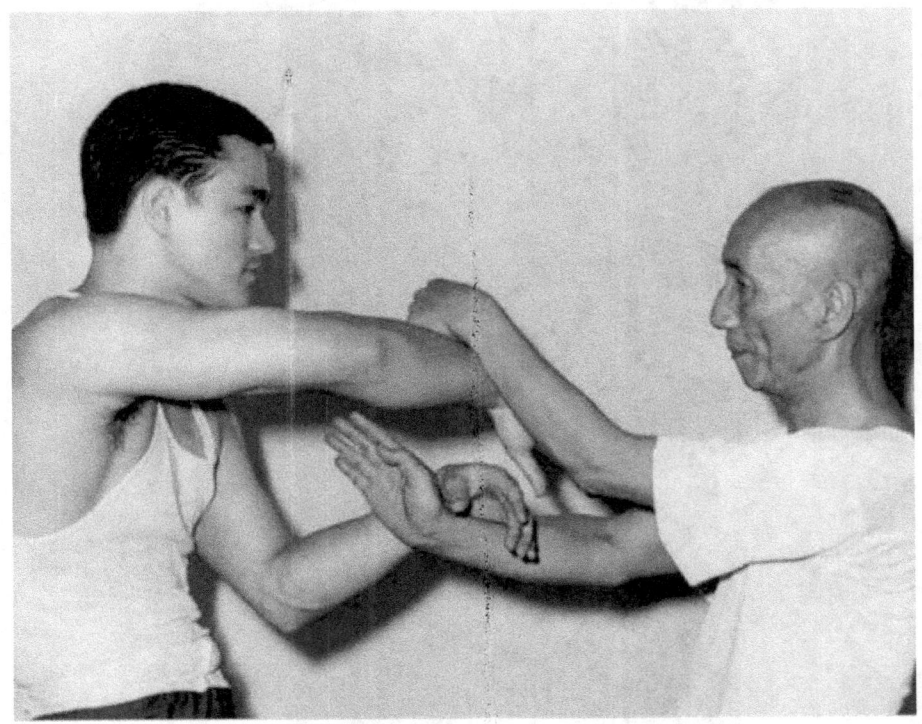

A JEET KUNE DO REUNION

Jerry Poteet & Dan Lee

by Fran Joseph

In early 1967, Bruce Lee opened a martial arts school in Los Angeles' Chinatown. Daniel Lee and Jerry Poteet were the first two students admitted to the 628 College Street school and both trained with him as members of a select group that also included Dan Inosanto, Steve Golden, Bob Bremer and Pete Jacobs. This original "core" group was fortunate to train with Lee not only in public classes, but also in private sessions twice a week (Wednesday evenings at Bruces house and closed-door sessions on Saturday mornings in Chinatown).
These two of Bruce Lee's original students fondly look back on a time in their martial arts careers when one man had all the answers.

Dan and Jerry, what was the training program like in Chinatown?

JERRY POTEET *Footwork. We devoted much time to movement, especially lateral mobility. Of course, structure was very important, and Bruce insisted on hitting with vertical fist from the right lead. For the first three months we cultivated only the front hand. Once, when we were working on front-hand drills, Bruce caught me using my rear hand and he said, "That was very good, Jerry. But not now; in time." His reason for stopping me was that he didn't want me to feel the power of the rear hand, and therefore neglect developing the front hand.*

Bruce felt the front hand, being closest to the target, was going to be doing 80 percent of the hitting, so it had to be developed to perfection. Instead of adding techniques or movements, he wanted us to refine the ones that were efficient.

Although I had excelled in kenpo, Bruce made me feel very slow. Once, when he was teaching me pak sao (slapping or clearing the opponent's arm), he ridiculed my telegraphic motions by turning his back on me and walking away before I finished my movement. It was quite a lesson in humility. I did, however, get to feel Bruce's pak sao, and even though I resisted, Bruce's energy exploded through my arm and knocked me off balance. Also, I'd never come across anyone who talked about awareness, but Bruce had developed a set of drills to enhance this attribute. In fact, when I asked him much later, "What will you do when you grow old and lose the endurance?" he said, "I expect that my awareness will increase as did my instructor's, Yip Man." With that, I was able to cut another man's speed in half. We were all friends in the group, and we shared with each other. We

knew the value of what we were receiving, since we had previous training to balance it against. I think Bruce enjoyed seeing our appreciation and each of us received supplementary training programs from him. His idea was to train the body to perform at its maximum, since the mind would always push it past the "breaking point." He had the ability to bring out the intensity in me, so that I was giving it my total effort at all times.

DANIEL LEE *Fitness was very important. Much time was spent "fine-tuning" punches and kicks. Bruce used to tell us that our punches and kicks were the "tools of the trade," just as a hammer and nails were a carpenter's tools. He told us that we should make every tool a masterpiece. We devoted*

a great deal of time to kicking the bags, and Bruce would watch us and provide a critique of our performance. His suggestions were tailored to each individual, so that each could overcome our shortcomings. He also emphasized liming and rhythm training. Occasionally, he would play music and have us study the rhythm of movement, and be able to fit into the space between the beats.

What characteristics or qualities did Bruce look for in his students?

DANIEL LEE *Moral character. Bruce spent a lifetime developing this art, so he did not want to pass it on to people of dubious character. As a result, he screened students quite carefully (although he did show his art to those who did not want to train extensively with him). He looked for a willingness to train, respect for him as a teacher and sincerity. Over the years, those who were truly influenced and touched by him still uphold his name and honor his requests not to commercialize his art.*

JERRY POTEET *Bruce had two requirements: physical ability and moral*

character. Even if you had the ability, without the character you would not be accepted. According to Bruce, the ultimate fighting machine was someone who possessed maximum physical ability and who was insane, who had "no thought of self." He felt that in our training we might have to "walk through the door of insanity," and without good character, we wouldn't be able to come back through.

What was your first impression of Bruce Lee?

DANIEL LEE I saw Bruce for the first time at the Long Beach Internationals in 1964, where he was demonstrating his art. I was in awe of the speed of his punches and kicks and the power he generated, yet his movements were so graceful and fluid, and seemed effortless. I was also impressed at his confidence in conveying his art to the audience. Later on in his class, Bruce was able to convert us to see what he saw, that we were so trained and conditioned in our rigid responses that our responses were predictable. He said that after years of training in a routine and feeling comfortable in it, that he could touch us at will because he knew our rhythm and could "fit in" with it. He could penetrate us at any time.

JERRY POTEET Now that I look back, when Bruce was teaching he would stop the class and re-emphasize what he wanted, and you'd repeat it again and again until he was satisfied. In a way, he was like a choreographer who is dissatisfied with anything less than precision. Most of the time he'd say,

"The key is to relax, don't push so hard."

What was the most difficult aspect of training?

DANIEL LEE During the first year, it was getting rid of all my preconditioned responses. For example, when someone threw a punch at me, I had developed a certain set of responses that were predictable. I was unaware of this, until Bruce exposed me to the fact that being too comfortable in something was to my detriment. In this way, he explained, your strongest defense could be your downfall.

What is your fondest memory of Bruce Lee?

DANIEL LEE On one occasion while we were working out in Chinatown, James Lee, my senior in JKD who was visiting from Oakland, observed the class. After the session, Bruce came over to me with a smile on his face and put his hand on my shoulder. "Dan," he said, "do you know what James said about you?" Bruce told me that James said, "You know, Bruce, that guy's really got it." I figured he probably felt I had trained very diligently and had a good level of timing and rhythm. I felt very honored and proud when I heard that from Bruce.

JERRY POTEET Since Bruce was multi-faceted, he showed different sides to different people. I saw the practical jokes side of the man. I'd been delving deeper and deeper into the Taoist philosophy and questioning Bruce constantly. Well, one Saturday morning after a workout, he really strung me along. As we were leaving the school, he walked up, put his arm around me and said very seriously, "Jerry, do you know what one of the hardest things to do is?" And I'm thinking he's going to lay a heavy truth on me, but

after a dramatic pause, he said, "One of the hardest things to do is to get that extra step on some guy on the street you've just exchanged blows with, to chase him and kick him in the butt." On another occasion, I was looking at the titles on the bookshelves in his library. Both hands were behind my back so I wouldn't be tempted to touch them. (Bruce hated his books to be disturbed. In fact, there was a sign on the bookshelf that read, "Do not touch.") Suddenly, from the doorway Bruce called out my name and I turned to see a three-sectional staff flying through the air toward me. I reacted with a yell as it caught me full in the face, and then I realized it was made of foam rubber. Bruce roared at my reaction, and I said, "Okay, you've

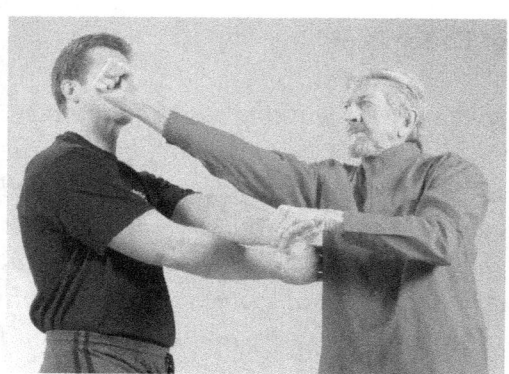

had your fun now let me have mine." Bruce knew I was dying to glance at the comments he made in the margins of his books so he said, "All right, but make sure you put every book back in its place." The joke was still on me, however, because as soon as I opened a book I realized all his comments were written in Chinese.

What concepts or principles did Bruce Lee stress?

JERRY POTEET *Simplicity, economy of motion and efficiency. On Wednesday evenings after a workout at Bruce's house, we'd cover philosophy, especially the Taoist principles of yin and yang, and the "fitting in" principle. We learned the application of these principles by performing energy, or sensitivity drills which were incorporated into the HIA (hand immobilization attack) phase of training, and ultimately, to all phases of combat and life.*
DANIEL LEE *What makes Bruce Lee great is that he was not only a dedicated martial artist training his body, but he was also a thinker, a philosopher. He told me once that he went to the University of Washington to ma-*

jor in philosophy so he could experience his martial arts through the eyes of a philosopher. To make an art unique, it must have a philosophical foundation. Bruce Lee saw his JKD principles in the Chinese Taoist philosophy, the relationship of yin and yang. It was this principle of "softness" of pliability overcoming hardness, the water principle of never clinging to one aspect, that gave substance to his art. That is the philosophy of tai chi, which is the one art that has endured in China, although there have been many other styles throughout the years. Bruce stressed these principles of pliability, that one should never be always on the attack, that one should also wait to sense the opponent's energy and then counter it, like water flowing and fitting into any space. This approach is opposed to making your own strategy and attacking like a wild bull without any consideration for your opponent's rhythm, liming, speed and size. The more I studied, the more I began to realize where Bruce's thoughts came from. JKD really is philosophy in action.

It would seem for you the Chinese principles or concepts are fundamental in your approach to JKD and martial arts.

DANIEL LEE *I agree with Bruce that the pliable or springing energy is critical, and I have been developing it in my tai chi training and in my combat. These Chinese concepts that have been influential in JKD are: the wing chun principles of economy and efficiency, the tai chi sensitivity training, Taoism, and of course, the philosophy of Sun-tzu.*

Is this why you believe tai chi and JKD enhance each other?

DANIEL LEE *In my own life they complement each other beautifully. Bruce emphasized feeling and emotional involvement, or combat readiness. However, one cannot have that feeling all the time; one must also find a time of repose. Through the harmonious movements of tai chi, I find the peace of mind and contentment that other martial arts have failed to provide. Even in my JKD, in combat, I still remain totally calm, free of anger. In this state of mind, you can remain calm and plan your strategy, even if you've been hit or hurt, rather than blindly retaliating. I found that this is where my interest lies: to leach people this level of centering to cope with their stressful lines. I do expose the combative elements of "yielding" to some of my advanced students who have had martial arts training.*

What are your hopes for the future of JKD?

JERRY POTEET *That the art be a stairway to understanding. Let's use it to understand ourselves and each other.*
DANIEL LEE *Every branch of martial arts has been influenced in some way by Bruce Lee's philosophy, although Bruce would object to JKD being used in the marketplace as a label. I wish we could move on, and continually develop and flourish in the art, yet not deviate from Bruce's guidelines. I would like to see the people who studied originally with Bruce get together*

at least once a year to exchange information and expound on his "Tao of Jeel Kune Do." We could share our knowledge and experience some of these basic, underlying principles. We should have a time of remembrance for Bruce Lee so that his art and philosophy will continue for the next generation and the future. Each student, based on his own inclinations, will develop according to JKD principles. I, for one, am very much influenced by the Chinese philosophy upon which Bruce built his art. I continued to study Bruce's "Tao of Jeet Kune Do," which was his analysis and insights into the martial way. Through Bruce, we have been liberated; even though we study other arts, we must avoid meaningless drills and routines where it becomes a stylized form.

This is not what Bruce was after. He said there was a process of constantly shedding techniques, that we should not be bound by drills so that we can confront a combat situation that is constantly changing. As Bruce said, "I am nothing but echo to a sound, I don't prepare what I plan to do." That is why I don't believe in constant drilling in technique; it binds you and makes you more predictable in your response. In combat training, you have to train with all kinds of partners, big and small, fast and slow. What may work for one type of opponent may not be appropriate for another. Sun-tzu said, "Know yourself and know your enemy, and you can become invincible." Therefore, JKD is not about working a fixed technique, but rather feeling the opponent's energy, his reactions, determining his weaknesses, then applying your particular skill to the individual. ☯

THE EVOLUTION OF TRAINING IN JKD

by Ted Wong & Tommy Wong

One major misconception that many martial artists believe is that jeet kune do is nothing more than a modified wing chun system with the addition of some long-range kicks from the northern gung fu (kung fu) styles, But JKD involves much more than this simple generalization, it is the end product of Bruce Lee's martial arts evolution, including a whole change in approach and attitude to the fighting arts.

One would notice that Lee's training closely followed his evolution in the martial arts. By observing the evolution of his training regimen, one would discover Bruce Lee's transition from wing chun to jeet kune do, thereby understanding where Lee came from, where he went, and where he might have gone had he lived.

WING CHUN PROWESS

When Bruce Lee came to the United States, he continued to diligently practice the wing chun techniques he learned in Hong Kong, Through his perseverance, he attained a high level in wing chun and became an exceptional practitioner of the art. At the time, Lee stayed true to the traditional training in wing chun by performing the wing chun forms many times, by practicing chi sao and many trapping drills with partners, and by working on the wing chun wooden dummy.

He also spent time on developing the strength. in his upper body required to trap effectively. Increasing the strength in his arms and shoulders would help Lee perform chi sao more effectively. This, included weight training to increase his forearm size and wrist strength utilized in the wing chun short-range punch as well as doing fingertip push-ups for the wing chun finger jab technique. Through his understanding that chi sao was used to cultivate a constant energy flow, Bruce Lee also performed some isometric exercises that would develop this flow.

It should be mentioned that although he professed that the strong side of the body should always be in front during a confrontation because of the advanced positions of the limbs, Bruce Lee caught that both the left and right sides would both be cultivated for combat.

This was because an unexpected fight may occur while the practitioner is in any position. In addition, jeet kune do endorses the coordination of the whole body, including the arms and shoulders, to move as one unit so maximum power can be achieved relative to one's body size and weight.

DIFFERENT WORKOUTS

After his famous altercation in Oakland during the mid-1960s, Bruce Lee found himself unusually winded, thus he increased his endurance workout by running more, using the stationary bicycle, jumping rope, and shadow boxing. At the same time, Lee began to change his approach to the martial arts, and this reflected in his training. One example is that with his new emphasis on adaptability, realism, and functionality, Bruce Les de-emphasized the practice of prearranged forms training, since it did not effectively and efficiently prepare a student for combat.
Instead, contact drills and full-contact sparring became increasingly important.
When Lee began to integrate some of the longer-range kicks, his training emphasis moved toward general physical conditioning for overall body strength and stamina since kicking would be more taxing on the cardiovascular system. As kicking was to be used more often, leg strength became particularly important, so kicking the shield, doing leg raises and squats with weights, and stretching for flexibility became regular exercises. Furthermore, as Bruce Lee became more and more influenced by boxing, many of the training and conditio-

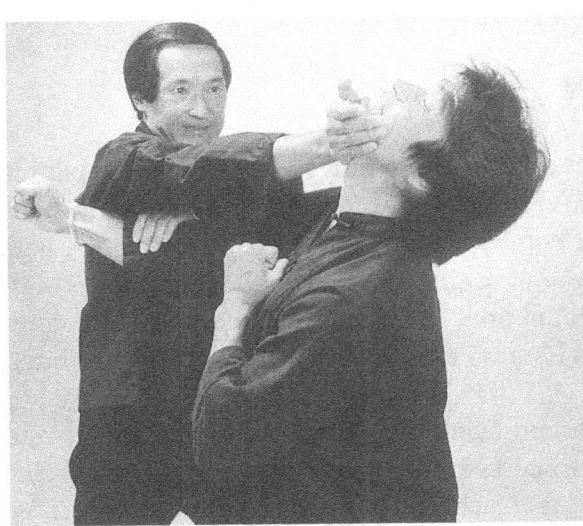

ning exercises from that sport became heavily adopted such as using the heavy bag, the top and bottom bag, and the focus pad. However, Lee would not only use these devices with hands, but also his feet.

With Lee's emphasis on longer-range fighting, distance and mobility became key issues. Countless hours were spent on developing smooth and rapid footwork to bridge and maintain distance, thus allowing Lee to quickly get in and out of a confrontation. Drills were used that developed one's chasing ability so that one could effectively catch one's fleeing opponent, Therefore, speed also became extremely important.

Such issues as initial movement, non-telegraphic motion, economy of motion, efficiency, and the lead hand/foot became vital in jeet kune do. With this additional speed, Bruce Lee could cleanly hit an opponent from a distance of six feet or more.

ANOTHER DIRECTION

Thanks to this emphasis on other fighting ranges, Lee began to taper his wing chun training more and more. For example, since he sought to increase his skill in the other combative ranges besides the trapping range (kicking, punching, and grappling), Bruce Lee would naturally begin to practice wing chun less frequently. Eventually, chi sao and wing chun wooden dummy workouts became non-existent in Bruce Lee's training by the late sixties.

Along with working on certain techniques such as the front hand lead punch and the sidekick, Bruce Lee began to isolate and work specific muscles that were used in these techniques, so that the training became more specialized to increase the performance of particular techniques. Next, Lee would consider different possibilities for improving the techniques. Finally, he would actually change the technique to make it better or more versatile for himself. This is really what jeet kune do is all about: the self-discovery of one's self through the process of simplification.

Bruce Lee never adopted another martial art (technique or training method) simply because it was good, but rather if it complemented what he was already doing. In addition, if Lee adopted something from another martial art, he would have modified it so much to fit him that it would not resemble the original art at all. If Lee had lived, he would most likely have developed exercises and training methods that would help him maintain the peak physical condition that the earlier achieved.

Bruce Lee stressed simplicity in his fighting. It is not how much knowledge or how many techniques one knows that will make him a better fighter, but rather how well one can use this knowledge and these techniques, What Bruce Lee called "hacking away the unessentials" was his way of streamlining his fighting arsenal to its bare essentials. This was to cut down on the confusion that one encounters when trying to figure out what response would be most appropriate to a given situation.

As a result, one would notice that JKD has very few techniques in its arsenal when compared to other martial arts. Jeet kune do is all about doing what is instinctual and natural. It is simply about being yourself.

EQUIPMENT TRAINING

Bruce Lee was one of the first martial artists to utilize many pieces of training equipment to hone his combative skill. In line with his convictions that realistic training and sparring were the most effective ways of cultivating fighting prowess, Bruce Lee sought training devices which would allow realistic practice and drilling.

Effective training equipment would be able to continually withstand Lee's full-power kicks and punches without breaking or falling apart, giving Lee the appropriate "feeling" when he hit it, while allowing Lee to use it with a partner so that a human element was involved.

Bruce Lee felt that the standard heavy bag is one of the best pieces of training equipment for developing power, stamina, and conditioning. He also had an extra-large heavy bag so that he could develop even more tremendous power by throwing full-power kicks into it. Lee would often hold the kicking shield for a new acquaintance who was unaware that Lee would later want to kick the shield.

Another way that Lee conditioned the body was by receiving blows from the medicine ball. The speed bag and the top and bottom bag were used to develop rhythm, timing, and distance in Lee's punches and kicks, Another of Lee's favorite pieces of training equipment was the focus gloves because it requires the use of a partner, it is extremely versatile, and it develops great accuracy in punches and kicks. He even punched paper suspended by a string to increase his timing and accuracy. Lee also constantly conditioned his hands by punching his small straw pad, his gravel and sandbox, and his famous three-canvas bags.

The men who were principally responsible for building much of the innovative equipment were James Lee, George Lee (in Oakland), and Herb Jackson (in Los Angeles), all of whom were Lee's students, George Lee and Herb Jackson built and modified most of the mobile equipment that Bruce Lee used, such as the protective gear, focus gloves, and various kicking shields, Bruce Lee used three kinds of kicking shields: a modified football tackle shield, a kicking board made of wood with handles attached to the back, and a thick, five-foot tall wooden shield that was held with seatbelts over the shoulder. Jackson, a construction engineer, padded the back of the latter kicking shield so that the person holding the shield would be protected from Bruce Lee's powerful kicks.

James Lee, a welder by trade, ingeniously utilized heavy automobile parts in the unique training equipment he built so that they were durable and flexible. For instance, his so-called "thousand-way fighting dummy" was supported by a strong spring from behind so that it would spring back after being kicked. His use of springs on the arms of his modified fighting dummy. on his finger jab and head target devices, and on his foot obstruction and shin-kick apparatus made it so that the targets would be flexible and bend, thereby giving

a more realistic feeling on the equipment. With all of the additional realistic training that Lee received from the use of his equipment, it is no wonder that he obtained such unmatched fighting skill. ☯

BRUCE LEE'S PERSONAL CHINATOWN WORKOUT

by Jerry Poteet & Fran Joseph

Few were lucky enough to study with Bruce Lee, and even fewer shared techniques during his development of jeet kune do. Jerry Poteet, however, not only spent time with Bruce, but he was given a personalized workout program.

Are you really ready to be a jeet kune do practitioner? Unlike many other methods of martial arts study, jeet kune do requires the dedication necessary to train at home on a daily basis; a commitment to honing your skills through supplemental training apart from classes, seminars, or lessons. In other words, jeet kune do training requires that you push yourself farther than you ever have before.

Back in the late '60s, when I was fortunate enough to be part of a small group of martial artists training with Bruce Lee, I realized that I was going to need an "edge" if I was to excel in Bruce's art of jeet kune do. Although I'd had three years training in kenpo karate, I found myself ill-prepared to make the transition to jeet kune do. In contrast to my previous martial arts study, where I had attempted to conform to the classical system, Bruce's training emphasized the development and self-expression of the individual. He constantly stressed that we were not to imitate him. but cultivate our own skills to the highest possible degree.

After a particularly frustrating workout, I asked my instructor what I could do to speed my progress, and he replied, "I'll have something for you at the next workout session." True to his word, when I arrived for class he handed me a personalized training program, and encouraged me to use it as a day-to-day home supplemental workout, along with basic "tool sharpening," as Bruce called kicks and punches. Several times during the course of my study with Bruce, I found myself "inspired" in the middle of the night, and got out of bed and stepped into my home gym. Once there, I would attempt to "problem-solve," whether it was on the wing chun dummy, the top and bottom bag, the roman chair, etc. In fact, I have found this program so effective that I still use it today and, like my instructor, I prefer to teach on a semiprivate basis so that I can personally monitor each student's needs and progress.

Starting with daily mobility, the only piece of equipment you need is a mirror. The push-shuffle, which resembles boxing footwork, is used primarily for "closing the gap," or bridging the distance between you and your opponent. The pendulum step is derived from fencing, and is used to close the distance with a kick. Lateral footwork is employed primarily to avoid the opponent's incoming attack, yet stay in close enough range to counterstrike.

Moving on to supplemental training, Bruce believed in training specific muscle groups, and thus emphasized developing those muscles (deltoid, triceps and forearm) that are utilized when actually delivering a punch. Note that in the program Bruce recommends padding the weight so that you are simultaneously developing your grip. Reverse curls done every other day build the forearms and elongate the biceps, while the wrist roller, when done properly, should produce a "burn" in the forearms. Also, you can include one that Bruce performed daily. This supplemental exercise requires only a broom, long stick, or staff: Hold the stick behind your head, resting it on each shoulder. Twist the body until you are in a right or left lead. This waist-twisting exercise is used to bring about the waist, shoulders and back motion into the delivery of a punch. The staff can also be used for isometric training. Employing a progressive exercise in three stages, this supplemental workout develops tremendous forward energy, which is used in delivering punches.

However, a day-to-day jeet kune do program must incorporate impact training. Making solid contact with hands and legs on a heavy bag, top and bottom bag, air shield, or if you have a training partner, focus mitts, are essential aspects of a jeet kune do workout. It is important that once a degree of proficiency is obtained, the equipment be used in an unpredictable, "spontaneous" manner, with the ranges and rhythm constantly changing, and not in a set pattern. Bruce once mentioned to me that he employed a variety of objects to hit so he would not become bored doing countless repetitions on the same surface. In fact, he once pulled a practical joke on me by asking me to hit his three "bean bags". The first one, which was filled with beans, was relatively easy, and gave me a false sense of confidence. The next bag was filled with sand, and I felt quite pleased with myself for flitting it soundly. With Bruce's encouragement, I hit the third bag, and yelped in pain. Chuckling, Bruce explained that this bag was filled with steel balls. The bean bags are used in jeet kune do training to develop a devastating close-range punch, with short rapid strikes controlling everything in their path. While most martial arts would have to rely on grappling or wrestling at close range, the jeet kune do exponent can explode with punches thrown from a distance of only six inches thanks to training on the wall-mounted bags. In any case, no matter what surface you hit (Bruce even hung a piece of paper from a chain), it is important to include impact training in your daily workout.

The optimum jeet kune do training program would include three days of supplemental workouts, and three days with a partner. Starting at kicking range, the shin guards can be used to apply the concept of the "longest weapon to the nearest target." Both partners wear shin guards, and when one advances, the other attacks by kicking his shin as he steps in. This phase of "impact-training" demonstrates the "stop-hit" concept of jeet kune do, since you are stopping, or interrupting, your opponent's attack before it is completed. The shin guards can also be used to train the foot-obstruct. When your partner moves to deliver a kick, you obstruct, or "stutter" his motion by simply raising your leg. Finally, the shin guards can be used to work kicks in hand range, such as the oblique kick.

If you have a partner, the focus mitts can be used to cultivate virtually every kick, punch and strike. Unlike the heavy bag or the air shield, which are used primarily for endurance through aerobic repetition (you can make gross motions and still have impact), the focus gloves are used for precision hitting and kicking, since the target is much smaller. Bruce was the first to recognize the advantage of training with the mitts, not only to represent constantly moving targets, but also to develop "focused," and therefore, explosive power in kicks and punches.

A workout partner is absolutely essential for the energy training phase of jeet kune do, since the development of sensitivity can only be acquired by contact with a partner who is continually changing the pressure in his movements. If you have some version of a wing chun dummy at home, you can use it to develop a heavy "bridging" action on the arms, and to practice the pulling (lap sao), trapping (pak sao) and punching with full contact. In contrast to a human training partner who would most likely be unwilling to absorb the punishment of daily full-contact trapping and hitting, the dummy can be used to bring about a progression of speed and power at a very close range. Although most martial artists do not have extensive equipment at home, for the serious jeet kune do practitioner, it is a requirement for building the skills essential to the arts. Therefore, the expense and use of home space is not a luxury, but a necessity. Much of Bruce's cat-like movement came from a rigorous stretching program, which he detailed on my workout sheet. When he presented it to me, I enthusiastically looked at his recommendations, until my eyes caught "alternate splits on chair." Noticing the incredulous look on my face, Bruce shot me a glance and said "something to shoot for." That was how Bruce was, but he never expected anything from his students that he couldn't do himself. ☯

THE ART OF JEET KUNE DO: FAST, POWERFUL AND DECEPTIVE

by Rodger Shimatsu

Dan Inosanto is a quiet-spoken and dedicated martial artist teaching the art of Jeet Kune Do in Los Angeles area. With a broad background in the fighting arts, he reveals some basic in Kung Fu and Karate training.

JEET KUNE DO

"LINE UP TEN PUNTERS and let them perform their kicking style without the football. Can you honestly judge who is the better kicker, or which is the better kick, by just studying their form? The real test of a punt is how far and accurately the football can be kicked. And yet, this is exactly what many seals of Karate and Kung Fu are doing—they are teaching how to kick without the football. In other words, deluding their students as well as themselves, Karate and Kung Fu instructors are attempting to teach how to fight without actually fighting," Inosanto says,

This is an ex-kenpo instructor speaking-out on his first love, Karate. He's a 33-year-old man who has studied Jujitsu, Kenpo, Kung Fu and Karate. He now studies Jeet Kune Do (pronounced "jeet-koon-doe") under Bruce Lee. This is Dan Inosanto exploding some hard-hitting thoughts and provoking ideas upon the Karate scene today.

A physical education teacher in the Los Angeles area, Inosanto is a quiet-mannered man. He's not a loud talker and is reluctant to offend others. He's married and lives with his wife and three-year-old child (with one more on the way) in a modern house in Carson, California.

It is obvious Inosanto is dedicated to the martial arts and on first impression he seems to like everything about them. Once the surface is scratched, however, one finds Inosanto has some very definite ideas on what's good and bad in the martial arts. His delivery is soft and his voice subdued, but after the interview, it feels like a huge tank has rumbled past, shaking the very foundation of one's philosophy of karate.

Having studied many styles, Inosanto has a broad background in the martial arts; it began when he was in the paratroopers and started taking the Army's self-defense course in jujitsu in 1959. The next year he graduated to karate. The style he and the others in that loose group of enthusiasts were taught depended on which instructor was teaching that day and where he had studied. The course was a crazy blend of styles: Japanese, Korean or Okinawan.

At that time he was stationed at Fort Campbell in the Strategic Army Corps and his group studied Karate three to five times a week under the sponsorship of Henry Slomanski. Reflecting on his Karate training while in the Army, Inosanto said, "The exposure to the various schools in the beginning taught me not to be one-sided because everyone had their own philosophies and each school seemed to have its good points and bad points."

'After Inosanto was discharged from the paratroopers, he moved to the Southern California area where he began taking Kenpo. Why did he choose kenpo, was the question. "I was very impressed with a kenpo student I met at Fort Campbell—I can't remember his name off hand. He wasn't stiff and he seemed freer with his movements, He was graceful, smooth and fast. He had studied kenpo in Hawaii and had a brown belt. I liked the way he moved and decided to take up kenpo when I got out of the service.

"In 1961, I started taking kenpo from Ed Parker at his Pasadena school. At that time, kenpo reached my expectations of what I was seeking in karate. I was looking for self-defense and also a body conditioning sport. I guess I got carried away with it, I became fascinated by the martial arts field and how there could be so many different ways of fighting."

CLIQUE-ISH KARATE FACTIONS

Even with the variety of fighting arts, especially in karate, Inosanto found himself in a quandary. "I was puzzled by the attitudes of the instructors and their schools here in Southern California. At Fort Campbell we were learning many different styles at the same time and we felt this was good. There was a give and take of information concerning karate. The various instructors came together to try to help one another. In Los Angeles it was a different story. I never realized how clique-ish Karate factions could be. I couldn't understand this and it made me even more curious about Karate as a whole. I couldn't believe instructors could be so hostile to one another and refuse to share knowledge.

截拳道

"When I first began taking Kenpo, the instructors and students there would run down the Japanese stylists. So I went to a Japanese Karate school out of curiosity and there they ran down the other Karate styles I was studying. Looking back at it as a whole, Shotokan puts a lot of emphasis on power, while in Kenpo they put their stock in speed."
As in football there ae various ways to run with the ball and Dan Inosanto used this analogy to drive home his point. "Take the three types of runners in football. A good runner can either have speed, power or deceptiveness. The runner can use any 'two combinations of the three, but very rarely can one be found with all three outstanding characteristics. Karate schools may stress as many as two, but it's hard to find a school that stresses all three: speed, power and deceptiveness.
"It wasn't until I started learning Jeet Kune Do under Bruce Lee, I found a style that used all three important aspects of fighting—a style that was fast, powerful and deceptive. Bruce Lee was able to take all the pieces of the Karate puzzle I was wrestling with in my own mind and make them

fit together in an integrated system, It seemed to me the other Karate and Kung Fu schools were trying to fit everyone into a size 38 coat, regardless of an individual's size, speed, build, reaction-time reflexes or anything.

"In boxing, everyone can't be a Marciano because everyone doesn't have the rugged build needed to wade in and take a punch, or have the ability to give one. Not everyone can be a Cassius Clay because they don't have his speed or his deceptive coordination. Looking at each person as an individual, it's not possible to take a 98-pound weakling and make him into another Marciano or Clay.

"Karate in general doesn't take the individual into consideration because the system stresses everyone must do the same things in the exact same way. The Karate student becomes a factory product—a molded replica of the instructor. The student sometimes comes out good, sometimes bad, sometimes better than the instructor, but it's hit-or-miss depending on the individual."

EXCELL OUTSIDE OF STYLE

To Dan Inosanto the individual is very important because, he says, "A man doesn't excel because of his style. It's only when a man can go outside of the bounds set by his system that he excells. If a martial artist can practice in a style without being bound and limited to his particular school, then and only then can he be liberated to fit in with any type of opponent. A great majority of instructors, however, bind their practitioners and brain-wash them into believing only their school of training is best. This is especially true of Kung Fu."

Dan Inosanto met Bruce Lee in 1964 at the first International Karate Championships. He got to know Bruce pretty well in the few weeks they traveled from one dojo to another all over California. During this period, Inosanto was introduced to Bruce Lee's philosophy. He wanted to study under him but Lee had to return to the Orient, so Inosanto began taking Kung Fu from other instructors in the Los Angeles area. He tried different schools, often studying at two to three schools at the same time. He soon discovered what his training was a far from what Bruce Lee was

talking and teaching. "To me," Inosanto says "what they were teaching – the forms, the blocking, the stances, etc. are posturings – wasn't realistic. The means to get good self-defense became the ends. The posture and form of the body are the ultimate end and not necessarily the efficiency in a real combat situation.
Their teachings didn't seem to have any direct relationship to self-defense, although it probably taught me to be graceful and helped with my coordination, posture and smooth, correct body movements."

ENLIGHTENING BUT FRUSTATING

Bruce Lee returned to the United States to star as Kato in the television series "The Green Hornet." Concurrently he opened two kwoon (schools), one in Los Angeles, the other in Oakland, California. Dan began studying under Bruce in L.A. and he recalls it as frustrating but enlightening. "I had been practicing and instructing in a kenpo Karate style for some years and I felt, at that point, it gave me the most freedom and variety of moves. By that time, I had stumbled across many partial truths and I had become more aware of workable and unworkable techniques. Being a die-hard kenpo man, I found myself confused and frustrated. I began to actually rebel against Jeet Kune Do.
"I was bound by loyalty to my former instructor and to his style. Looking back on it, I really didn't want to see the truth in self-defense. I began to mentally criticize the informal and "unstylized" way JKD (Jeet Kune Do) moved, kicked, punched and trained. Yet, I found myself using what I had learned and liking it better than kenpo, finding it more functional, powerful, faster, freer, and above all the easiest style to express."
Just what is Jeet Kune Do? Dan says it is the art of "fitting-in" with all types of opponents and a way of expressing oneself in combat. Many of Bruce Lee's students are former Karate and Kung Fu stylists and they maintain JKD's style-less style of combat is 50 to 100 years ahead of its time. Dan anticipates Karate will continue to progress and will someday reach the beginning stages of ideas and principles set forth by Bruce Lee today. As explained, Jeet Kune Do is not an organization or even a style

in which students can affiliate. The principles of JKD are stated simply as self-defense, because everything is so dependent on what the opponent will do. It's almost like an exchange of ideas between two combatants with the communication being done with offensive and defensive techniques instead of words. The action must flow like a conversation and the two combatants must be in tune with each other as the fighting reaches its climax and one or the other is taken down, knocked out, or placed in an otherwise helpless situation.

LIKENED TO KICKBOXING

Spectators watching a Jeet Kune Do practice session come away with differing views. The sparring has been described as vicious but polished street fighting. At other times, it looks like boxing, sometimes Wrestling and even Thai kickboxing. The kicks resemble karate, but in a more informal, livelier and freer manner. The practitioners use 12 or 16-ounce gloves and they are encouraged to punch and kick below the waist, especially to the shin, knee and thigh areas.

Comparing Jeet Kune Do to other fighting arts, Dan observes, "Karate is mainly a stylized form of punching, kicking and striking. Judo is a throwing, grappling and choking sport. Wrestling is grappling and boxing is a punching sport. All of these arts or sports are highly effective in their range of distance, What boxers call the "in-fighting" range is never reached in Karate tournament free styling because the referee usually separates the combatants before they reach this stage of fighting. But in reality, isn't this where real fighting begins?

"If a good boxer learns Jeet Kune Do's bridging (transition and moving-in techniques), he needs only his hands to be effective. A proficient wrestler, using Jeet Kune Do's techniques, can tie-up the majority of the classical martial artists. If the wrestler is sharp with his grappling range, he will be more than effective. An experienced fencer, if he learns Jeet Kune Do techniques, can become very skilled with his outside range.

"A great many karateka have the tendency to belittle, degrade and look down on judo, boxing and wrestling as being inferior to karate. To me it is like a football coach who uses and believes in his split-T formation, then starts to belittle other formations and styles such as the T, wing-T, slot-T, or the I formations. A good football coach, even if he believes in his own style of play, will study and learn how to defend against those offenses. I believe a good martial artist should likewise prepare for the wild street fighter, the wrestler, the slugger, the judoka."

To illustrate the importance of preparing for all types fighting situations, Dan likes to quote Bruce Lee, who in turn quoted Sun Tzu's book The Art of War, written around 500 B.C., "Know your enemy and know yourself and you can fight a hundred battles without disaster."

Explaining this statement, Dan affirms, "Some people think they know themselves but in reality they only know their weak points and not their strong points, or vice versa. Others are intelligent in knowing themselves, but ignorant in knowing other."

"To quote a certain football coach, "Every system of football has strong points and weak points in its structure. Every football coach believes in his methods of training and drilling. The training and drills should be as close to reality as possible and all drills

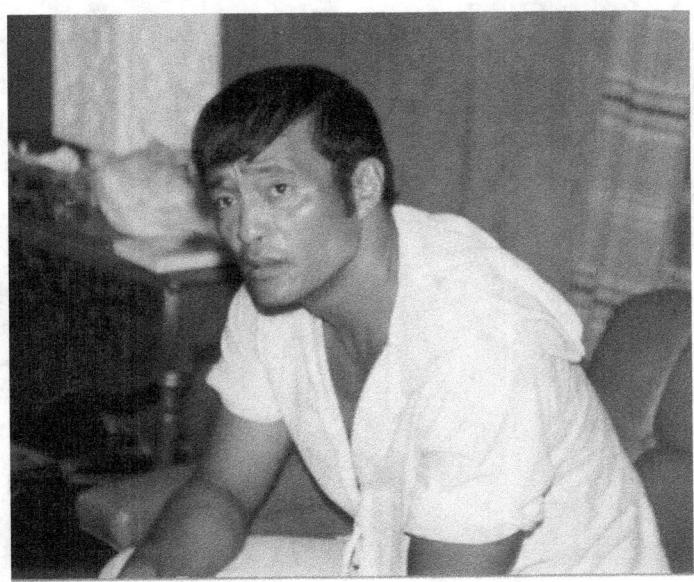

should be as close to game-like conditions as possible'" he adds.
The quiet spoken Bruce Lee student and Jeet Kune Do instructor always kept his conversation in low tone. He never seemed excited or tight with his expressions. It was ironic how Dan Inosanto could demolish this writer's beliefs in such a quote that seems to sum up his own philosophy and the principles of Bruce Lee's Jeet Kune Do: "Totality and freedom of expression toward the ultimate reality of combat should be the goal of martial artists. To achieve this, absorb what is useful; reject what is useless; add what is specifically your own." ○

THE REAL SECRET OF JKD: MAKING BRUCE LEE'S NOTES WORK FOR YOU

by Chris Kent

"There's no denying that the elbow is one of the many tools used in JKD, because Bruce Lee even lists it in his notes which were later published as The Tao of Jeet Kune Do. But is there anywhere in the text that tells you how to throw the elbow?"

Most of the time those who have read the book think about it for a minute and then shake their heads no. They're surprised when I tell them, sure it does. I then go on to explain that, no, it doesn't tell you that an elbow should be thrown in a 63 degree diagonal downward arc and that your other hand should be placed in the middle of your forehead, et cetera. But what it does do is give you the underlying principles that define and govern the use of the technique–principles such as the blow should be non-telegraphic and delivered with an economy of motion while maintaining good defensive coverage, and that you should recover quickly in order to either continue the attack or to defend, if necessary. So while it may not give an exact technical description or breakdown, it does tell how to throw an elbow or a punch or kick or any technique, for that matter.

In order to get the most out of JKD it is essential to know how to make Bruce Lee's notes work for you–how to bring them to life and use them to help you achieve your fullest potential as a martial artist, regardless of the particular style or method you may practice.

Bruce Lee's notes have been likened to guideposts, or clues, that can lead an individual to their own self-expression in the martial arts. But guideposts do a person little or no good if they don't know how to read or interpret them correctly. So the first thing that needs to be understood is how to study Lee's notes. This is not as easy as it sounds. When reading Bruce Lee's notes, three intrinsic principles should guide your study. These principles may, in the beginning, require several separate readings but in time can be done concurrently:

1) Understand the notes: You need to comprehend thoroughly and perceive clearly the nature of what you're reading. What are the particular notes you are studying saying?

2) Interpret the notes: The word "interpret" in this case means, "to bring out or explain the meaning of something." In other words, what do the notes you're studying mean? In martial arts it seems that many times people rush to the application stage of Lee's teachings and bypass the interpretation stage. They want to know what the technique means to them before they understand what Lee intended it to mean.

3) Evaluate the notes: To evaluate something means to judge or determine its worth or quality. In other words, is the given principle right or wrong for them? Is it valid or not? Unfortunately, many people tend to skip over the first two principles and jump right into evaluating Lee's notes. They judge a particular concept to be right or wrong before they understand what it says or before they interpret its meaning.

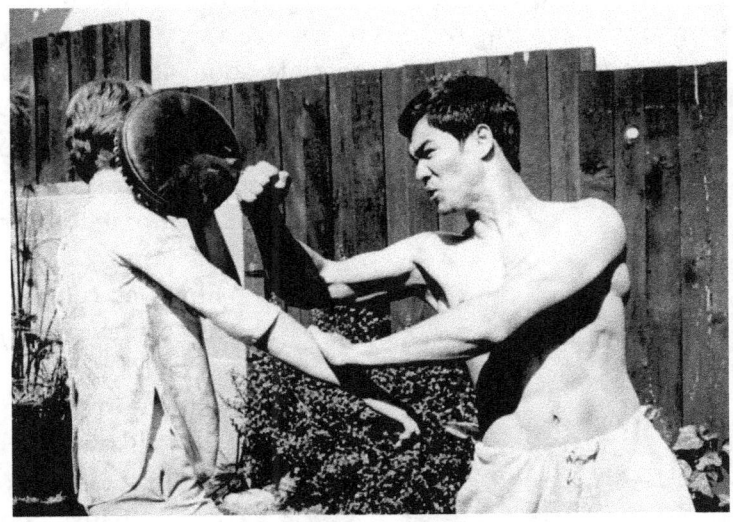

The above three intrinsic principles are, however, by themselves, inadequate. To study Bruce Lee's notes successfully and get the most out of them, a person also needs three important extrinsic aids:

1) Experience: Experience is the only way to interpret and relate what has been read. A person who has little or no experience in martial arts and/or philosophy is going to be at a distinct disadvantage understanding, interpreting and evaluating Bruce's notes. I may be able to tell you what I like or don't like about a particular painting by a master like Van Gogh, but I will not be able to interpret and evaluate it like a person who has an education and background in fine arts. Experience that has been understood and reflected upon informs and enlightens your study.

2) Other books: Books that precede or advance the subject you're studying can be very significant. Very often books or notes can have greater meaning when they are read in relation to other writings. I have had the privilege of perusing the books in Bruce Lee's personal library at great length. But I have also established my own library which includes books on martial arts, Western fencing, physical fitness, kinesiology, philosophy and psychology. Studying and analyzing these books has helped to increase my understanding of Lee's notes. Lee always approached a subject wanting to know as much as possible about it and with an open mind ready to absorb new information. If he were alive today, there is no doubt that he would avail himself of the most up-to-date information including books, videos, films, et cetera., related to whatever subject interested him or that he was studying. We should all do likewise.

3) Live discussion: The final intrinsic aid is live discussion; which means the interaction that occurs among individuals as they pursue a particular course of study. When you discuss and debate certain issues, techniques or philosophical attitudes relating to JKD, many times new insights emerge that might have never occurred without this type of exchange.

As important as it is to successfully research Lee's notes, however, it is equally important to know how to use them. The first step of this process is to read Lee's notes without trying to fit them into established categories. The goal here is to simply grasp the content of the material, the essence of what is being presented, and to understand it. Expect to hear new things in new ways when you read the notes at different times and don't be concerned if you don't get some things in the first reading. It may take several readings before you fully comprehend something. All of us have had the experience of reading something over and over and then, all of a sudden, understanding what it means. This "Wow, now I get it!" experience of understanding catapults us onto a new level of growth and freedom. You might find it useful each time you read the notes to use a differently colored pen to mark certain things that stand out to you. It is also helpful to keep a notebook or journal handy to jot down thoughts and impressions that occur while reading.

The next step is to investigate why Lee drew a particular essence from an art or why he chose to absorb something into his own art. It's important here to recognize the difference between absorbing and simply adding. Bruce did not add something simply for the sake of adding it. To "absorb" means "to take in and incorporate; to assimilate." To "add" means, "to take in and unite so as to increase the number, number, size, et cetera." Ask yourself, "What is it about this particular technique or principle that Bruce Lee felt was useful or valid to what he was doing?" Analyze it by breaking it down into its parts and examining it to find out its function or interrelationship with other material in Lee's notes.

The third step is to apply what you're studying. Theory without application means nothing. You've got to take the material you're investigating onto the floor and test it. You need to see if and how well it works under pressure and in realistic situations. Keep in mind, too, that just because you may not be able to do it or use it at that particular moment, it doesn't mean that it's not valid, or that it's no good. If your instructor shows you how to do a spinning rear kick and then you try it and miss the target completely, don't immediately respond with, "Oh that's stupid. It doesn't work."

截拳道

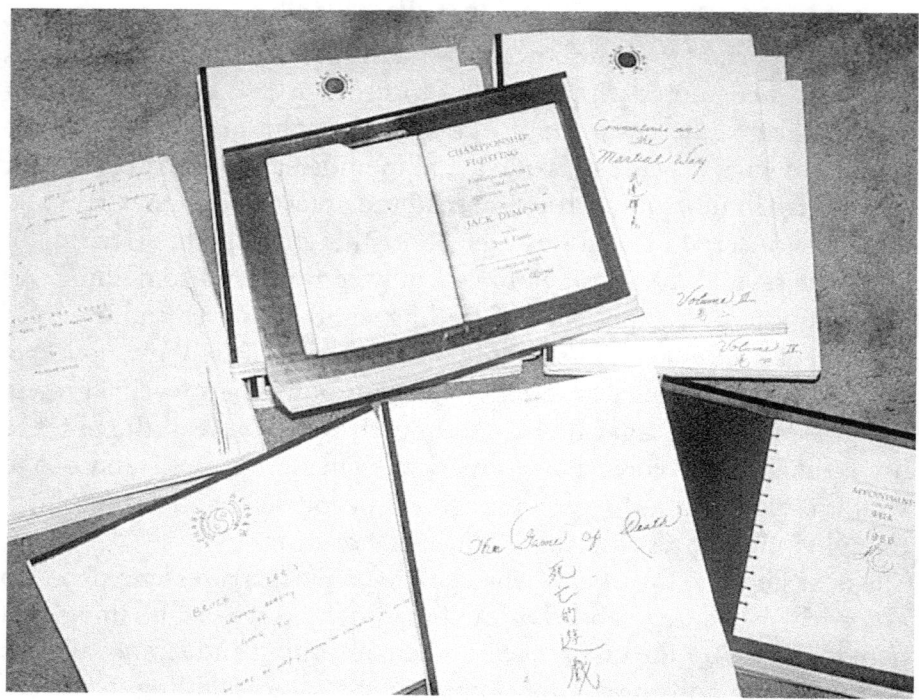

The final step is evaluation, in which you judge the value of the material for a given purpose. Ask yourself, "Is this particular principle or technique valid or not? How does it relate to me? Does it have an application to what I'm doing?" If, for example, the particular style of martial art you practice doesn't believe in the use of hand immobilization attacks, then sensitivity training such as chi sao may have no application for you. Keep in mind, though, that just because something might not have an application for you, it doesn't mean it won't have an application for someone else. The following are some potential pitfalls you should try to avoid when studying and/or using Bruce Lee's notes:

1) Simply memorizing and regurgitating Lee's words, ideas, et cetera. Anybody can repeat someone else's words by rote. Remember, it's not how much fixed knowledge or information you have accumulated, it's what you can use and apply that counts.

2) Taking the material in Bruce's notes to be the "Bible" of martial arts. Some people approach JKD very dogmatically and with the fundamentalist view that "If it's not in The Tao of JKD, or if it's not in Bruce's writings, then it's not JKD. This is the very antithesis of Lee's teachings. Bruce was a seeker of truth. To him, each thing he wrote down represented a truth, not the truth. No one has a monopoly on truth. There is no "one way."
3) Thinking that Bruce's notes are all there is to his way of martial arts.
4) Adding your own interpretation to Bruce Lee's material. I am not saying do not interpret Bruce's material. I am simply reminding you to keep things in proper context. Many times people read something with an eye towards finding support for what they, themselves, are doing. For example, in Bruce's notes it states, "Investigate into fighting from ground…develop such mastery that one can fight safely from ground." But Lee doesn't make a point of telling you to study any particular style of ground-fighting or martial art which includes ground-fighting. The point is to hear what Bruce Lee is saying, not what we want him to say.
5) Solidifying Bruce's guideposts into laws. Bruce changed his mind about publishing his notes when he came to the realization that trying to

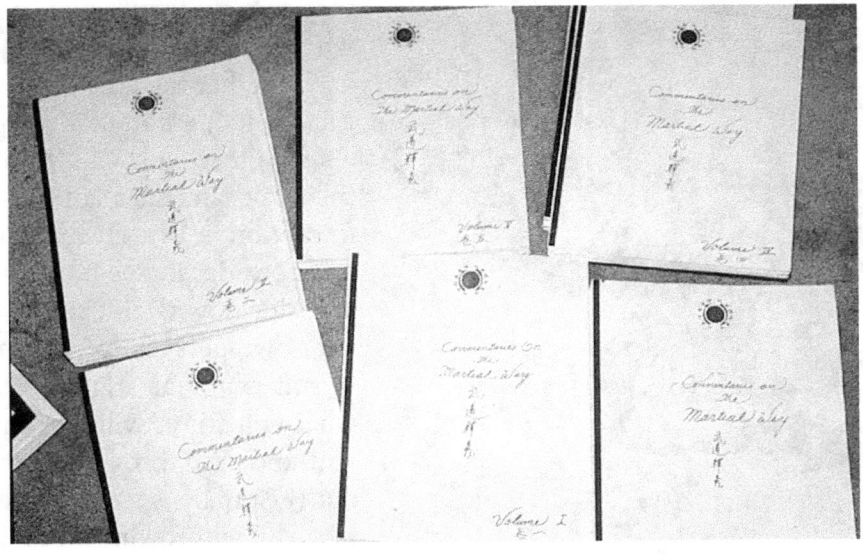

encapsulate fighting into words was like trying to capture something on paper that is alive and constantly changing. It was, he concluded, "like attempting to tie a pound of water into a manageable shape." Don't calcify what should remain alive and growing.

6) Starting from a conclusion. Remember, to taste someone else's tea you must first empty your cup of preconceived ideas, notions, et cetera. Begin with an open mind.

Bruce Lee's notes are like an extension of Bruce himself. They describe the direction of his studies and shed light on his own process of intellectual growth and development as a martial artist. As such, they can serve as a pipeline to his ways of thinking, feeling, and researching. Bruce's notes can also act as a navigational guide, like a compass, which can help direct you to where you want to be as a martial artist. If you know

how to use a compass, even if the terrain changes, a road becomes blocked, or a detour arises, you can still remain on course toward your ultimate destination. In order to do that, however, you must know where it is that you want to go and whether the goal is physical, mental, emotional or spiritual. Once you know that, then you can take all of the information in Bruce Lee's notes and consider it, debate it, turn it upside down, look at it from your own perspective, refine it to suit you, rearrange it, keep what you think will work for you, and even throw some of it out (just make sure you know why you're throwing it out).

THE JEET KUNE DO ARCHIVES

Each of the following fighting sequences, while not specifically scripted by Bruce Lee in The Tao of June Kune Do, still follows his precepts and principles. Another JKD practitioner, given the same exact confrontational situation, would probably come up with an entirely different fighting sequence to deal with the opponent. I'm sure Bruce, himself, would have handled the situation differently. Does the fact that different people are using different techniques mean that someone is "wrong" and someone is "right" in their approach? Not at all. It simply means that we are doing JKD, which is to respond to a situation by using what works best for each of us. Lee's notes make this very clear.

Don't allow anyone to simply hand the truth to you. Take an experiential attitude and find out for yourself what works for you. See Bruce Lee's notes as a literary work in progress, not as something which was finished or completed. Remember, "If you understand it and can use it, it belongs to no one; it's yours." ◯

DAN INOSANTO

JUN FAN: LIBERATION PART 1

For a time while he was a student at the University of Washington (circa 1962), Bruce seriously contemplated a nationwide chain of kung-fu schools. Several years later, when his spiraling "Kato" fame would have certainly censured the success of such vesture, he discarded the idea, saying this was not the way to bring out the art. And then as his movie career started to break, he realized here was the proper medium for enlightening the public to the true meaning behind the martial disciplines.
In the intervening years, though, Bruce did establish three kwoon in Seattle, Oakland, and Los Angeles. Yet all were no signs anywhere on the outside so identify them,
When Bruce first came to America from Hong Kong, he didn't waste any time in adjusting his system to fit the new environment. Indeed, he was astutely aware the compact movements and close--range tactics of Wing Chun, which were ideal for the overcrow-

ded conditions in the Far East, were ill-raised to the sprawling metropolitan areas of San Francisco and Seattle – his first two stops.

To further illustrate the profound impact environment can have on one's fighting method; I would mentions there exists a style of Filipino sword fighting which teaches its practitioners to respond to as encounter by immediately dropping to the ground is a settled posture.

Ridiculous, you say? Sure, if the assault takes place on solid footing, such as a parking lot or a deserted street corner. But there is as usually heavy rainfall in the region where this style comes from, which leaves the ground so madly and slippery that after the first stroke the practitioner invariably slips anyway.

As he began to realize wing chun placed too much emphasis on close-range or in-fighting (hand techniques) fighting. Bruce incorporated some of the more refused kicks of the Northern Chinese style. And it is this hybrid form of wing chun we refer to today as jun fan.

Originally, though, the term jun fan was used to designate the school – not art – of Bruce lee. You see, Jun Fan Gung Fu latitude was the name Bruce gave to the see commercial establishment in Seattle, Oakland, and Los Angeles, and later on meaning again shifted somewhat to mean "the place where jeet kune do trains." Then once jet kune do was firmly established as in entity is itself, jun fan was locked upon as the art that Bruce taught in Seattle and Oakland – which was more wing chun oriented with additional kicking techniques. Jeet kune do, then, is really a liberated form of jun fan, it encompasses much more. But jun fan is still part of the total art. You can't separate the two.

His wife, Linda, recalls Bruce started impromptu teaching in the Seattle area even before he was officially enrolled at the University of Washington. Blessed with superior talent and a dynamic personality, it's not surprising he attracted a highly visible –if small – group of devotes. Among them was a Japanese American named Taky Kimura, then well into his 30s (Bruce was not yet 20). Taky recalled how he first because acquainted with Bruce and his art.

"I was taking judo around 1959. And I got hurt two or three times so it was pretty frustrating. In fact, I was running around with my arm is a sing when one of the follows that knew Bruce dropped by the supermarket where I was working. He told me he'd meet his young man from Hong Kong who was phenomenal" Of course, I took it with a grain of salt because by that time I'd seen a little bit of everything and I couldn't believe there was anything more to be sees. During that time these guy were working out in backyards and in public parks. So, I went to one of the athletic field down by the university, and that's where I first met him. I was so impressed when he unleashed his power and speed that I asked if I could join the group and for about a year we met for several hours on Sunday. After class we would go to a Chinese restaurant and listen to Bruce philosophy over a cup of tea.

By this time, too, Bruce was becoming increasingly distasted with his setup at Ruby Chow's. A Seattle restaurant owner and promises figure in local politics, she had contested to let him stay in one of the rooms above her restaurant in exchange for his services as a busboy and waiter. But, as Taky recalls, "Ruby Chow could be a very domineering price and, in fact, Bruce could be too. So I think there was a little personality clash, and he recognized it was time to get out of there. But Bruce was also a very proud young man and felt he had to make it on his own rather than become a burden on his father by having him send money. And since he was endowed with all this knowledge of martial arts, the guy is the group he was training gathered together and decided to open up a school and try to get some money for him."

Taky also remembers trying to impress upon the young instructor in spite of his age, he was Brue's most dedicated and determined student – and how it eventually paid off. "I was working twice as hard as the other guys," he explains "because I was much older than these. One day I was looking out of the corner of my eye to see if this made any impression on Bruce. Of Course, he knew exactly what I was doing and heard him say to one of the other guys "He'll sever make it." Naturally this drove me to try that much harder. And even though I was very clumsy. I think he saw I was very dedicated and sincere in what I was trying to do.

"Then he started to work with me and kind look me aside and above me not a lot of extra things. The next thing I knew he was grooming me to be his assistant. As time wore on, I did become his assistant instructor, and more or less conducted all his classes.

The first school was down in Chinatown, simply because, I suppose, we were more familiar with that area than anywhere else and it was a smaller group at that time. Shortly the rather, we recognized the limitations of the Chinatown location and since he was going to the university, we felt there would be more potential out that way.

So the Jun Fan Gung Fu Institute was relocated along University Way, prospecting Bruce and assistant to step up the demonstration they had been giving on campus and at various fraternity become it began of drumming up additional business initially they were quite successful and maintained what Taky terms "plash" headquarters in a ground floor studio that was part of a brand new apartment complex. The excellent fee was $22 per month and $17 for juniors.

During one of Bruce's early demonstrations, a Japanese karate black belt took exception to hit outspoken opinions and ideas and issued a challenge. Bruce tried to explain it was not his intention to downgrade any particular system but rather to dairy his own methods,. But the karate expert persisted in demanding a bout, telling the sizable crowd that Bruce didn't "know anything. Don't listen to this guy." So Bruce was forced to accept the challenge, and the two departed for a nearby handball court.

The challenge wasted first to establish certain ground rules, such as so punching to the lead or pros, and going against his usual practice.

Bruce accommodation him to as acceptable degree. Still the outcome of the brief (11 seconds) match was server in doubt. The karate man opened with a strong kick which Bruce effortlessly avoided before punching his opponent from one end of the court so the other. When it was all over, the challenge lay in a pool of blood. And, as Taky explains, Bruce was quite magnanimous about the whole affair. The karate guy was out of school for a whole work after the fight and when he cause back, he sold all his friends he'd been in a car accident. Rather than embarrass him any further, Bruce just let to go at that"

JUN FAN: LIBERATION PART 2

Taky Kimura says the Jun Fan Institute continued until around 196, or about the time of Bruce Lee's marriage to pretty blade coed Linda Emery. By then there was a considerable turnover of students, and Bruce decided the best thing to do would be to return to Chinatown with a small core dedication followers. "It was a good move at that point," explains Taky, "because shortly after that he left Seattle and I wouldn't have been able to keep up that big place by myself.

"Bruce and I were discussing it one day after he had moved to California, and we decided not to promote the school as such. He said; "Why don't you just close it down? After all, what's life about than to have some close friends around who you trust?" So I continued on that basis. Today, we operate only as a very exclusive private club."

Less than a year after the close of the Seattle kwoon, the new yards had moved into James Lee's house in Oakland. A widely recognized martial artist in his own right, James was probably the first classically trained kung-fu man in America to recognize and appreciate Bruce's extraordinary ability. In fact, it was at James' suggestion that Bruce had been asked to appear only months before at Ed Parker's Intentional Karate Championship, which proved to be major turning point in his career.

Actually it was fate that originally brought James and Bruce together near the end of 1962.

As it turns out, the pair was introduced through James' relatives who had been taking dancing lessons from Bruce on and off since his arrival from Hong Kong in the 1950s. (Bruce's stay in San Francisco was a short one. He supported himself by teaching the cha cha before accepting Ruby Chow's offer of steady employment). Allen Joe, who grew up with James and was a good friend of Bruce's, explains, "James' brother Robert was taking dancing lessons and during intermissions, Bruce gave a demonstration of wing chun. So he went home and told James that Bruce had put on a pretty good show. At that time James paid so attention; we were taking over classical style and felt like hotshots in kung-fu. Then James said to me, "Since you're going to Seattle"- this was for the World's Fair in 1962 – 'why don't you check this guy out and see how good he is?'

"When I got to Seattle," Allen Joe conceives, "I looked him up at Ruby Chow's restaurant. I waited until after I that sight, then finally he showed up. I was sitting there having a smooch, and in walked Bruce all dressed up real sharp. No smile. He meant have been wondering what in the heck I was doing there. So right away I mentioned Bob's same and be relaxed. We started talking kung-fu and went out back where he told me to through my classical motions. Then be said real calmly. That's so good. Now try it again." And I went flying all over the place. I was really impressed. After that he went through his routine on the wooden dummy (mock jong), which he had set up in the parking lot behind the restaurant. And I was even more impressed watching him work on the dummy. He was so smooch that everything I had learned seemed stiff and clumsy in comparison.

"After I returned home, Bruce wrote me a letter, and about two weeks later, James wrote him and he came Dows for visit. Ever since then he and James became good friends. Bruce started teaching James his version of wing chun, and James said: "Allen, this guy is good. He's unreal" that was the beginning. Then James and Bruce continued training together and eventually opened a gym."

The gym Allen Joe refers to because the second Jun Fan Institute. (It was located on Broadway and has long since been torn down and replaced by a Pontiac dealership). Like Bruce, James had little patience for sties in the martial arts commonly who still chung to the outmoded belief that the secret of kung-fu should not be revealed to non-Chinese. Both men agreed to accept students from all races in their kwoon, which caused resentment and antagonism among some of the die-hand traditionalisms. Bruce felt by creating his own method he could avoid the fierce interschool rivalries which had been a way of life in Hong Kong. This was only wishful thinking, however. And one oof the first experts to attempt to put Bruce in his place was a kung-fu master from across the Bay in San Francisco's Chinatown.

Until the clash with the Bay Area man. Bruce had for the most part been

context to improve and expand his original wing chun style. All that changes, though, when he begun to dissect the fight and realized that his rather lack hunter performance (the fight should have lasted only seconds) was due in large measure to his thick-headed adherence to a certain style. In addition, as Bruce confessed to me some years later, he was usually winded near the end which proved to him he was in less--than-per feet shape. So partly because he recognized once and for all limitations of wing chun, and partly out of a growing appreciation of the need for proper conditioning – Bruce began to intensify his search for the ultimate reality in combat. And if there was one thing he had training, it was that the myriad forms of martial arts relied on styles that were essentially incomplete. Or as Linda Lee succinctly observes in her fascinating and informative book, "Bruce Lee; The Man Only I Knew."
 "Each had its own forms, movements and so on and each practitioner went into battle believing he had all the answer and for that reason he (Bruce) refused to call jeet kune do a "style" which he felt would be to limit it. As it was therefore, it possessed neither rules, a set number of forms or movements nor a set number of techniques."

THE BIRTH OF JKD

It all began in the early part of 1968 while Bruce Lee and I were driving along in the car. We were talking about fencing. Western fencing, Bruce said the most efficient means of countering in fencing was stop-hit. A stop- hit is when you do not parry and then counter; it's all done in one step. When the opponent attacks, you intercept his move with a thrust or hit of your own. It is designed to score a hit in the midst of the attacker's action, and is the highest and most economical of all the counters.
Then Bruce said, "We should call our method the 'stop-hitting fist style,' or the "intercepting fist style,"
"What would that be in Chinese?" I asked.
Jeet kune do means the way of stopping fist, or the way of the intercep-

ting fist. So, instead of blocking and then hitting, our main concept is to dispense with blocking completely, and instead to intercept and hit. We realize this cannot be done all the time, but this is the main theme.

Up until 1967 our method was called "jun fan" kung-fu, which was modification of various techniques from northern praying mantis, southern praying mantis, choy li fut, eagle claw. Western boxing hung gar. Thai boxing, wrestling, judo, jujitsu and several northern kung-fu styles. It is obvious that wing chun was the nucleus and all the other methods evolved around it.

It was during this time that Bruce developed his particular styles of kicking, modified from the northern styles of kung-fu and gravity improved by the way he trained for it.

In later years be became sorry he never coined the seem jeet kune do because he felt that it, too, was limiting, and according to Bruce. "There is no such thing as a style if you totally understand the roots of combat."

The term "JKD" came about naturally, because Bruce used to abbreviate much of his material, such as "HIA," "ABC," "ABD," "SAA," PIA."

One day I said to him, "This JKD is fantastic."

He said, "Hey, I like this term JKD," and he used it as a shortcut for jeet kune do. In our personal conversations, we used "JKD" as a term for something very good, out of this world, unique, or very fast" So, for instance, we could be driving along and see a restaurant we liked and say,

"Yeah, the food at that place is JKD."

Or,

"That movie I saw last night was JKD"

Or,

"Mmmmm, his singing is JKD."

Or,

"Wow, that painting is JKD"

However, Bruce also said, "JKD is just a name, don't fuss over it"

AS EXPLANATION OF THE JKD EMBLEM

Instead of opposing force by force, a JKD man complete his opponent's movement by "accepting" his flow of energy as he aims it, and defeats him by "borrowing" his own force. To reconcile oneself to the changing movement of the opponent, a JKD man should first understand the true meaning of yin/yang, the basic structure of JKD.

JKD is based on the symbol of the yin and yang, a pair of mutually complementary and interdependent in this universe. In the symbol; the yin and yang are interlocking parts of on whole, each containing the qualities of its complementariness. Etymologically, the characters of yin and yang mean darkness and light. The ancient character of yin, the dark part of the circle, it a drawing of clouds and hill. Yin can represent anything in the universe, such as negativeness, passiveness, gentleness, internal, insubstantially, femaleness, moon, darkness and light. The other complementary half of the circle is yang, which in its ancients form is anything as positiveness, activeness, firmness, external, substantially, maleness, sun, brightness and day.

The common mistake of most martial artists is to identify these two forces, yin and yang, as dualistic (thus the so-called soft style and the firm style). Yin/yang is one in separate force of one unceasing interplay of movement. They are conceived of as essentially one, or as two consisting forces of one indivisible whole. They are neither cause nor effect, but should be looked at as sound and echo, or light and shadow. If this oneness is viewed as two separate entities, realization of the ultimate reality of JKD won't be achieved. In reality, things are whole and cannot be separate into two parts. When I say the heat makes me perspire, the heat and perspiring are just one process as they are coexistent and the one could not exist but for the other. If a person riding a bicycle wishes to go somewhere, he cannot pump on both pedals at the same time. To go forward, he has to pump on one pedal and release other. So the movement of gong forward requires this oneness of pumping and releasing and vice versa, each being the cause and result of the other. Things do have their complementariness, and complementariness coexist. Instead of mutually exclusive, they are mutually dependant and are a function of each other.

In the yin/yang symbol there is a white spot on the black part and a black spot on the white one. This is to illustrate the balance in life, for nothing extremes, be it pure yin (gentleness) or pure yang (firmness). Notice the stiffest tree is most easily cracked, while the bamboo or willows survive by bending with the wind. Is JKD, yang (firmness) should be concealed in yin (gentleness) and yin in yang. Thus, a JKD man should be soft yet not yielding, firm not hard.

WING CHUN: THE NUCLEUS OF BRUCE LEE'S ART

In setting up his art, Bruce Lee seems to have acknowledged that there is nothing to permanent as change. Down through the years some things stayed the same, but there was continual modification. For example, when I first met Bruce back in 1964, he had by then considerably altered his original style, wing chun.

Upon returning to the Starters from Hong Kong at the age of 18 (Lee was born in San Francisco), he began almost immediately to adjust the angles, stances and footwork of wing chu because it was all his experimentation, which he called jun fan (a variation of his Chinese name), was the art that was taught at the schools he opened in Seattle and Oakland in the early sixties. And though he considered this new art to be more fluid and direct than its predecessor. Bruce always expressed a very high opinion of wing chun. Indeed, even after he had taken it a step further to create jeet kune do, he would still say, . . . I would like to stress that through my present style is more totally alive and efficient. I owe my achievement to my previous training in the wing chun style, a great style."

Based on the theory that the shortest distance between two point is a straight line, wing chun lacks the elongated, flowing motions that are a part of most other forms of kung-fu. The centerline, as imaginary line that runs down the center of the body, forms the basis of wing chun movements – the axis around which the blocks and strikes revolve, wing chun practitioners are taught when in combat to have their centerline directly opposite the opponent's chin.

The immovable elbow theory, the four concerns and his sil die dar (simultaneous block and attack), contribute to the over economy of movement which is characteristics of wing chun. The first of these concepts – which holds that the hand and forearm can move in any direction, but the elbow must remain in position about three inches in front of the body – defines the boundary lines for proper utilization of wing chun techniques.

The boundaries of the four corners are identical to those of the immovable elbows; the eyebrows at the top, the groin area at the bottom and the region just past the shoulders on either side. Also, the By-Jong is divided into four areas, or gates as they called. And within each gaze there is a forward and rear area.

Lin sil die dar, though quite simple is theory, is harder to implement in practice. As the natural sendency is to either retreat or try to block an attack, this concept can only be mastered after much training and discipline.

The simplicity of wing chun is reflected in the total number of forms (kuns) in the style-three! In one way or another, all wing chun techniques are contained within the siu lim tao ("little idea"), the chum kil ("searching for the bridge") or the bil jee ("shooting fingers").

Wig chun taining starts with siu lim tao, the basic foundation of the that will follow, and progresses through chum kil and bil jee, in that order. Along the way, the student is also taught the chi soo (sticky hands") exercise. This exercise, based on the dynamic balance of opposing forces (yin and yang), heightens the student's sensitivity in his hands and area to the point where he can detect the intentions of his opponent by feel.

Finally, after the three forms and chi soo have been mastered, the student applies what he has learned in the 108 movements of the mook jong (wooden dummy). A training method unique is all the martial arts, the 108 movements simulate every conceivable situation and stand as the pinnacle of wing chun training – all previous knowledge contained and applied therein.

Although Bruce's father had introduced him to the graceful flowing movements of chai chi when he was just a youngster in Hong Kong, he did not begin training in earnest until he was about 13. As the story goes, he decided to take up wing chun out of a feeling of insecurity that arose once he had established a reputation as a gang leader and street fighter. "I kept wondering" "he once confident to many of his close friends, "what would happen to me if my gang was not around when I met a rival gang." So in the fifties Bruce became a student of the famed master. Yip Man, then patriarch of the wing chun school in Hong Kong – and he would go to any length to further his instruction. One of his favorite ploys, for example, was to arrive at the training hall long before any of the other students. And then at they began to show up for class, they would be greeted by Bruce who would assure himself of a private lesson by shaking his head and telling them, "The old man's not n. No class today. "He also had friends in other styles, which gave him an opportunity to broaden his horizons as energetic Chinese youths practiced tirelessly after school and even during recess.

During his senior year in high school Bruce developed a fascination for busing and decided to enter an amateur contest.

An uncommonly fierce competitor, his being crowed the high school champion of Hong Kong is only surprising in light of the fact that he had never that he had never before put on a glove!

Yet the real purpose of the countless hours he spent sharpening his techniques with Yip Man's senior students and friends in either styles, as well as the experience he got in the unfamiliar confines of the ring, was purely structural: according to Bruce, the ideal proving grounds for combat remained the ever-dangerous backstreets and alleyways of Hong Kong.

Taking into account the myriad styles of kung-fu that were – and still are – taught openly in Hong Kong, why did Bruce select wing chun? From all indication I have gathered over the years, there were three things he liked especially about wing chun: 1) its economical structure; 2) its directness; and 3) its emphasis on energy or sensitivity training (chi sao).

In any event, I think it is safe to say that wing chun does in fact form the nucleus of jeet kune do. For early with a basic foundation that is already stripped down practically to the essentials could be have made such rapid and amazing strides in the development of his own art.

JEET KUNE DO: WHAT'S IN A NAME?

People are still trying to define jeet kune do in terms of a distinct style, (i.e, Bruce Lee's kung-fu, Bruce Lee's karate, Bruce Lee's kickboxing or Bruce Lee's street fighting) To label JKD as Bruce Lee's martial art is to miss completely its meaning, its concepts simply cannot be confined within a system. To understand this, a martial artist must transcend the duality of the "for" and "against" and reach unity without distinction. The understanding of JKD is a direct institution of this unity. Truth cannot be perceived until we have come to a full understanding of ourselves and our potential. According to Lee, knowledge in the martial arts ultimately means self-knowledge.

Jeet kune do is not a new style of karate or kung-fu. Bruce Lee did not invent a new style, or composite, or modify any style to set it apart from any existing method. His main concept was to free his followers from clinging to style, pattern or mold.

It must be emphasized jeet kune do is merely a name – a mirror in which we see ourselves. There is some sort of progressive approach to its training, but as Lee said, "To create a method of fighting is pretty much like putting a pound of water into wrapping paper and shaping it."

Structurally, many people tend to mistake JKD for a composite style because of its efficiency. At any given time, JKD can resemble Thai boxing; wing chun, wrestling or karate. Its weaponry resembles Filipino escrima and kali and, at long range, it might resemble northern Chinese kung-fu or tae kwon do.

According to Lee, the efficiency of style depends upon circumstances and range of distance. The important factor is not technique, but the range of its effectiveness. Just as a hand grenade is used at 50 yards, a dagger is used in close. A knife, for example, would be better weapon than a staff in a fight in a telephone booth.

Jeet kune do is outside as well as inside of all particular structures. Because JKD makes no claim to being s style, some people conclude that perhaps it is being natural or simply is different. Again, this is not the case, for JKD is at once "this" and "not this."

A good JKD practitioner resists in direct institution. According to Lee, a style should server be like a bible with principles and laws which can server be violated. There will always be a difference with regard to quality of training, physical makeup, level of understanding, environmental conditioning and likes and dislikes. According to Lee, truth is a "pathless road;" thus JKD is not an organization or an institution of which one can be a member. "Either you understand or you don't, and that is that," he said.

Martial arts, like life itself, are a constant un-rhythmic movement, as well as are very important. Finally, a jeet kune do man who says JKD is exclusively JKD is simply "not with it, "He is still "hung up" on his own self-closing resistance, anchored to reactionary patterns and, naturally, is still bound by another modified pattern and can move only within its limits. He has not learned that the truth exists outside all molds and patterns. Awareness is never exclusive. To quote Bruce, "Jeet kune do is just a name, a boat to get one across the river. Once across, it is get to be discarded and not to be carried on one's back."

Students should be taught experiences rather than technique. In other words, a karate practitioner who has sever boxed before needs to experience sparring with a boxer. What he learns from this experience is strictly up to him. According to Bruce, a teacher is not a giver of truth; merely a guide to the truth and the student must discover this truth himself.

The total picture Lee wanted to present to his pupil was that above everything else he must find his own way. He always said, "Your truth is not my truth, and my truth is not yours." Bruce did not have a blueprint, but rather a series of guidelines to lead you to proficiency. Using equipment, there was a systematic approach in which you develop speed, distance, power, timing, coordination, endurance and footwork. Jeet kune do, for Bruce, was neither as end unto itself, nor was merely a by-product; it was a means of itself-discovery. In other words, it was a prescription for personal growth; it was as investigation of freedom – freedom to act naturally and effectively not only in combat, but in life. In life, it means to absorb what is useful, to reject what is yours own. To fully understand JKD you must experience judo, jujutsu, alkido, Western boxing, some kickboxing style, Chinese systems of sensitivity such as wing chun, the elements of kali, escrima and arnis, with the elements of penjak silat, Thai boxing, French savase, and understand all the strength and weaknesses of each. It is not necessary to study all of these arts, only to understand the highs and lows of each. It would be impossible to study every style in detail, but if you can get the essence you can capture the style. Or, as Bruce used to say, "I hope martial artists are more interested in the root of martial arts and not the different decorative branches. Flowers or leaves. It is futile to argue as to which single leaf, which design of branches, or which attractive flower you like; when you understand the root, you understand all it's blossoming.

There is a distance at which Western boxing is superior to any kicking style, whether it be Korean karate or northern Chinese style of kicking. There is a distance and a time when wing chun can be superior to Western boxing; likewise where Western boxing is superior to wing chun; likewise where tai chi chuan can be superior to wing chun; and likewise where wrestling can offsets tai chi chuan.

Neither art is inferior/superior to say other. This is the oject of jeet kune do; to be bound but no style and in combat to use no style as style, to use no way as way, to use no system as system, to have no limitation as your limit in achieving your against one. Is other words, it just "it" as in the Zen maxim; "In the landscape of spring these is neither better nor worse. The flowering branches grow, some short, some long." Draw from everything with so boundaries to limit you.

The principles of jeet kune do can relate to any interest or vocation is one's life.

截拳道

Martial art was the field in which Bruce Lee was most interested. However, his technique could be applied to any aspect of life. In addition, the knowledge derived from any one field can help the individual in every other field. The principles of jeet kune do involve using certain ideas, techniques and approaches to life whenever appropriate.

Former World Welterweight boxing champion Sugar Ray Leonard once told Playboy magazine what he learned from Bruce Lee movies.

"One of the guys who influenced me the most wasn't boxer. I always loved the catlike reflexes and the artistry of Bruce Lee, and I wanted to do in boxing what he was able to do in karate. I wanted watching his movies way before he became really popular in Enter the Dragon, and I patterned myself after him in a lot of ways.

To start with, Lee was always in control and very confident. He'd lay back and be gentleman, and he wasn't really outspoken, but all along he knew that whenever he wanted to, he could kick any guy's butt. He had lightening reflexes and he could move and think and just pick his opponents apart. In a sense, my left jab comes from him. My hands are still not as strong as I wanted them to be, and other watching Lee, I became much more precise about landing my jabs on an opponent's nose or be teen his eyes. I also got some moves – both offensive and defensive – from him. For instance, he'd let a punch come within a fraction of an inch of face and then he'd slip it and pop a guy. Lee was as artist and, like him; I try to go beyond the fundamentals of my sport. I wasn't the public to actually see a knockout in the making, starting from the moment I begin setting up as opponent, start picking my shoes and then – POW! – finish him off. I want my fights to be seen as plays that have a beginning, middle and an end.

The notion of change is essential to jeet kune do. The concept advocates learning experiencing and evolving. Jeet kune do will continue to grow as long as any one person is using its approach toward discovery. The vitality of JKD – in a way - existed long before Bruce Lee and will continue long after Bruce Lee. Bruce Lee himself is not important. What his presence, as a symbol, may lead others to aspire to is what counts. If his influence as a figure who "followed his path" can help another to discover his own path, Lee's purpose has been achieved. Perhaps this is Bruce Lee's greatest gift to our world – the son stop gift of freshness and as open-minded approach to knowledge.

WAS BRUCE LEE ANTI-FORM?

A misconception exists that people who study jeet kune do are anti-form. Nothing could be further from the truth. They have as understand of form, and as such can practice a freelance version. It is like having "no form as the form."

Learning proper body mechanics is the main reason for form. Also important is learning to identify and interpret what natural body weapons are produced when doing the form. This was Bruce Lee's philosophy is practicing the form with no form. It doesn't mean he practiced form without form. Having "no form "is ignorance. Having "no as the form" it transcendences.

Many people ask me why Bruce was anti-form, why he hated the practice of form. Let me clear up this misconception once and for all. Bruce often said to me, "The lesser expression can be found in the greater, but the greater is not found in the lesser, "Simply put, form in part of your personal expression, but your personal expression is not always developed through the practice of form.

Bruce was among better forms men man I've seen in my years in martial arts. I saw Bruce perform classical Chinese gung-fu sees with beauty, precision and power. I saw him perform sets from eboy li fut, Southern praying mantis, northern praying mantis, tai chi chuan, and different style that employ kicks. Bruce Lee had as appreciation for classical forms, but separated this part from his martial art training. He felt form should be labeled "martial arts gymnastics," and not be included in martial arts terminology.

Bruce soon dropped the practice of classical forms and replaced them with forms that were set, yet they were not set. It was more of a freelance self-expression type of shadowboxing. While Bruce practices form, it was more of the free-expression variety, using his imagination on different types of opponents and situations. He used this practice to develop agility, balance, and dexterity, economy of motion, flexibility, grace, endurance, power, spread, imagination and mobility. It was also helpful in developing familiarization and identification of body tools and the line they could travel. Timing, rhythm and reaction time to a stimulus and sensitivity are often hard to develop through the use of forms. Because they all need an opponent to be effective, Bruce believed training was lost through the practice of classical forms.

In the early stages of Bruce's training, he went through forms to understand forms. I don't think he advocated the complete denial of classical forms. However, he was trying to say that if you stay with form for the sake of form and cannot separate the practice of form from the actual reality, that will soon become a detriment to your martial art efficiency. A good martial artist should be able to separate what is used for ring combat, what is beneficial for tournament competition and what constitutes good exercise. Bruce often maintained that forms have their place. What he was trying to say, however, was that some martial arts instructors of the 1960s placed so much emphasis on forms – their appearance, complexities, difficulty, length and power – they lost sight of the original purpose, which was as an aid to combat efficiency.

I like Bruce's concept of shadowboxing, which is more of a freelance version. However, sometimes there are movements like wooden dummy techniques I like to perform over and over in a set pattern. I also practice the forms from the Villabrille–Largusa system of kali which are split into two areas, a set pattern of predetermined movements, and a personal, creative freelance form against imaginary opponents. I also like to practice tai chi chuan on a daily basis. And I practice pentjak silat traditional forms.

Like my Indonesian pentjak silat instructor Paul de Thouars, I feel you can fight with form if you understand the usage of the form. This is a concept I stress to my JKD students. If you separate the practice of form from the reality of combat you will have no problems. The utilization of good form is paramount in any martial art as long as it brings about the most economical and proficient mechanical motion of the body in combat. This is why the movement of form should be as close as possible to reality.

Form definitely has a place in martial arts training. It is beneficial if it categorizers and serves as an encyclopedia or dictionary of movement as Ed Parker often stresses in kenpo karate. The key is not to be "bound" by form. As an example, most of us in the jeet kune do family appreciate the classical forms of wushu, even if most of us don't physically practice these forms. The majority of jeet kune do practitioners prefer to freelance. It is not that we are enough to suit our personal needs.

BRUCE LEE'S RX FOR PERSONAL GROWTH

I have received a tremendous amount of mail on Bruce Le and I will try to answer some of the most often-asked questions.

I have said it over and over, but I will say it again. Jeet kune do is NOT a style, it is NOT an end unto itself, and it is NOT merely a byproduct. To Lee it was a means of self-discovery. He called it a prescription for personal growth. It was an investigation of freedom – freedom to act naturally and effectively, not only in combat, but in life itself. He also said like many other discipline, the martial arts demand self-knowledge. He devoted a lifetime to the development of an all-encompassing martial art philosophy. Technical knowledge of martial art does not master you the perfection of the art. You have to drive deeply into its "inner spirit" Lee's many years of dedication training and discipline had conceived him the real purpose for studying a martial art was for self-improvement, and "fighting skill" was merely a luxurious byproduct. However, is the beginning, I believe Lee's main thrust was to attain perfection in "fighting skill" But is his quest be realized the real purpose was self-improvement. In searching for the ultimate truth and reality in combat. Lee discovered certain "truths" for himself, both in combat and in life.

He refused to organize or canonize them into set rules or formulas. As he often said to me, "My truth will not be your truth." It was important to Lee, when he instructed me, that I join him in the "problem-solving." He wanted me to develop what he termed a "discerning mind." He understood a "precept" is only understood is so far as it is "experienced" and lived in the present. As Lee often said, "A teacher functions as a pointer to the truth."

Lee had no desire to focus to found a new style. He was not "pope" of the art. He merely wished to free his students from the "bondage" of style, pattern and doctrine. Lee also rejected the action that learning is a "process of accumulation." He said, "that is reality, it is the opposite." He gave the analogy of sculpture, who instead of adding day to his subject, would chisel away the day until the essence was revealed. His jeet kune do concept involved a daily "decrease" rather than as "increase."

According to him, "truth" could only be realized when you had discarded all the "untruths" or "unessential's," as Bruce called them.

In my opinions, learning skill is as accumulation of knowledge, the "sum total" of life experience. My knowledge first comes from the creator because he gave us life. To understand life, we must experience it in its many complex stages. Only other you have had many experiences can you "chisel" away the many unessential's.

Whatever you call it, "truth" or the understanding of knowledge," only you can answer the questions. That is why it is important to "know" yourself. The lack of understanding and immaturity lies in the ignorance of yourself. Therefore, to understand yourself is the beginning of wisdom. You are an expert on yourself. Our total self, both socially, is the result of out total experiences, knowledge and behavior. In essence, each of us is literally the sum total of our past. We have to use the accumulation of previous knowledge as a guide so we may achieve greater heights. To be bound by previous knowledge is the way of the "mindless and enclave." To be inspired by previously accumulation knowledge is the way of the "enlightened man."

Sometimes people get preoccupied with "semantics" They have not used experience as a learning device. Regardless of what everyone says, the learning experience is necessary. Bruce often quoted Krishnamurti: "Learning about yourself is always in the present, and knowledge is always in the past. But if you are learning all the time, learning every minute, learning by watching and listening, learning by seeing and doing, you will find that learning is constant movement without the past. "if you analyze this writing, you still have to experience every minute, and experience every succeed that you are listening, watching, seeing and doing.

These experiences teach you how to live in the present. To quote Krishnamurti again: "To understand anything, you must live with it, otherwise it, you must know all its context, its nature, its structure, its movement." To understand fully this statement, it is necessary to have previously accumulated knowledge.

Many things sound "nice" when spoken, but once put in practical application it doesn't work. Though learning is in the present because you are experiencing it, that experience soon becomes a past experience, which makes you more knowledgeable. I have seen people "spout off," that knowledge is without past experience – that it is it the present. After watching them very poorly, either in boxing or kickboxing, I realize had they had the knowledge from past experience, they would have fired much better physically and mentally. That is why a "veterans" football player is more knowledgeable than a "rookie" football player, why a "veteran" police officer is more knowledgeable than "rookie" police officer, why a "veteran" teacher is more knowledgeable than a "rookie" teacher. Their knowledge comes from previously accumulated learning experiences. Yet it is true every moment brings a new living situation in which one must immediately learn from it. But one can better cope with it if he has knowledge to flow from moment to moment.

Remember, without the past, there would be no present, and without the present, there would be no future.

Even Bruce accumulated knowledge before he chiseled away the unessentials. There was much trial and error through experience of what was functional for him, and what was functional for his students. For example, when I first introduced Bruce to the football shield as a kicking shielding in 1964, he rejected its usage, because at the time he preferred to train solely on the heavy bag. I asked him to experiment with it, and maybe he would find it useful. After two weeks, through experience, and trial and error, he discovered many different kneeing, elbowing, kicking and close-range punching uses for it. He further developed various drills on the football forum pads and focus gloves. These drills changed from time to time, because experience taught him how to perfect and streamline what he was seeking.

If I am honest with myself, I have no desire to be the "leader" or so-called "pope" of the jeet kune do clan. My main concern is to grow-physically, morally, spiritually, mentally, and socially – using the martial arts as a vehicle, I like to share the knowledge with all the deserving people, and in turn hope people will share their knowledge and "truth" with me so I may continue to grow. I hope my students will appreciate the skill and knowledge of all discipline without being prejudiced toward other style, pattern, or doctrines. Then they will never say "this style is better than that style," or ground jiu-jitsu is better than standing jiu-jitsu or a boxing jab is superior to a boxing cross"

I want no one to take my word as "gospel" but experience the moment by moment "flow of life." In closing I would like to share this quote from Indonesian pentjak silat. "That no matter what man has achieved, physically, mentally or spiritually, he will always be both below and beneath the creator. And that knowledge here on earth is a constant, new learning experience."

WHAT'S A "GOOD" TECHNIQUE?

People always are asking, "Which technique is superior and will one technique beat another?" I also have been asked to write as article on what makes a technique "good." To be honest with public and myself, technique is something that takes internalization. You first have to know your capabilities. You have to know what technique is appropriate for each situation and environment. You have to ascertain the ability of your opponent within the first seconds of a confrontation.

With this comes as understanding of the functional techniques used in the different ranges of combat and defense. You must have command of your body in the execution of various techniques at long range, middle range and close range. You should have the understanding the technique on the ground and standing up. Reaction time, reflex, timing, and conditioning all are important factors in combat and self-defense. Courage and determination also are prime factors is a successful outcome of any combat or self-defense situation. Performing under pressure is the heat of combat or any self-defense situation greatly affects the outcome of the concentration.

Sometimes courage plays as even greater role over the "mastery" and execution of a proper technique which is performed with great determination and will is equally as important as the choice of technique. For example, a person might defend himself with as "unaesthetic" looking kick, with bad form and posture. But the individual will be successful because of his determination. He made the kick work.

Being in balance while using different techniques is important. A person should be knowledgeable in the use of the trapping and grappling technique, both standing and on the ground, and not just in kicking and punching.

Even the use and education of various weapon, ranging from the stiff and flexible to projectile weapon, is important and can contribute to the successful outcome of an encounter.

There have been many magazine articles comparing different styles and systems, such as how to "counter" or defend against a number of various attacks, including the reverse punch, a swing, a straight kick, a round kick, a lapel grab or choke. These comparisons only depict an "ideal" situation, a "role model" to follow in a controlled or ideal situation. In actual combat or a self-defense situation, too many "outside factors" can influence the outcome of the situation. Many techniques only show movements for a single direct attack. Very few comparisons show what to do in a combination-attack situation. One should learn how to counter hand combination, kicking combinations, hand-to-kicking combinations, kicking-to-hand combinations, and hand combinations techniques to grappling techniques. This is where the arts lies- how to do deal with an opponent when he is attacking you in combination. And your opponent almost always sill attack you in combination. Seldom will you "take out" or "finish off" your opponent in one single technique, unless you are so superior. As soon as the first move is countered, another attack will follow, followed by another and yet another.

If you have six styles and you research each style in relation to how it would counter kicks and punches, you would begin to see similarities. It is unimportant to know how a Korean, Japanese or Okinawan stylist would counter a kick or punch. I would want to know what works best for me, whether the technique comes from a Korean, Japanese or Okinawan, or Chinese system.

If you take one song and teach it to 50 people; all will sing the song in a different manner. Some will sound good, some not no good. Yet it is still the same song. You can give the playbook of the Dallas Cowboys to 50 different high school teams. Some teams will lead the league, some will finish in the middle and some will be last. You can teach the technique to 50 different people. Some will execute the technique well, some not so well. Yet it is still same technique.

Technique is an important part of any confrontation. But remember, the spirit and determination of the individual is as important as the technique itself.

KNOWING WHEN TO BREAK AWAY

The traditional training methods and techniques and the classic styles and writings link the modern practitioner to the wisdom and knowledge of martial arts pioneers. It must be remembered these byproducts are merely as end result. And like any product it must change with the times to remain current.

To quote Bruce Lee, "To be bound by a traditional martial art style or styles is the way of an enslaved and mindless martial artist, but to be inspired by the traditional martial art and so achieve further heights is the way of genius." Here lie one of Bruce Lee's greatest contributions to the martial arts.

To him, martial art knowledge and learning were separate entities. According to Lee, martial art knowledge is the past while martial art learning is the present. There must be constant movement with relation to the outward elements of the present. I'm not saying what you learned yesterday cannot be used today; I am implying the present often brings forth many problem-solving situations that were not covered in your education as a martial artist.

I often relied on institution in my problem-solving situations, whether they be in the realm of class, self-defense or just the general lack of knowledge or skill. It must be remembered that martial art knowledge, while indispensable as a foundation, can never give you that complete, final inner "knowledge." Intuition is in the present, and comes without thought. It is "sudden knowing." Intuition is from above and beyond. For me it is a source greater than conscious self. Intuition is free from past reason, emotion and memory, and comes with astounding accuracy and lightening speed. The results always astound me.

One of Lee's favorite saying was, "One can function freely and totally if he is beyond systems." A second-class martial artist blindly follows his instructors and accepts his pattern, and as a result his action and, more importantly, his thinking become mechanical. His response to situations is automatic, which makes his choices even narrower.

It is easier to follow rather than to explore the unknown or create from the unknown, and most people, including myself, seem secure in this thinking.

Some of the more daring and knowledge seeking martial artists have explored, experimented and created better training methods and techniques. Other, however, are context to cling to the security of a traditional knowledge, style or system.

In some cases, when these techniques, forms and training methods are taught, students never consider improving or changing the methods because they maintain tradition it sacred and immovable. Everything handed down is taken as "gospel" because the founder said it was the truth. But truth is relative to the environment, situation and time element. What was the traditional and accepted way in one time period might not be the accepted way in the next period.

In the area of track and field, for instance, the "known" way, the "traditional" way, the "accepted" way, and the "time-proven" way has changed as new training methods and techniques were implemented. Since man has always sought constant improvement, it has been necessary to go against the traditional methods or teachings to prove a point.

Somehow, the practitioner must link the knowledge of the first pioneer with modern day demands. They should use the knowledge of the past as a foundation for the future.

Just look at how the height of the high jump has improved from the early 1900s to today. From the scissor technique and the western roll to the straddle jump and the "Roxbury flop," athletics have used a variety of methods to constantly improve their performance. Lee's suppose those practitioners would have followed the "accepted" way or the "traditional" way. Would there have been such improvement? Probably not.

Take the pole vault event. At ease time, the record of less than 16 feet stood for almost a quarter-century. But in the last two months, a Russian has soared to over 19 feet, 3 inches. Why? Because he is just the latest in a number of athletics who broke from the traditional way of training and used new technology to succeed. The biggest change was the elimination of the aluminum pole in favor of the fiberglass variety.

Sometimes it only takes the determination of the one individual to change thinking. Parry O'Brien was noted for changing and revolutionizing the shot pot technique. At time, however, many coaches scoffed at his method. Now it has become the accept way of thinking.

Roger Bannister, for example, changed revolutionizing and improved the training methods for miles. During his career, most track and sub four-minute mile. But once Bannister broke the barrier, others followed his lead. Had Bannister not changes his traditional way of training, we probably would not have as many sub four-minute millers.

Forty years ago, the traditional way to shoot a basketball was underhand with two hands. Then the shot progressed to an overhand two-handed shot. Enter Hank Lusetti of Stanford University who revolutionized basketball with one-handed set shot. Today you have sky hooks, jump shots off the dribble, reverse layups and slam-dunks that start at the foul line. But in Lusetti's day, the leading basketball coaches in the country criticized his method. It just shows what building and experiencing on tradition can accomplish.

In every field of endeavor, there were people who were discontent with the "accepted" way or the "traditional" way. Only by improving upon the accepted practice could they achieve higher results. For the martial arts to improve, its practitioners practice, and still keep their respect for their founders" styles.

THE SHAPING OF A MARTIAL ARTS STUDENT

When I was first learning the martial arts, many things were puzzling to me. I could never understand why there was so much testing of a prospective student in the "traditional" martial art way. And I could never understand why old-time martial arts teachers passed out their knowledge with such care and hesitation. I have known some very high-caliber instructors, and to a man each refused to divulge their complete knowledge. In fact, they sometimes held back as much as 60 process of their experience. Knowledge, you see, is power, and power should be passed out discriminately. For which power, whether it be physical or political, comes responsibility.

I can understand now why discipline and respect played such an important part in the development of a martial arts student. He must be discipline from the beginning. Like a young tree that must be shaped and straightened from the start, so too must a martial artist be molded from the outset. It is much more difficult to reshape or re-straighten once the martial artist has reached maturity.

I have been told by many martial arts instructors that by giving knowledge too fast, you tend to spoil a student; and by giving knowledge too slowly, you may bore him. Many of the instructors choose to test a student over a long period of time. This way, the knowledge is passed into the correct hands.

If you talk with many instructors today, they will tell you of splits and dissension among various schools and martial arts organizations. It is very unfortunate that every major martial arts organization, style, school or club has incurred some type of split or dissension among its top students. Splits also have occurred between senior students and their instructors. This can cause a great deal of pain and suffering. Loyalty and open-mindedness are rare qualities. Developing a martial arts student is an art unto itself. It is a martial arts "two-way street" Good instructors produce a good students, and good students produce good instructors. The problem comes when one good student tries to get ahead of another student, with each vying for the attention of the instructor, the knowledge of the instructor, and the special status and rank within the organization or school. Sometimes these problems arise because certain students want notoriety, sometimes because there is a disagreement over material and techniques, or the progression of those materials and techniques.

And there is always the possibility a rift can develop from a personality conflict. A gap is created and dissension occurs. These are many ways to keep this problem in check. Instructors should realize everyone has his path of truth. What occurs can be overlooked if one can see the beauty of each path. As Bruce Lee once stated, "A teacher is guide only and a pointer to the truth." I have realized my students are never really my students. I do not own them, and I have never wanted them to be like myself in terms of technology or concept. But I would like them to follow my philosophy of love, respect, proper ethnics, conduct and discipline. My idea of what constitutes a good teacher comes from the writings of Kahil Gibran in the book Prophet;

"No man can reveal to you aught but that which already lies half asleep in the downing of your knowledge.

The teacher who walks in the shadow of the temple, among his followers,

gives not of his wisdom but rather of his faith and his lovingness.
If he is indeed wise he does not bid you enter the house of his wisdom, but rather leads you to threshold of your mind.
For the vision of one man lends not its wings to another man.
And even as each one you stand alone in God's knowledge, so must each one of you be alone in his knowledge of God and in his understanding the earth."
In martial art training, you lead and guide them to think for themselves. Let them express themselves. The expression of the self is the "art" within correct guidelines.
A martial arts teacher is a leader. Bruce Lee introduced me to a book entitled "The Way of Life," according to Lao Tzu. The book combines one of my favorite quotes, for it correctly identifies what my martial arts philosophy should be. I have tried to use this as guide.
"A leader is best when people barely know that he exists, Not so good when people obey and acclaim him
Worst when they despise him.
"Fail to honor people. They fail to honor you."
But a good teacher, who talks little when his work is done, his aim fulfilled. They will all say, we did this ourselves."
I want my students to say, "We developed ourselves," At the same time, I want them to respectfully acknowledge that their development was due in part, and made possible by, all their former martial arts instructors. In essence, my students are my children are the martial arts. Kahil Gibran may have said it best;
"Your Children are not your children. They are the sons and daughters of Life are keeping for itself.
They come through you but not from you. And though they are with you yet they belong not to you.
You may give them your love but not your thoughts,
For they have their own thoughts.
You may house their bodies but not their souls.
For their souls dwell in the house of tomorrow, which you cannot visit, not even in your dreams.

You may strive to be like them, but seek not to make them like you.
For life goes not backwards nor tarries with yesterday.
You are the bows from which yours children as living arrows are sent forth.
The archer sees the mark upon the path of the infinite, and
He beads you with His might that His arrows may go swift and far.
Let your bending in the archer's hand be for gladness;
For even as He loves the arrow that flies so He loves also the bow that is stable."

SEEING IS BELIEVING

Teaching is an art. Throughout history, man has taken expert in his specialized field and made him a "teacher| if his specialty was music, they made him a music teacher. If he specialized in art, they made him an art teacher. However, being an expert in one thing does not necessarily mean you can teach. Teaching is a subtle art, and being able to teach different levels of people is an art unto itself.
And so it is with martial arts. I have had many great martial arts instructors who possessed the technical and fighting skills. Of these instructor, I would say only half understand the principles of teaching. One book I would highly recommend to any teacher would be Colin Rose's "Accelerated Learning," published in Great Britain. This book was given to me by Greg Rhodes, an English student and friend. To quote Rose, "Historically, most teaching has been undertaken by those who were the best at the subject – the person best at French became the French teacher. But the person was not necessarily the most skilled at the principles of teaching. You employ an architect to design you house, because his specialty in the principle of construction, but a builder to actually carry out the plans, because he is adapt at the practice".
In a similar way, psychologies have begun to define the principles behind learning, and these finding have led to a quite different approach to le-

arning. Conventional teaching has assumed that learning should involve determined concentration and frequent repetition.

We now know that this style of learning is not efficient, because it causes unnecessary services and tends to involve just one-half of the brain. Accelerated learning, in contrast, teaches you how to achieve a pleasantly relaxed, yet receptive state of mind, and presents information in new ways that actively involve both the left and right brains.

Bruce Lee, for example, was a great fighter and great technician. He also was very knowledgeable in the martial art field, and with this be possessed the necessary skills to explain his art to a varying degree of students on three different teaching level, physical, mental, and emotional. On a one-to-one situation, Bruce Lee was a master teacher, maturing the physical, mental and emotional progress of a student into one complete person. As a teacher, I always wanted to be like him, and I try to emulate his methods. These are very few instructors like Bruce, he could motivate, while making it fun to learn, yet it was physically using and emotionally intense and draining at the same time. He could always present information is new ways that actively involved both the left and the right side of the brain. The left side of the brain specializes I analyzing information in sequence, while the right side processes the information into one overall thought.

Lee always stressed creativity and originality with me, and often pushed me into becoming more actively involved in martial art research. Some people feel while JKD is good as a fighting art concept, it fields to satisfy the emotional seeks of the practitioner. I found that the JKD concept of training gives concernment and peace of mind in so many ways. He Geek concept of educating the whole person is definitely integrated into the training progress.

John LaCoste, Paul de Thouars, Floro Villabrille and Bruce Lee always stressed the value of imagination and creative visualization in martial art training, not just the physical art and the physical technique. Napoleons said, "Imagination rules the World." Einmeis said, "Imagination of knowledge," Mind training in martial arts is very important element, just as the holistic approach in healing treats the "whole" patient, not just the body.

Villabrille visualized winning his matches long before he entered the ring. The strength of the mind is illustrated in the 1964 story of man who had accidentally rapped himself inside a refrigeration car. When the man was discovered, he had all the physical symptoms of being freezes to death. They did not realize, however, that at no time had the refrigeration unit been turned on, nor was he ever close to dying. The man believed so strongly that he was going to be frozen, his mind produced the physical effects, and be "froze to death. "The mind controls the body. In London a hypnotist touched the arm of female subject and told her his touch was that of a "red hot poker." Her lymphatic system caused her to flinch in pain, and an immediate red welt appeared on her arm.

An instructor should encourage his students to use the power of imagination and creative visualization to achieve their goal not only is martial art training but also in everyday life.

EXTREME PREJUDICE

It has always been my goal that through martial art all cultures could be appreciated and unified in the spirit of brotherhood. This might be considered idealistic in today's world with all the existing problems we have among races, cultures and countries. I hope that through the media of martial art brotherhood, instructors will try to unite different groups, cultures, races, and even countries.

Sometimes it is very frustrating, for even within one group there is pretty jealousy and dissension. Most people will say I'm a dreamer, but through the study of martial arts from different cultures. If everyone would do his small part, the world would be a better place in which to live.

What is disturbing is that even within the same ethnic group, such as the Filipino martial arts, some instructors breed base and disrespect for other groups in their art. Some instructors "brainwash" their students into appreciating only their system. It is so wonder their students reflect their arrogant behavior toward other systems, and that their attitude and behavior only breed hate, misunderstanding and contempt among groups.

If a style or system is superior, it need not ridicule or malign other group. A fighter within any system understands that victory and defeat is a matter of so many existing factors.

Even in pro football and pro basketball the top team might be beaten on any given day by any other team. Among fighters, there should be respect for each skills and training methods.

Just as a superior singer seed not put down a third-grader attempting a simple tune, "great" martial artist trying to do his thing. Yet in the martial arts some instructors castigate other systems at every turns. People in the martial arts should realize there are different levels of achievement, skills and understanding, and remember there will always be people above and below you.

Remember, man is a living, creating individual and he is always more important than any established style and dogma which is limited by nature.

Even the skill and technique which Bruce Lee used to great advantage will not necessarily work for others. The body and rhythm of that individual will require methods which are unique to that person. To briefly follow Bruce Lee's teaching is to improve oneself is that personal method. It is perhaps this issue which has resulted in the greatest disharmony since Bruce Lee's death. Division and competition have resulted, even among those who trained and learned from Bruce, James Lee, Taky Kimura and myself. Basically, the very fact that Bruce tried so hard to eliminate has started all over again among some of his followers. It truly hard to understand the lesson of "do what is right for you."

Yet Bruce himself often said, "A teacher or model cannot give truth – he can only guide you to the truth. Do not take the fighter to be the moon of fix your gaze so constantly on the finger that as so miss all the beautiful sights of heaven." If the followers of the jeet kune do concept and jun fan gung-fu groups were truly to understand this essential, they would not look to Bruce Lee for the most important answers they would look inside themselves for the greatest wisdom. Bruce Lee himself is not important; what is important is that he served as symbol for the people to follow. This is what counts. If it helps inspire another to discover his own path, the purpose of Bruce's life as martial artist has been achieved.

The concepts of jeet kune do deal with what is right for the moment, not what is right in general. In other words, there is no better or worse discipline. Any discipline could be right for any given situation.

Bruce Lee's goal was that all cultures be unified through the medium of martial arts. His goal was to create a standard of excellence for the progress and evolution of all martial arts regardless of country or origin. This is my goal as a martial art instructor and this is the concept I advocate.

BRUCE "NOT" THE TRUTH

"What is jeet kune do about?
It has been written a hundred times and probably said a thousand times. Nothing I can say will change this. Truth cannot be perceived until we have come to a full understanding of ourselves and our potential. According to Bruce Lee, knowledge in the martial arts ultimately means self-knowledge.

Therefore, being able to jab, cross, hook, bob and weave, slip right and slip left does not qualify a person as a jeet kune do expert. Being able to side kick, round kick, straight kick and spin kick does not qualify a person as a JKD practitioner. Nor does performing various chokes, strangles and arm-locks qualify one as a JKD expert. Performing all the jeet kune do sets on the wing chun dummy, and being able to do all the trapping of jun fan wing chun cannot qualify on as a JKD expert. Going through "the ranks" at the Inosanto Academy of Martial Arts cannot assure you of the knowledge you are supposed to process as a JKD practitioner.

Being trained in JKD class itself does not assure you of being knowledge it JKD matters.

In fact, I will say those trained by Bruce Lee himself cannot really say know all about JKD. Of those who were trained by Bruce, each picked up something from him, but it was a partial segment of all that he was trying to teach us as a totality. Herein lies the danger. Some have taught this partial truth as JKD, and what I fear is that their students will develop an "elitist" attitude that they are better than the rest of the martial art community because of what Bruce taught them. It must be remembered that JKD is a process of learning, it is a not a product. Like a style, this process must be experience and experimented with until you understand yourself.

Jeet kune do for Bruce was neither an end unto itself, nor was it merely a byproduct it was a means of self-discovery. In other words, it was a prescription for personal growth, an investigation of freedom to act naturally and effectively not only in combat, but in life. It means "to absorb what is useful, to reject what is useless and to add specifically what is your own." The total picture Bruce Lee wanted to present to his pupil was that above everything else he must find his own way. He always said, "Your truth is not my truth, and my truth is not yours." It must be remembered that JKD makes no claim so being a style, so some people conclude perhaps it is being started or simply indifferent. Again, this is not nor the case, for JKD is at once "this" and "not this."

Bruce Lee hoped to "free" his students from the "bondage" of styles, pattern and systems. He did not want his words to be law. He wanted to one to take his advice as "gospel." He knew that a man in the martial arts is first and foremost a man. And as a living, creative individual, the man was always more important than any "created" system or style.

Truth is always universal, and to as extent almost every style or system is self-limiting. It is important to remember that Bruce Lee was a "pointer" to the truth and not the truth itself.

I can only say those who have descended from the "Bruce Lee class" will being up the art in many different ways, and follow many different paths. They will develop and go in many different directions, both in their techniques and philosophical outlook is trying to preserve the teaching of Bruce Lee. This is good as long as they do not insist their way is the

way that Bruce would have wanted his art to develop. For no one truly knows, had Bruce lived, how he himself would have progressed, changed, developed or continued in his concepts of his jeet kune do.

KEEPING AN OPEN MIND

Keeping an open mind in the martial arts and learning to appreciate other martial artists and their styles is extremely valuable for growth. In my training under Bruce Lee, he often told me "a fighter can only view a fight, style or system, according to the limits of his conditioning." A boxer, Wrestler, or any martial artist who is trained in a particular method, will see the fight according to the limits of his particular conditioning. Every attempt to describe the fight is his partial idea of the total fight depending on the practitioner's likes or dislikes. Combat is definitely not something that is dictated by your conditioning as a Japanese, Chinese, Okinawan, Korean, Filipino, Thai, Burmese, or Indonesian martial artist.

As Bruce Lee so eloquently said, "True observation begins when one is devoid of its set pattern, and freedom of expression occurs when one is beyond system." One cannot express himself fully - and the important word here is "fully" – when one is exposed only to partial structure or style of combat.

A true historian, if writing an accurate account of the Civil War, must be exposed to the propaganda and background of both the North and South. The historian must not be partial to either the North or South if he is to give an unbiased, objective account of the Civil War.

The evolution and training of the martial artist should be treated in the same manner.

As Bruce Lee often stated "Be not for or against a particular form of combat or style." To quote an old Zen saying, "For in the landscape of spring, there is neither better nor worse. The flowering branches grow some short and some long."

Styles borrow from each other and expand and construct like the universe. But each student makes style workable only by individual needs. Instructors remove and add elements to the style they teach. Students may add things to a style that were thrown out by their instructors. These are no styles; I prefer to use the terms: method" or "systems" of training. Style is something individualized.

All systems, regardless of their country's origin, have their good and bad points. All have capability to let the practitioner grow physically, mentally, emotionally and spiritually, using the martial arts as a vehicle, "his is the martial arts" greatest gift. The system, style or vehicle you choose masters only if you grow.

I believe in the premise that no style system, race or nationality can have a monopoly on all that is functional and worthy in the martial arts.

I have been in the martial arts for several decades, yet it never ceases to amaze me how much I do not know. But I have found myself thinking I am like fish in a small pond; that this pond is the only one in the world and not realizing there are other ponds, lakes, streams, rivers and oceans where bigger fish swim.

Keeping an open mind in the martial arts is extremely important for continued growth.

It must be remembered that keeping as open mind allows you to learn from many sources. Learning allows you to learn from many contacts, experiences and facets of your life. The assimilation of learning is called "knowledge," and the proper use of knowledge is called "wisdom."

In my book, "Absorb What Is Useful," I say that knowledge in the martial arts can come from field outside the area. Knowledge can come from your elders, your juniors, your peers, your students, your teacher, and even from your mistakes.

I have met many teachers in the martial arts who I greatly admire. Each has a certain greatness that is unique to him and his discipline.

It is a pity when I hear a karate man say there is nothing to learn from a jujitsu man or an aikido man or a wrestler. I'm sure if they met people like Gene LeBell, Wally Jay or Dan Furuya, to name just a few, they would defenitely change minds.

I have often heard people say the Chinese arts are flashy, but the style is for show and not fighting. But meeting a Chinese martial artist, the caliber of Chicago's Wai Lun Choi, who teaches the Six Harmonies and the Eight Method system, would definitely change their minds.

There are some narrow-mind and opinionated people who say the only valid and true martial arts styles are found in Japan, Korea and Okinawa. This is wrong. For after meeting people like Dr. Muag Gyi (bando system) from Burma, Pendekar Paul De Thouars (pentjak silat system) from Indonesia, Chai Sirisute (muay thai) or Thailand, and Floro Villabrille (kali/ecsrima) of Philipines-Hawaii, I could never believe such narrow-mindedness.

After witnessing these men perform it is obvious there is so very much that can be learned.

In the early 50s and 60s, most martial artists were either prejudiced against other methods or too proud to learn another style. It is a pity because you can learn from every contact you make. You owe your allegiance to truth, knowledge and personal growth. Some people give their allegiance to their style or instructor. This is a noble gesture, as long as it doesn't restrict your quest for total knowledge. You owe your allegiance to personal growth, rather than a particular style system or person.

I personally encourage my students to study and look into other systems and instructors, as long as they respect all parties. No art, person, or culture is extramurally better than the other. A Rolls Royce is no better than a canoe in the jungles of the Amazon. I try to bring instructors from many different styles into my classes as guest teachers to help my students grow. No system has it all. Each system has something to offer and together they yield a better, better-rounded martial artist.

It is important for an instructor to remain a student, to constantly seek better ways of training and execution. It is important to be creative, to experiment and seek help in areas where you lack expertise. Even a teacher with a doctorate in U.S history needs help in getting information about Southern Asian history.

The goal of the martial arts is not for the destruction of an opponent, but rather for self-growth and self-perfection. The practice of a martial art should be a practice of love for the preservation life, for the preservation of body and for the preservation of family and friends.

THE TRUE QUEST

Every martial artist has been asked, "Why do you practice the martial arts?" People often ask why I practice martial arts and why have I made them my avocations as well as my vocation. Martial arts has become of the least understood discipline in the world. And the uninitiated are always asking the same questions:

With all the violence and killing in the world, aren't you adding to the mayhem? What value does martial art have in our society? What do martial art practitioners contribute to our society?

I have always believed that there are two sides to a coin. My philosophy is that the quest of a true martial artist is to preserve life, not destroy it. A martial art practitioner should always be holistic in his approach, and should develop not only his fighting skills, but whether it is on a national level or as individual level, should be part of everyone's education. All the training in the world can't make you secure from every form of violence. The objective is to train the body to preserve you own life and the lives of your loved ones. Sometimes in trying to preserve ourselves, our culture, or our beliefs, we may be found to fight, and the taking of life may be unavoidable. However, the destruction of life must never be our primary objective.

Throughout history, an army and a warrior class has always existed. Europe had its Knights, Spartans in ancient Greece placed a high regard on military training and skills as well as philosophy. The Roman Empire had its Roman legion to preserve its culture. In China, the Sil Lum Temple stressed scholarship, religion and martial art skill by combining self-defense training with a sophisticated system of moral ethics.

I am an American-born Filipino. As such, the Filipino martial arts serve as a vehicle to self-understanding. Holistically, I am more effective. By

teaching the Filipino martial arts, I hope so somehow do my small part to bridge the gap of understanding between people. Hopefully, if people can appreciate certain facts of the Filipino martial art, they can appreciate other aspects of the Filipino culture; they can appreciate certain aspects of other cultures as well, using the martial arts as a vehicle to this understanding. This understanding may help bring people closer together, and hopefully someday we may live together in harmony and peace.

FOLLOW YOUR HEART

As Bruce Lee often said, "Jeet kune do can become intelligent only in the process of self-discovery." It must be remembered that for Bruce Lee, jeet kune do was not an end until itself, but merely a by-product. Jeet kune do was to serve as a means of self-discovery. In other words, jeet kune do was to serve as a prescription for personal growth. It was the research of freedom, to act naturally and effectively, not only in mortal combat, but in life itself. Bruce Lee realized that art lives where there is absolute freedom. He also realized that like in other arts, training in the martial arts demands self-knowledge. Character can be shaped in any way or form to make it more beautiful and symmetrical.
Bruce spent his lifetime in the development of an all-encompassing martial art philosophy. He knew that mere technical knowledge of the martial arts was not enough to make a man a "master." He knew that one in the martial arts must penetrate deeply into its inner spirit. Training and discipline in his many years convinced him that the real purpose of studying the martial arts was "self-improvement." In researching for the ultimate "truths" on combat he discovered certain "truths" about the meaning of life, but he refused to set them into "set" rules and "set" laws. He often told me, "Remember Dan, my truth will not be your truth." It was Bruce's idea not just to instruct me, but to inspire me to think along with him. He wanted me to develop what he might have termed a "dis-

cerning" mind. He impressed upon me that "the truth is only the whole truth, immortal as it is experienced and lived in the present." He said to me that unless I could join him in problem solving, I could never understand what he was trying to convey to me. It was up to me to research and research, to experiment and experience his concepts and to actively participate in the quest. Only by doing this would I truly understand his concepts in the martial arts.

He explained, "a teacher serves only as a pointer to the truth, not as the giver of the truth." Before I met Bruce I sincerely believed that learning was a process of the accumulation of knowledge. Bruce Lee used the analogy of a sculptor, who instead of adding day to his piece of work, kept chiseling away until the "essence" was revealed. Bruce Lee stated that jeet kune do is a daily decreasing, rather than a daily increasing.

As he often said, "Truth can only be realized when you have discarded the untruths and the non-essentials" I agree with him, but I still believe that learning is a process of the important is the accumulation of repeated experiences. I also believe in serve discarding any knowledge.

What may be useful for you may not be useful for your students, and what may be useful for your student may not be useful for you; for knowledge is relative to the user and the practitioner.

Bruce's "key" thing, and it has been said many times, is that he hoped to "free" his students from the "bondage" of styles, pattern and systems. He did not want his word to be law. He wanted no one to take his advice as "gospel" He knew that man in the martial arts is first and foremost a man. And as a living creature and creative individual, the man was always more important than any "created" system or style.

Truth is always universal, and to as extent almost every style or system is self-limited. It important to remember that Bruce Lee was a "pointer" to the truth and not the truth itself.

In closing, I would like to leave you with this poem that I wrote in 1979.

截拳道

We are all climbing different paths through the mountain of life,
And we all have experienced much hardship and strife.
There are many paths through the mountain of life.
And some climbs can be felt like the point of a knife.
Some paths are short and others are long
Who can say which path is right or wrong?
The beauty of truth is that each path has its own song
And if you listen closely you will find where you belong.
So climb your own path true and strong
But respect all other truths, for your way for them could be wrong.

A BURNING DESIRE TO LEARN

In the martial arts, learning is an art in and of itself, learning is an art unto itself. To learn you must experience. Experience is still one of the best teachers.

Understanding comes from experience. This is why school-teachers set up learning experiences as part of their lesson plans. Learning will take place despite the ability of the teacher to teach and despite methods used by the teacher or school. Learning takes place best where there is a "burning desire to learn." No matter how an instructor can motivate his student, no matter how well an instructor can impart his knowledge and subject matter, it is still the student who must possess that "will" and "burning" desire to learn, to experience, to problem solve and strive for perfections to quench that thirst for the unknown. Multi-faceted learning takes place simultaneously on the physical level, the mental level and the spiritual level. Often moral lessons are learned along the way.

Many old fashioned instructors still look for that thirst, that hunger in their students. A young, prospective student once came to learn from a well-known martial arts master. The master told this young student to come back in a week's time if he "really" wanted to learn, because he only taught students who were serious. The student left and returned

a week later. And again the master informed the young student that if he "really" wanted to learn he would leave and return next week. The patient student left and returned in a week's time. He was again told by the master to leave and return in a week. This procedure went on for six weeks. On the seventh visit, the master again repeated the same thing to the student, but this time the student replied. "Master, this is my seventh visit, and again you tell me I must leave and return in a week's time. Tell me what am I lacking?" The master replied, "I am trying to build a "thirst" for knowledge, which is necessary in learning the martial arts." The student replied, " I do not understand." The master said, "Follow me if you really want to know and understand."
The young student followed the master to the back of his living quarters. Beyond the house was Small River. Upon coming to the river the master told the young student that now he would "understand" what he meant. The master grabbed the young student\s head and shoved it under water. He held the student's head under for a long period. The student struggled, but could not free himself. Just when he thought he could hold his breath no longer, the old master rescued the student and asked the young man what he had experienced. The frustrated and obviously upset student said that he still did not know what the master meant; only that he old man had nearly drowned him, and his lungs felts as if they were going to burst. He said he felt a "burning" desire to breathe. The old master replied, "Exactly! You had a "burning" desire to breathe. When your desire to learn and train is as strong as your desire to breathe you will be ready to learn the martial arts.
That "desire" was increased because the student's head was held underwater where the appreciation for the air was most apparent. The old master told the student if he withheld drinking water from him for a number of days, the student would build up a "thirst" for water.
Of course, this story constitutes as extreme case. But it does illustrate that consciousness is heightened when we are temporarily deprived of an instructor and his knowledge. This experience helps increase productive learning because a better appreciation level has been reached.

A COMMERCIAL MESSAGE

Many martial art instructors, including myself, sometimes feel a little guilty about accepting money for teaching. This is because when we were coming through the ranks, it was drilled into us that a "good" and "true" martial artist is not supposed to receive money for teaching. He was not to get a "big" sum of money or get "rich" off his discipline.

Some martial artists would often tell me that a certain individual was not a "good" practitioner because he took a "big" sum of money for his demonstration or his instruction. Some people equate commercialization with not being a good martial artist. I feel strongly that you can receive money for your teaching and still be a "good" martial artist and a "good" instructor. Let's look at a few examples that prove a martial artist doesn't have to be poor to be good.

Do we say entertainers such as Frank Sinatra, Dionne Warwick or Donna Summer are not "true" artists in the field of music simply because they sing and perform for a free? Are they any less great talents because they receive money for their skills and talents? Do we say physician is not a "true" physician because he receives money for his services? Do we say that he is commercializing medicine just because he gets paid for his services? Would we say a football player is any less a football player because he draws a salary and accepts money for playing football? Or is professional basketball player any less a basketball player because he receives money for playing basketball? What about a baseball player? Can you imagine going up to a professional baseball player and telling him that he is not a "true" baseball player because he receives money for playing? Can you picture going up to Chris Evert-Lloyd and saying, "You are not a good and true" tennis player because you accept money for playing tennis? "Or would you tell dentist that if he were a "true" dentist and humanitarian he would work on your teeth for free? Would you go up to an outstanding boxer such as Muhammad Ali and say he is not a "true" boxer because he received money for fighting in the ring? Would you go up to a professional wrestler and tell him he should wrestle for the "pleasure" of the sport and not receive any monetary gain? Would you tell a lawyer he should offer his services free of charge to serve humanity, or he is not a "true" lawyer? Do we question or tell a school teacher if he were really a dedicated and "true" teacher he would teach for free because payment would constitute commercialization? Can we really go and tell the writer that if he were a "true" writer he would write a book or movie script for free and not for any payment?

Martial arts is still one of the few "backward" areas where as individual can get highly criticized of my students "slide" on the payment of their dues mainly because of financial hardship. Many times this practice hurt my financial status, and made it extremely difficult to pay my bills, let alone pay the rent for the academy. But if I had to do it over again, I would probably do the same thing.

A truly good martial arts instructor may well be worth more that he could ever be paid. For there are hidden benefits derived from martial art training. How can you place a monetary value on one a whole talents are so instrumental in the development of student\s character and confidence? What price tag do you put on the spiritual and mental growth which comes through training and self-awareness?

It is important to remember that martial arts instruction is a profession, and that anyone who has the talent should be paid. Many "good" or "true" martial artists can afford the luxury of teaching the art as a hobby, so they do not depend on monthly dues to pay the bills. They have alternative sources of income and do not need the money they would otherwise charge their students. They should be respected no more or no less than the instructor who must charge for his services.

A good martial arts instructor can be a combination of many things – from a big brother and father figure to close friend and counselor. Such talents and skills need not go unrewarded.

The greatest satisfaction from teaching the martial arts obviously is not monetary; rather it is in seeing a student grow mentally, spiritually and physically. These are the "true" rewards of the martial arts instructor.

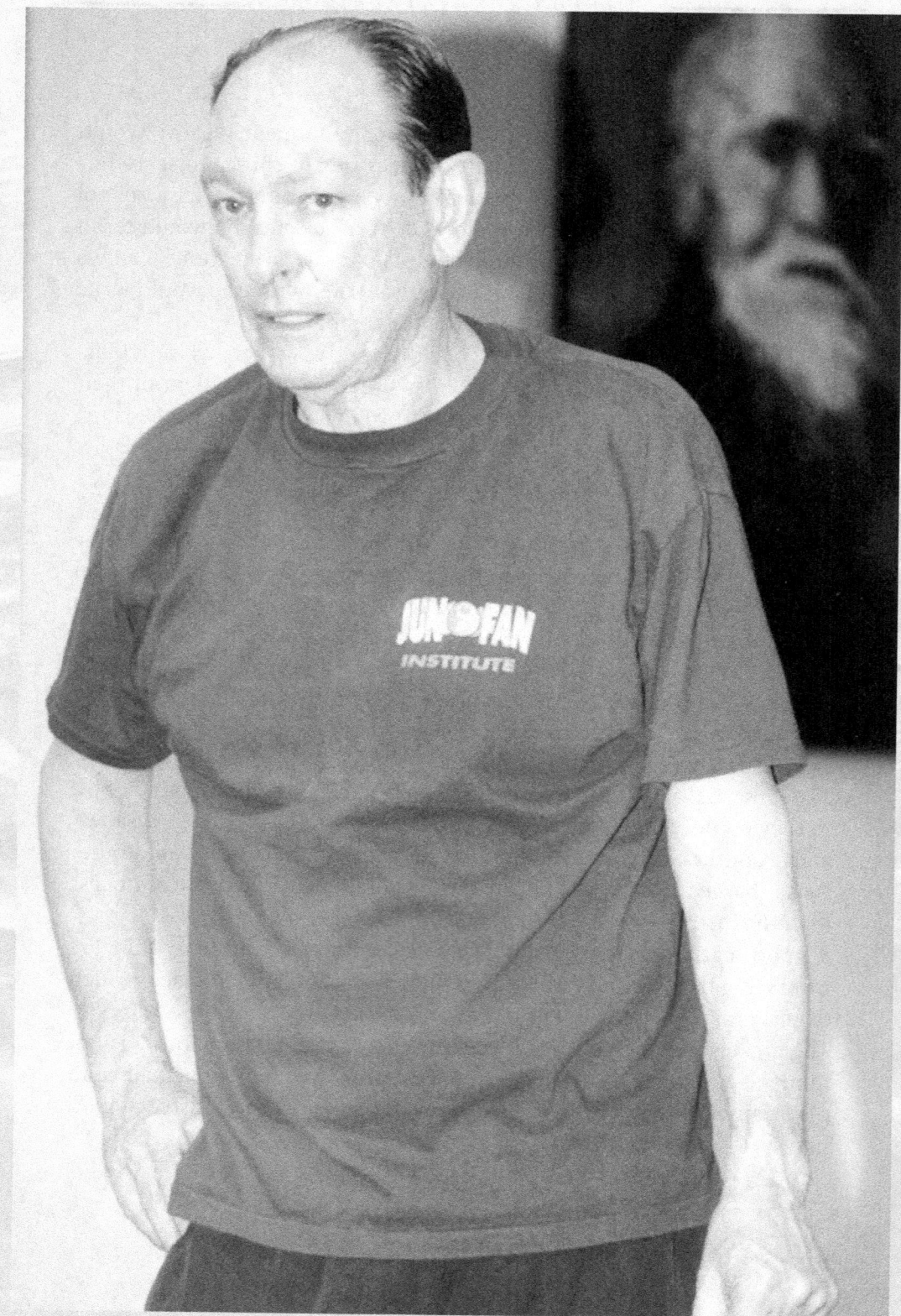

TIM TACKETT

JKD PHILOSOPHY AND TECHNIQUE

JUN FAN GUNG-FU - On March 27, 1981, jun fan gung-fu/jeet kune was inducted into the Kaushu Federation of the Republic of china, making it a legitimate and recognized martial art such as tai chi, etc. (It is a recognized art, not a style.)

In this there are four levels:

Elders – Direct descendants of Bruce Lee (Dan Inosanto, Taky Kimura, etc.)

Pal Sho – Direct descendants of elders (Chris Kent, Tim Tackett, Ted Lucaylucay, Cass Magda, etc.)

Affiliates – Those who ae trained by the above but not necessarily on a full-time basis. (People such as Rick Faye, Dick Harrell, etc.)

Participants and Liaisons – People not affiliated with jun fan but who aid in its perpetuation or who act as advisors. (People such as Lucky Lucaylucay, Bert Poe.)

Jun fan is the foundation from which jeet kune do eventually evolved. It is what Bruce Lee taught and referred to as his "martial way" before the term jeet kune do came into existence. If JKD is a way of thinking, training, researching, and experimenting, the jun fan martial arts are a primary vehicle to get you there.

Jun fan training consists of:
- Punching and striking techniques;
- Kicking and kneeing techniques;
- Joint locking techniques;
- Choking and strangling techniques; and
- Grappling, throwing, takedown, and sweeping techniques.

Jun fan gang-fu consists of:
- Wing chun (jun fan);
- Gang-fu (jun fan);
- Kickboxing (jun fan);
- Chin na; and
- Jun fan weaponry.

Each of the aspects of the jun fan martial arts, while being a separate entity, is also part of the "whole" and most be able to be linked with all of the other aspects. The linking of the various facets is one of the most important aspects of the socal jun fan program, and one of which a tremendous amount of training is aimed.
A point should be made about the term "modified." Modifications were never made just for the sake of change, or simply because something looked pretty or better. Modification is jun fan evolved gradually, through a constant process of trial and error, and experimentation. A technique was modified only because it did not theoretically accomplish what Bruce felt it should, and nothing was changed unless a genuine improvement could be demonstrated.
And jun fan is still evolving. Throughout the years since Lee's death, training methods from other martial arts such as many Thai, savate, prentak

silat etc, have been synthesized into the jun fan curriculum so improve constantly.

The following excerpts are from an article written by Dan Inosanto:

"To Bruce Lee, martial art knowledge and martial art learning were two separate realities. According to Lee, martial art knowledge is of the past and martial art learning is in the present"

"The traditional training methods and the traditional techniques along with the classic styles and the classic martial arts writings provide us a link to the wisdom and knowledge of the early pioneering practitioners and founders of the martial arts."

"The knowledge and wisdom of these founders are in and of themselves just a product, and like any product it must change with the times or the environment."

"To quote Bruce Lee, "To be bound by traditional martial art style or styles is the way of the mindless, enslaved martial artist, but to be inspired by the traditional martial art and so achieve further heights is the way of genius.""

TRAINING FOR KEEPS

Training is the process of preparation of a martial artist for the highest levels of performance. It comprises all the learning processes and elements, including self-teaching, which are aimed at improving one's overall abilities. Therefore, the training process should be organized with a lot foresight. The better the process, the better the results you should achieve. Planning calls for the creative work of the instructor based on comprehensive knowledge and training methods. The trainer must consider in a creative manner the connection between that organization of training and the development of personality and performance.

Failing to understand how the various elements in jun fan are bound up into a single "Whole" makes it impossible to master the methods of its practical structuring and planting. It then dissolves into a haphazard accumulation of various pieces of a puzzle without any idea as to what the finished picture will look like. Without this correlation of elements, the various components of jun fan, such as punching, kicking, trapping and grappling will sit as separate links.

The main tasks, which should be seen and tackled as a whole during a martial artist's training are:

Developing personality – Developing positive attitudes, good habits, self-discipline.

Conditioning – Development of stamina, power, speed. Building essential prerequisites of high efficiency.

Technique and coordination training – Enables the martial artist to make economical and optimum use of his physical condition.

Tactical training – Enables a martial artist so make optimum use of his physical condition and psychological capacity, is responding effectively so an opponent's strengths and weaknesses and in adapting to any situation.

Mental training – Development of the martial artist's intellectual faculties, improvement of training knowledge and principles, and creativity applying such knowledge to training.

PERIODIZATION OF TRAINING

When you look at the various technical components which are integral in jun fan, such as Western boxing, kickboxing, hand trapping and grappling, you may wonder how to fit all the various facets into a cohesive training program that assures continual growth. Integrating the components is achieved by using a training principle which in athletics is referred so as "periodization in training." Periodization is the continuous sequence of periodic cycles or phases in the process of building up a standard of performance. With so many different functions (speed, endurance, power, technique, etc.) it becomes practical and sometimes necessary so concentrate on some of these functions at certain periods.

In periodization, the training year is broken down into several major periods, each several months long. These are then broken down into smaller phases of anywhere between one to several weeks. These can again be broken down into weekly and even daily cycles. These small cycles serve as building blocks from which the average training cycles are built. Each is connected with the previous and following one. The phases or cycles apply to each various aspect, such as boxing and follow a pattern from general to specific. Let's look at as example for how a single year might be broken down into three phases of training:

Phase I
This phase would consist of general conditioning, cardiovascular training, muscle strength training, combined with improving the functional level of individual performance factors (basic weapon development, footwork and mobility, etc.). This phase is paramount as it sets the base for all future work, both general and specific. Inadequate preparation at this stage is a prescription for future problems.

Phase II
Involves transforming the performance factors which have been developed in the previous phase into new higher and more complex standards of performance. Combustive attitude and technical problems are stressed while maintaining the level of physical condition achieved in the prior phase.

Phase III
This phase is concerned with the elimination of known weaknesses, correction of faults stabilization of the newly acquired skills and abilities, and the engagement in sparring. How long each phase should be depends on how many technical or tactical skills and techniques have to be learned, and the level of the student. Training is, to a great extent, an individual matter. Performance is the sum of numerous factors, which can vary from individual to individual, even if ultimately the same results

are achieved. A martial artist deficient in power may compensate for it by superior techniques; inferior technique may be compensated for by aggressiveness. For this reason it is very important to identify and fully mobilize each individual's potentials.

Individual training sessions

The entire training process is comprised of a multitude of separate training sessions. The structure of a separate training session should be such that it is an integral link in the social training chain, and aimed at achieving a maximum training effect in the particular aspect(s) being worked on in that session.
The breakdown of a typical training session might look like:

A. Loosening up – Getting rid of any muscular tension, attaining to prepare of the lessons.

B. Warming up - General - Increase cardiac output, mobilize circulatory system, increase lung ventilation and raise body temperature. Mainly simple and familiar exercises to keep the student moving without interruption – jogging, skipping rope, cycling. The intensity is gradually increased.
Specialized – Here the martial artist prepares for the main phase by getting accustomed to certain movements he will use (shadowboxing, shadow kickboxing etc.)

C. Main phase – Training to help promote the development of or consolidate the martial artist's level of performance. It is broken into two sections: Technical training, the process of learning or perfecting technical elements. This demands utmost concentration and that is possible only if the martial artist is fresh and is an optimum ready state. Speed and power should be developed in this half, perhaps in conjunction with technical skills.

D. Final Phase – Recovery phase. Relaxation exercises, loosening up the muscles, relaxing concentration, breathing exercises – all to help promote recovery.

DEFENSIVE TOOLS

There is a basic theory in fighting which states. "For every move there is a counter." Attack has been given priority is JKD, and is important, but so is defense. Defensive techniques can negate an opponent's attack and place you in a position to counter. The learning of defensive skills is necessary, and should include as wide a varies of defensive techniques as possible.

One of the main theories of defense in JKD is that the best form of defense is a good offense. Rather than attempting to block a kick or punch, the idea is to try to intercept it with your own kick or punch. This way even if the opponent's attack should score, at least there is an exchange. This requires a continual alertness and awareness of the opponent and his movements.

However, intercepting may not always be possible or appropriate. Perhaps one's awareness is off, you may not have time, then one's skill in defense may well make the difference between success and failure.

The basic methods of defense are listed, from the least to most efficient:

Distance - Simply getting out of the way of the attack and allowing it to miss its target. This usually means that you will not be able to counterattack without first reclosing the distance.

Blocking and Hitting – What is known as "touch and go." In this case, the attack is halted with a definite blocking motion, and then the counterattack is launched.

Parrying and Hitting – Differentiated from the previous method by the fact that rather than a pure block, a parry is used to dissolve or redirect the attack, then the counterattack is thrown.

Evasiveness – Includes such body motions as slipping, ducking, bobbing and weaving to avoid an attack by misplacement, while remaining in range to counter.

Intercepting – The opponent's attack is intercepted by the defender's own counter attack, nullifying the original attack.

As stated before, the method of defense chosen may depend upon the circumstances under which an attack is delivered. Sometimes distance may be more appropriate than interception, and vice versa. If you understand all the variables, you have a wider selection to choose from and will not be limited.

TAKING COMMAND

Bruce Lee's kickboxing phase began in 1965 when he moved to Los Angeles from Oakland to pursue his acting career. Prior to that time he was Jun Fan/wing chun oriented.

Dan Inosanto was among a headful of students that Bruce taught privately in his living room between 1965 and 1966. In late '66, Bruce began to conduct small semi-public gung-fun classes behind Wayne Chan's Pharmacy in Los Angeles' Chinatown. In 1967 the Chinatown school on College Street was opened. It was during this time that Bruce Lee's kickboxing era flourished.

The secret "closed-door sessions" were devoted to physical conditioning and tool development, utilizing all types of training equipment such as focus gloves, heavy bags, top and bottom bags and football shields. Everything was contact-oriented and sparring was the crucible, the ultimate testing ground that all the students had worked on in training. Basic trapping, sensitivity and various types of sparring were used (one--on-one, two vs. etc.) to develop timing and distance.

The arts influencing the kickboxing phase were diverse in structure and distance.

The arts influencing the kickboxing phase were diverse in structure and origin. Western boxing. Thai boxing, savate, northern and southern gung-fu kicking, sikaran, modified wing chun, among others, were used. The use of body armor was used for safety during full-contact sparring in the early days, but was gradually eliminated as the kickboxing progressed. Strict uniform dress codes never existed, with students wearing anything they wanted, even construction boots.

In 1970, Inosanto greatly influenced the curriculum by adding Filipino boxing (panantukan). There were two reasons for the addition: it added more sophistication to the Western boxing and, it added the ability to drill realistically and combatively without each student bushing the other's face in every workout. The Filipino training methods were developed from their stick-fighting methods to allow a student to "survive" in training.

Since then, many new training drills and methods were synthesized into the kickboxing curriculum. Like modern athletics, older methods are updated and changed where necessary, while fundamental principles remain. Students learn body mechanics and body motion and then "make it their own." What an individual chooses may be different – some favor hands over feet, some favor feet over hands, but they all learn to understand the strengths and weaknesses of each facet.

As in athletics, to comprehend what a martial artist does, to appreciate how he pursues his art, you must understand the art. You must speak the language. And the martial artist should communicate effectively in his chosen medium of expression. That is why jeet kune do has remained so long a mystery to so many languages. It is a strangely complex and mystifying animal. What is attempted here is to demystify it a little.

Like any formidable opponent, the animal must become known before it can be challenged with any surety of success. To know it, you must study and observe it. Not for weeks or months, but every day for years. Even with knowledge and training, more is required. Maturity and a deep comprehension of combating principles are necessary. The animal is cunning, continually changing, forever adopting.

What is time consuming is not so much the mastering of each element, but understanding and embracing the total concept. To the unknowledgeable observer JKD may only appear to be various separate elements such as boxing, wrestling, wing chun, loosely strong together to create one generalized martial art. But that is an illusion, and to embrace the illusion is to invite defeat. It is a single entry, both an art and a science, and understanding that in all its ramifications is the key to successfully engaging and doing battle with the animal. It must be understood. It must dictate the plan for training, and permeate every hour of the martial artist's study.

The animal is a whole with many parts, commitment to any single portion of which will detract from the rest.

So how does one go about studying the animal? The same way one would approach any athletic endeavor. Combative situations combine different elements, and change from moment to moment, strength the next, then resilience, the endurance.

Every combative skill has is technique, its motion that must be developed and perfected, the right move at the right time. In any physical movement there is always a most efficient and lively manner to carry it out; that is regarding leverage, balance and economical use of motion. It must first be learned, the same way one learns a lesson. But then it must be taken beyond that level. A martial artist thinks while learning, and that is how it should be. In an actual fight situation there will be little or no time for thoughts. By then each action must be second nature so the individual, the same way he brushes an annoying fly away from his face. This automaticity of response is what one seeks.

In a time of narrowing expertise and specialization, the KD practitioner is the super all-sounder – a martial artist whose specialty is the overall picture. Such an accomplishment requires a tremendous commitment of energy and training.

The incredible diversity of combat means that JKD training is intentionally general in scope. Particular emphasis may be placed on different aspects at different times to increase a student's awareness in these various arenas. But the essence is to understand a particular art to deal with it – not to become a "boxer" or a "wrestler". It is to enter into their realm, experience it, but not be caught up in it. Unfortunately this is where a lot of people fall into a trap and start to think that "boxing is where it's at." It is "a" truth, to "the" truth. All arts have advantages and disadvantages, none possesses everything.

A JKD practitioner cannot study ten times as hard or ten times as long as a martial artist who specializes in one method. He must train ten times as smart. The ultimate goal is to get as good as your genetic potential will allow in each of the elements – and to shift from one to another without stopping the mind to think about it. And sparring is the texting ground for the street.

The animal is yourself. The essence is to be in command of your body, to make it do what you want it to do when you want it to do it. That's what JKD is about, and what makes it "uniquely complicated simplicity."

EVALUATE YOUR TRAINING STANCE

Evaluation of training

Planning and evaluation of training constitute a unity. The purpose of evaluation is to check the progress being made in implementing the training plan and to find out how efficient the training methods and means of training are. The use of periodic clinics to check progress enhances the martial artist's overall training. Each check supplies the martial artist valuable information and feedback about their current performance level and abilities. He recognizes his own strength and weaknesses. Managed property, the use of such clinics and checks can spur the student on to putting more effort and determination into training.

A periodic clinic can be used to evaluate:
1. Basic fitness
2. Speed power
3. Agility

4. Flexibility
5. Awareness
6. On-guard positioning in attack and defense
7. Footwork
8. Attitude
9. Kicking and use of the leg – single/combination
10. Punching and striking – single/combination
11. Techniques – execution, protection aggressiveness

Continuous familiarization of the martial artist with the effects of the training and its influence on their development of efficiency and long--term conditioning is aimed at enabling the student to train on his own.

Technique

Technique can be defined as "the mechanical or formal part of an art." The development of technical skills and abilities required practice, attention and concentration, plus constant correction and refinement. Technique is to teach you coordination and proper body mechanics, but should not end there. The natural development of techniques will lead to the loss of conscious awareness after the individual motions have been learned so that the execution in practice or sparring becomes second nature. The idea is not to look for absolute flawless technique, but rather technique which is simple, mechanically sound, and individually suited so that martial artist. In the learning of motor skills there are three characteristic phases. They are:
Developing a rough coordination; learning the motor action.
Developing a refined coordination; perfecting the motor action.
Stabilizing the refined coordination and developing its availability in varying circumstances; stabilizing the motor action.

Mental training and attitude

The mental aspects of training are another essential ingredient in Jun

Fan martial arts. This is why training methods are utilized which combine physical preparation (tool development, overall conditioning) with psychological preparation (willpower, perseverance, etc.)
Throughout training the student should be trained to act with deliberation, self-reliance, skill and perseverance in coping with training tasks. Mental concentration is required to attain optimum development. Too many students work out without being prepared boy mentally and physically. It should be impressed upon every beginner to develop keen observation skills and to mentally register a particular opponent's reactions under specific circumstances.

Developing mental attitude through sparring

In the course of training, situations similar to combat can be simulated. However, these situations can only be appropriate in real situations. In a real fight the available energy sources are often more quickly exhausted than during training. One's fighting experience, emotional and physical states all enter into it.
Only in sparring is it possible to develop to the fullest the ability to compete to the best advantage against an opponent, to exhaust your strength and energy reserves with maximum economy and sense of purpose, and to master the inner excitement and "surpass oneself." Above all, the mental qualities specific to fighting can only become evident in difficult sparring session. For this reason it is necessary for the martial artist to gain plenty of sparring experience, and to also spar against unknown opponents. If you just spar against opponents who are known to you, you may develop stereotyped responses which may cause you trouble when you meet something unusual or unexpected. By participating against varied opponents the martial artist develops the ability to adapt quickly to different conditions.

SPEED TRAINING

The quality of speed can be broken down into two categories: reaction speed and movement speed. Each of these types of speed can be broken down into many minor variations, such as visual awareness speed, alternation speed, footwork speed, hand-trapping speed, etc. However, these are subcategories of either, speed of your motor reaction or speed of your movement. It is also very diverse. A fighter may have fist hand motion but slow footwork. Likewise, another may have slower reaction speed but compensates for it with faster perceptual speed. Thus, to say an individual is fast and another slow in an oversimplified generalization. A lot of one's speed is also inherent. However, various aspects of speed can be increased in everyone to some degree. Let's take an in-depth look at each type of speed.

Movement speed

Movement speed can be defined as the ability to generate bodily movements in the shortest possible time – be it a simple or complex movement. Motor speed can be a deciding factor in one's fighting abilities.

Some of the essential prerequisites for speed are:

- Mobility of nervous processes – Fine-tuned neuromuscular skills and abilities.
- Power performance – The ability to explode from one's neutral position.
- Muscle flexibility and elasticity – Necessary for full range of motion and to cut down muscular resistance which can slow a movement.
- Proper focus of one's attention.
- Willpower

Many factors other than basic speed abilities also condition movement speed. Those are such things as strength, endurance, coordination, or technical skill.

Any punching or kicking movement is basically a ballistic motion (like a bullet). On the way to its target the weapon is being acted on by inertia. Even as your arm or leg is extending on its way outward, the antagonistic muscles are preparing to fire and slow the movement or stop it to prevent you from injuring yourself. If it doesn't then you may end up hyperextending the join. Even so you must keep the antagonistic muscles as relaxed as possible to truly "explode" a punch. In this case, the more powerful the explosion of your initial movement, the faster the punch or kick will travel.

Reaction speed

Reaction speed, like movement speed, is also conditioned by other factors. These include: Proper focus and concentration on the object to be responded to; fatigue (physical or mental); and awareness (visual, aural, (not clear). It can also be divided into simple motor reaction; and complex motor reaction. A simple reaction may be all that is required against a single attacking motion, whereas a complex one may be necessary against a combination attacking motion.
Most of the reactions prevalent in martial arts are complex in that, because of constant and sudden changes in situation or actions, the martial artist has to select from several possible actions one that is adequate to the situation.

Speed improvement

There are two ways two improve one's speed. There are:
- Increase the positive factors – improve strength power, endurance and awareness.
- Decrease the negative aspects – improve neuromuscular coordination (skill) or improve flexibility.

The basis for improving speed is to include a strictly regulated session devoted to installing movement speed or developing reaction speed in your training program. And during the workout the martial artist must attempt to reach his highest speed or surpass it by the highest possible neuromuscular coordination which corresponds to the physical action being trained. The technique which is being trained must also have been mastered and stabilized at medium speeds first to ensure proper body mechanics.

The four basic consideration to be included in a speed training workout are:

- Amount of work – The amount of work at maximum speed which best develops speed is relatively small per session because of the high demands on the neuromuscular system.
- Intervals – the rest intervals between reposition should ensure an optimum recovery level of the performance level.
- Psychology – High demands should be placed on the martial artist in the session to induce a strong application of willpower.
- Safety – Full fitness should be ensured before training sessions are used to isolate and develop speed, as such work places high demands on the muscles, tenders and ligaments. A careful warmup including stretching and relaxation exercises is a must, and training should be stopped in the event of muscle pains or cramps. Physical freshness is also necessary, and speed work should not be done following tiring activities.

Movement speed improvement method

This is the recurrent execution of a particular action aiming at the maximum movement speed. Any of the timing devices on the market today have great merit as they help to develop movement as well as reaction speed.

Simple Reaction Speed Improvement – A recurrent reaction by the action to the suddenly appearing (predesigned) motion with the objective being to reduce the time taken to react. This can be practiced both isolated (with trainer and student stationary) and with the student having to

move with and relate to a moving opponent (trainer).
Complex Reaction Speed Improvement – The main way is the modeling in the course of training of integral situation in which the student must select the appropriate response. Gradually increasing the number of variants in action allowed to the other partner. Light sparring is also helpful.

Training methods

Reducing the spatial limits in which action takes place (sparring in a smaller ring).
Reducing the time limit allowed to execute actions (shortening the time of a sparring boat or the time it takes to complete a combination).
Using boxing gloves/wearing shoes of various weight (heavier, standard, lighter) when sparring.
Shadow boxing with weights. These must be small, five ounces to possibly one pound. The more weight you use the more your neuromuscular system will change and affect the "grooving" of the motion.
Increasing body weight through the use of weight vests, etc., that will not hamper proper body movements. Again the amount of weight must not be too high. In no way do we recommend "air" kicking with weights around the ankles.

TACTICS AND STRATEGY

As old fencing proverb states that "to hit a worthy opponent with a complex movement is satisfying and shoes one's mastery of techniques; to hit the same opponent by a simple movement is a sign of greatness." It is fine to go out and defeat an opponent with simple moves, but sometimes you may have to push it to the very edge and use every means at your disposal. Those means are tactics. Tactics allow you to utilize your capabilities economically and to their maximum

Tactical actions only become visible with physical actions. A physical solution is a complex activity composed equally of mental as well as physical abilities and skills. It is the result of productive and creative thought connected with an optimum use of physical capacities, technical skill, and mental qualities as well as the product of observation and analysis of a combative situation.

The decision to use any particular method of attack or attacking action is greatly influenced and in some ways even decided by the opponent. His physical size, mental attitude, method of fighting and technical skills all play integral parts in the situation. This is what Bruce Lee meant by "You are my technique. Your technique decides my technique."

Any tactical problem is first solved mentally and then physically. The mind's job is to find the best solution for the tactical task at hand in the shortest possible time on the basis of knowledge of one's own capacities and analysis of the situation. The fighter must be sure of his knowledge, physical skills and abilities, confident in his decision and convinced that these things are sufficient to translate his tactical solution into reality.

The prime prerequisite for high-level tactical training is that the martial artist must have complete command of his weapons systems (arms/legs, etc.) and their variants. Only when you don't have to consciously be concerned with such things as balance, freedom of movement, attacking and defensive motions, can you then concentrate on the more tactical elements. Think of anything you learned, riding a bicycle, for example. Remember when you first started how it seemed like so much to try and do at one time – pedaling, steering, balance and braking. But as you became more proficient, these action became almost unconscious and you were then free to look at all the things around you as you were riding. It is that same in martial arts.

While it is true that no opponent should be attacked unwisely without first having ascertained his reactions with probing attacks and feists, sometimes this is not possible. One may not have the time to decide, or one's choices may be limited because of extraneous circumstances. In this case, the better trained you ae the higher your chances of success. Likewise, the wider the variety of attacks, counterattacks, fighting methods (many Thai, savate, karate, etc.) that you have been exposed to in training, the less chance you stand of being surprised by unfamiliar motions.

The mental and physical process of a tactical action
1. Perception and analysis of the situation.
2. Consideration of the solution of the specific tactical task
3. Physical execution of the tactical action.

Guidelines for tactical training
1. Train your powers of observation and analytical skills. Boxers watch films of other boxers, football teams watch videotapes of other teams. Observe other fighting methods and even other students you train with; seek out and mentally record any idiosyncrasies. Analyze and "tune" yourself up to what actions and counteractions can be used to defeat them. Don't waste time with idle gossip between sparring boots – observe and be aware.
2. Develop and maintain a high level of technical skills, physical capacities and mental abilities.
3. Organize your training program to include tactical training as an important part of the overall training process.
4. Stay loose and relaxed
5. Confident plus at all time. If you're hurt or tired, try not to show it.
6. Keep moving – well-lanced and economical motions.
7. Maintain a well-covered, balanced ready position.
8. As soon as the opponent comes into range – HIT!
9. Puzzle and confuse opponent – constant variety in attack and defense. Never do the same thing twice in succession.
10. Do exactly what the opponent doesn't want or expect you to do.
11. Whenever the opponent gets set to hit or kick – MOVE
12. Mass business when you hit, and hit confidently, not half-heartedly or timidly.
13. Maintain proper focus of attention – a "careful watchfulness" of opponent and his actions.

14. Never underestimate any opponent at any time

THE ATTACK

A compound attack is an offensive action that includes one or more feists before the final hit. A combination attack is comprised of several offensive actions each of which is intended to land. In both forms the attacking motions flow naturally from one to another, and are usually thrown to more than one target area. Progressive indirect attack is an example of a compound attack, whereas attack by combination would be a combination attack.
When using either a compound or combination attack, two basic factors need to be evaluated with regard to the particular combination of weapons used.

There are:
Using movements that are most economical for yourself. By using movements that don't require extreme changes in the on-guard position and major preparatory motions, you reduce the risk of being countered.
Using movements that are the most direct to the opponent in light of "between" combination of kicking tools and striking tools. Knowing which strikes "fit" together naturally and smoothly without major gaps during which the opponent can escape or counter-hit.
Therefore, train yourself to examine all combination in terms of:
Facilitating a speedy recovery to the on-guard position.
Attacking and defending from where you end up or are going to end up.

Timing the attack
The right time to attack is when your opponent cannot use distance to hit advantage and is therefore forced to parry your attack, or when your opponent makes the initial movement of his front foot in the step forward and it is impossible for him to suddenly change his mind.

There are two basic moments for attack:

- When your own will decides the time to attack.
- When it depends upon the opponent's movements or the failure of his actions. By preliminary probing we can ascertain the opponent's reactions – whether or not he uses distance, parries hard, tries to crash, etc. and the decides, without a moment's hesitation, the best type of attack.
- Once we have his information and are ready to attack, the following factors will increase the chances for success:
- Estimate the correct distance so your attack lands precisely on target and not too short or too far.
- Time your attack properly to catch the opponent in a moment of unpreparedness and regulate the speed of the attack to the speed of the opponent. In this way your attack will be "on time", neither too fast nor too slow.
- Maintain a loose "pliable" awareness – constantly watching the opponent and being alert to the opponent's attempts to stop hit, counterattack, etc.
- Try to keep the proper degree of relaxation in the muscles to be used so you can explode with your attack. If you're too tense you will move slower – so try to stay loose.

To reduce the risk of the opponent stop-hitting or countering you in the midst of your attack you should:
Maintain a well-covered position in attack.
Fire the weapon straight from the neutral-ready position without telegraphing your intentions by winding up, pulling back, etc. In other words, kick or strike without preparation,
Recover immediately to either:
Continue the attack.
Defend if necessary.

Minors vs. major blows

In boxing, the lead jab is not designed to knock an opponent out. Rather it is designed to set the range, offset the opponent, and set up the combinations of finishing blows. It is a minor blow, nor in terms of the extent of its use, but in terms of overall power. Minor blows can be described as those which are not ordinarily used as knockout or finishing blows. Minor blows are generally used for the following purposes:

To irritate and offset the opponent as he prepares to launch his attack. For example, a low kick to opponent's calf to irritate.

To set up a finishing blow by either opening a line, stunning momentarily, or affecting the opponent's balance. For example, a backhand flick.

To distract or offset the possibility of the opponent counter attacking in the midst of your attack.

Some strikes can be used as both minor and major blows. It depends upon the amount of force put behind the strike.

Negative and positive energy

Major and minor blows are both examples of positive energy blows in that energy is transferred from your strike to your opponent. With a major blow there is a lot of energy while there is less energy with a minor blow. The less energy that is transferred to your opponent in your fist strike, the faster the second strike will be. A negative energy strike is one in which little or no energy is transferred to your opponent. A negative energy attack can be used for the following purposes:

To set up a finishing blow by opening a line.

As a "feeler" to probe your opponent's defenses without using much commitment.

As a rangefinder to feel the proper range for a more positive energy attack.

COUNTERATTACK

Counterattack can be defined as an offensive or defensive-offensive action executed against the opponent's attack. The difference between counterattack and counter time again is that in counterattack the opponent initiates the action whereas in countertime you do.

Offensive counterattack – Stop hit/kick
Defensive-offensive counterattack – Time hit/kick
Parry and hit/kick

The stop hit/kick

The stop hit or kick is an offensive motion. It is not just sticking out an arm or leg and all the opponent to run into it when he attacks. The stop hit or kick must land before the opponent's final action and requires excellent judgment, precise timing and correct distance. Therefore it should be used sparingly, otherwise the opponent can draw your stop hit and counter it. If it is used judiciously and correctly, it can be extremely effective against an opponent who prepares for an attack with a step forward or attacks with feints and wide attacking actions.

The risk factor in using a stop hit becomes greater as the opponent's attack is developed further. A stop hit/kick may also be combined with footwork to secure the best distance.

You may use a stop hit with:
a. Advance
b. Retreat
c. Angulation
d. Stationary

Stop hit/kick drills

Below is a sample of progressive drills to train the stop hit or kick. To do these drills the trainer should wear boxing gloves, body armor, head gear, and shin pads, while the student wears boxing gloves. It is through drilling that you develop technique.
- Trainer – initiates a hand or foot attack. Defender stop hits or kicks
- Trainer – initiates any kick. Defender – stop hit or kick.
- Trainer – initiates any two kicks. Defender – uses distance against first kick, stop hit or kick on trainer's second kick.
- Trainer – uses any hand attack. Defender uses only stop kicks; only stop hits; uses stop hit or kick.
- Trainer – uses any hand or foot. Defender – stop hit or kicks – evades – stops or kicks.

The time hit/kick

A time hit/kick is a stop hit which lands while at the same time preventing the opponent's attack from arriving on target. It anticipates the line in which the attack will end, then closes the line of attack.

Time-hitting requires correct anticipation of the opponent's attacking intention; precise placing of the tool in the path of the final movement of attack; and precision in hitting the available target. If you try to time-hit too soon the opponent can switch his line of attack, and if you wait too long the opponent can score.

He response hit is a counterattack where you parry and attack an opponent before his attacking limb has recovered his guard. Usually used against a hand attack.

Double time

In a double-time counterattack you parry and then hit. In Jun Fan this is usually against a kicking attack or with a beat against a hand attack.

Of course in combat you don't tell yourself that you're going to do a stop hit, or a single time-hit, or a double time-hit, etc. You merely relate to your opponent and try to act as efficiently as possible. Which one of the above is the most efficient? Which one is the least efficient? What kind of follow-ups can you use after each one?

Jamming
Jamming can also be used to offset the opponent's attack and put you in position to counterattack. When you jam an attack you crash into the attacking line in a well-covered position, nullifying the attack and putting you in position to shift to close-range fighting or to shove your opponent out to kicking range.

Use of the parry in counterattack
The parry is a defensive motion used to detect an opponent's attack to reach the target. Like attacks and counterattacks, you have simple parries and compound or combination parries. The defensive parry should halt as soon as the attack is blocked. If not, it gives in extra "push" to the opponent's tool which he may use to his advantage by switching the attack into another line. Consider parrying as "closing" the door on an attack as opposed to "slamming" it shut.

Parrying can be made more efficient by including body positioning such as a slight lean or footwork such as side-stepping with it. When fighting an opponent who has superior skill or has a reach advantage, one may need to take a backward step when making the parry as opposed to drawing the arm back. This action helps you maintain a "buffer zone" between you and the opponent, and needs to be adjusted to the length of the opponent's attacking movement to ensure the required distance is maintained for a successful counterattack. When using multiple parries, each should be made smoothly and controlled, so that the succeeding parry can be executed with maximum speed and firmness. The final parry should not be made too soon, to avoid giving the opponent the chance to deceive it.

Defense against counterattacks
The best defense against counterattacks is basically to give the opponent as little opportunity as possible to use them.
Offensively, the best tactics are: using mainly simple attacks to offset the

validity of counterattacks; avoid overly complex attacks; be prepared automatically to offset any counterattack.

Defensively the best tactic is second intention using countertime, that is, an offensive action that follows the parrying of a counterattack.

To minimize the risk of counterattack you should:

- Feint to disturb your opponent's rhythm, offset him and cause him to lose movement in time.

- Change your body position during your attack by slipping, changing levels, having an elusive bend, and other evasive body actions.

Constantly vary your attacks and defense to make it difficult for an opponent to "read" you.

THE "EVERYDAY MIND"

Relaxation is one of the most important qualities. Both mental and physical relaxation are necessary for efficient learning of new tasks. If you are not mentally relaxed you will be too tense and nervous to really concentrate on learning a new skill or to focus on your opponent. Bruce Lee said that in combat you should have an "everyday mind," that is, a mind uncluttered with fear or anger. In combat you should be mentally relaxed. Then you can fire a punch or kick with emotional content. To be able to turn your adrenaline off and on as if you were turning on and off a light, he said, was the essence of a skilled combative mind. Many times an inexperienced fighter will be so nervous in the dressing room before a fight that he will have little left when he gets into the ring. He has in a real sense used up his adrenaline before he needed to sue it. As the fighter becomes more experienced, he learns to control his emotions. If you are attacked in the street, you will not have the time to use up your adrenaline. Your problem will be to control it. You will need to try and stay both mentally and physically relaxed, which is the essence of the "everyday mind." When you hit you need a strong enough image of something you hate so much that your adrenalin instantly fires giving great power to your strike. But you must practice this so it is controlled anger (emotional content) which can be turned off as easily as it is turned on. For each student this mental training is an important as the physical training. Since each individual is different no one can give you the proper sparring in the gym, but under the pressure of a real fight your training can go out the window in a burst of uncontrolled anger. In that case you may find yourself slagging wildly.

No one can teach you this combative mind, only experience. But is possible to work on it in the gym. For example, when you punch a heavy bag or kick the Thai pads try to do it with emotional content. This should be done after you've acquired the skill, not as you are learning it.

Mental training begins with relaxation exercises. The following exercise should be done at least 20 minutes a day until you can instantly relax anytime you need to. Mental and physical relaxation go hand in hand. If you are physically relaxed your mind will be also and vice versa. Tape the following two exercise until you can learn the by heart. Do them before you train;

Progressive muscle relaxation – This exercise takes practice but is quite easy once you get the hand of it. The idea is to find tease a muscle group so you will have an awareness of how muscles to feel the release of tension. You should do this exercise in a quiet room, stretched out on your back on a comfortable mat or rug. Breathe deeply. Then exhale slowly, feeling the relaxation of tension as you do so. Tease each major muscle group, then release the tension. Inhale as you tease, exhale as you relax. If you do this exercise faithfully, you will relax your muscles without tensing them first.

1. Flex your feet toward your head. Relax.
2. Press your feet downward, teasing your calves. Relax
3. Tighten your thighs and buttocks, pressing them to the floor. Relax.
4. Arch your back upward. Relax.
5. Tighten your stomach muscles. Relax
6. Breathe in deeply. Exhale slowly and relax.
7. Shrug your shoulders. Relax

8. Clench your fists. Relax
9. Bend your elbows up to tense your biceps. Relax.
10. Press your arms down to tense biceps and forearms. Relax.
11. Flex your neck. Relax.
12. Clench your jaw and lips. Relax.
13. Close your eyes tightly and frown. Relax.
14. Wrinkle your forehead. Relax.

Breath relaxation - On your tape for this exercise make sure you leave enough time to relax each part of your body before you move on. Lie on your back with your hands at your sides, palms down, and feet flat on the floor. When you are comfortable, breathe and concentrate on the image of riding your breath.
"Watch with your mind your breath going way out . . . Like a switchboard start to unplug your impulses . . . Breathe into what is tense and tension will go out with your breath. . . relax . . . so tension . . . ride your breath . . . relax your eyes . . . mouth . . . jaw. . . Let your tension out of your body with your breath as you ride it . . . shoulders . . . float into the ground . . . Relax your arms . . . hands . . . fingers . . . torso . . . ride your breath . . . Relax your thighs . . . tops of legs . . . calves . . . feet . . . toes . . . continue to ride your breath . . . You're now totally relaxed and floating . Let your thoughts happen. Don't pursue them."

YOUR BEST WEAPON

An attack is an offensive action made with the objective of scoring a hit on an opponent. This action may be single motion (simple attack) or comprised of several motions (compound/combination attack). It may be a direct attack is that it travels straight to the target via the most direct route. Or it may be indirect in which case while the attack begins in one line, it finishes in another.
The type of attack one uses is generally dictated by the form of defense

used by the opponent. Is he a runner? Does he attempt to parry or does he attack onto your attack? Likewise, the decision to use a particular offensive action is influenced by the opponent's technique and method of fighting (his on-guard position, the way he moves, his size, etc.). This is what Bruce meant when he stated, "My opponent's technique decides my techniques."

A main factor in attack is to try to take advantage of the opponent's weaknesses while avoiding his strengths. For example, if a man is a good kicker, when you stay out at long range you allow him to function in his area of strength. If you can close the distance and jam his kicking abilities, you avoid his strength. On the other hand, if the opponent is weak in grappling skills, you may seek to attack that area.

In jun fan there are five ways of attack:
- Single direct attack – From an on-guard position the attacker shoots a punch directly to the opponent's midsection with no attempt to disguise the motion.
- Attack by combination – The attacker bridges the gap with a low line kick, and follows up with a high backfist, low cross, lead uppercut punching combination.
- Progressive indirect attack – the attacker draws a preliminary reaction from the opponent by using a low cross false attack to close the distance. The attacker then deceives the reaction and scores in an open line.
- Attack by drawing – the attacker baits the opponent by appearing to lower his rear guard, then as the opponent kicks into the open line, the attacker angles his body and scores into the now open line.
- Hand Immobilization attack – the attacker fires a lead punch to gain an attachment. He then immobilizes the arm and scores.

Primary / Secondary attacks
Primary attacks are offensive actions initiated by oneself with the intention of landing using:
Pace – Using one's superior speed and accuracy with no attempt to disguise the attack.

Fraud – To deceive the opponent by appearing to attack in one particular line and upon drawing a reaction switching the attack to hit in an open line.
Force – Attacking a closed line with sufficient force to open it.

Secondary attacks are offensive actions intended to outmaneuver or retaliate against the attacks initiated by the opponent in one or another of their different stages:
Attack on the preparation – A Preparation is any preliminary movement a fighter makes to facilitate the development of his offensive action such as taking a step forward, or attempting to engage the opponent's arm. Such motions are sometimes referred to as "motions without intention" in that there is no actual offensive action involved. An attack on preparation must be done before the opponent starts his attack. The attacking action you use against the opponent starts his attack. Split-second timing differentiates between attack on preparation and counterattack. The attacking action you use against the opponent starts his attack. The attacking action you use against the opponent's preparation should be as simple as possible to give the opponent the least amount of time to reorganize.
Attack on development – An attacking action that arrests the opponent's action midway to the target.
Attack on completion – An attacking action made as the opponent's action is at full extension.

Simple attack
A simple attack is a single offensive action executed in one tempo with the objective of going to the target via the most direct route. Single direct attack and single angulated attack would be classified as simple attacks. Simple attacks are classified in two categories: direct and indirect.

A direct attack is made in the lien of engagement or an opposite line made by simply "beating the opponent to the punch" or catching his moment of vulnerability. The attack should be timed against the opponent.

Indirect attack is a single movement, the first half of which causes some reaction from the opponent so that the second half of the motion may be completed opposite the original line of engagement into an open line.

TED WONG

JEET KUNE DO: THE INTERCEPTING FIST

It has been 15 years since the passing of a good friend and martial arts instructor. During that time, I have stayed out of the limelight and taught only a few, select number of students. I have spent much of the time in further developing my own skills in the ever--changing, ever-developing, ever-evolving manner of JKD. And, I have done so more or less in isolation. But, it has been 15 years since Bruce's passing, and to prevent JKD, that is, JKD as he taught it to me, from becoming a lost art, I feel it is time to reveal some of the skills Bruce developed in the time that I spent with him.
Bruce was always fast to pick up on marital arts techniques, and by the early 1970s, his skill for both observation and execution had reached such a phenomenal level that very few people could keep up with him. Now, I trained with him – I lived, breathed, and trained with him on a daily basis during that time. We were him on a daily basis during that time. We were from similar cultural

backgrounds and we both thought in the same mother tongue language so we were able to communicate on a more personal level. We were also very close in height, weight and body size and we shared similar ranges of body motions and degrees of flexibility. And, even though he was the teacher and I was the student, every day we both were learning something new, something different. JKD training with him was indeed an ever-changing, ever-evolving, ever-developing process. For example, from week to week, his side kick would look and feel different. But nevertheless, Bruce's emphasis was always on efficiency, immediacy and above all, simplicity. His art was indeed "The direct expression of one's feelings with the minimum of movements and energy."

To start talking about JKD training, I should stress, right off the bat, the importance of the lead hand/foot weapon, that is, the lead punch/kick is the backbone of jeet kune do. To understand the art of JKD, one must completely understand this concept. Bruce always stressed placing the lead hand weapon forward. The lead punch, unlike the Western boxing jab, is a devastatingly powerful punch. The lead punch is delivered from an on-guard and is delivered non-telegraphically with no wastage of motion during its execution. The punch is propelled forward and explodes right through the target. As some readers might have seen in books, magazines or other sources, pictures of Bruce throwing a punch and myself holding a focus mitt depicts exactly that.

The punch is delivered in such a manner that the hand always moves first, before any other part of the body, namely, the foot. The punch also lands first, transferring all the energy of the entire body through the punch, before a single ounce of energy is transferred through the landing of the foot.

You can practice the lead punch with a partner. First, have you partner hold a focus mitt. Assume a fighting stance with the lead hand aimed toward the focus mitt. With no wasting of motion and no telegraphic movements, strike the pad and recoil back to the same starting position. Begin with a position that is at arm's length from the target, and gradually increase the speed of delivery as you warm up. As you hit the target faster and faster, have your partner move the focus mitt away the instant he detects your movement. This is more like actual combat and will also train your partner to read (or not read) your attack. Gradually, step further and further away from the target. Now, you must move in with the foot, but remember, the punch must move in before the foot and also land before the foot. This was Bruce's way of exploding through a target from a distance.

In many classical martial arts systems, the foot always precedes the hand in delivering a punch. In Bruce's JKD, it is the reverse. The hand always precedes the foot, and the punch explodes with the whole body weight behind it. In the months to come, I will introduce other techniques of JKD as well as other training methods. Bruce had so much to offer in the form of the art of JKD. Let us not allow it to perish forever with him.

THE ESSENCE OF JEET KUNE DO

Previously I discussed the importance of the lead/foot weapon in training in jeet kune do. Of equal importance is that during the execution of any punch/kick, there is no waste of motion or telegraphic movement. This is essential to what Bruce Lee called the totality of combat.

To Bruce, the totality of direct hand-to-hand combat meant all the possible approaches to combat. It did not and does not mean the sum of all the techniques of every "style" of martial arts ever invented. Totality is not the amalgamation of 16 or 32 or even 128 different martial arts systems. Since we must always keep in mind the importance of no wastage of motion and no telegraphic movement, it is, in fact, the very opposite – the hacking away of the unessential moves of all different "styles." Totality is not the accumulation of technique, but the simplification of technique to make each and every approach to combat the most direct and effective.

Jeet kune do is not a classical style. Its purpose is not to segregate, conditioner restrict. It does not hold the practitioner in bondage to one partial aspect of combat. The totality of combat is conditionless and bondless, since combat is never fixed, and is changing from moment to moment. Bruce created (derived) JKD to bring back the totality of combat. Bruce once described his martial arts efforts by comparing the to the work of a sculptor, a JKD practitioner does not keep adding techniques, but hacks away at the unessentials in his art so that the true spirit of the martial arts is expressed."

Furthermore, "Jeet kung do, ultimately, is not a matter of petty technique, but of highly developed personal spirituality and physique. It is not a question of developing what has already been developed, but recovering what has been left behind. These things have been with us, in us, all the time and have never been lost or distorted except by our misguided manipulation of them (in styles). In JKD, all technique is to be forgotten and the unconscious is to be left alone to handle the situation. The technique will assert its wonders automatically or spontaneously, but of spiritual insight and training."

Nevertheless, Bruce's approach was/is extremely thorough. He was amazingly efficient in looking at all possible angles of entry as well as all possible methods of striking. He broke down combat into four ranges: kicking, punching, trapping, and grappling. These ranges will be discussed in future issues. Bruce stressed the importance of mobility, and of remaining, at the same time, well oriented and in balance by keeping a firm hold on one's center of gravity; he stressed the importance of being alert and aware of one's surroundings at all times. He concentrated on developing speed, reaction time, and methods of delivery, on building power and stamina, and on staying physically fit. This was what Bruce meant by the totality of combat.

In training in JKD, one does not ask for more; one only asks for the essence.

THE JEET KUNE DO SHUFFLE

According to Bruce Lee, mobility is one of the most neglected attributes of martial arts training. The essence of combat is the art of mobility – to seek our target, while at the same time, avoid being one. In JKD, footwork should be easy, relaxed, and alive. Where traditional, classical horse stances are unnecessary and non-functional, and basically seek firmness in stillness, JKD finds firmness in motion. In fighting, you are required to move instantly in any direction. Therefore, springiness and alertness of footwork are essential.

A moving target is definitely harder to hit than one that is stationary. The more skilled a fighter is at footwork, the less he has to use his arms in avoiding getting hit. With skillful footwork, the JKD fighter can evade strikes and blows, swiftly cover distances, escape tight situations, and conserve energy, all while preparing his own course of attack. And, as with all else in jeet kune do, footwork tends to aim toward simplification with a minimum of movement. "Do not get carried away and dance all over the place like a fancy boxer." The idea is simply to get where you are safe and he is not.

Effective mobility helps you gauge your fighting distance within the four ranges: kicking, punching, trapping, and grappling. It allows you to glide in and out of the kicking range and it also dictates the fighting distance between you and your opponent. If your mobility is good, you can bridge these distances with greater speed and swiftness. If your mobility is bad, chances are your actions and distance will be dictated by your opponent. Mobility was developed by Bruce, as you have probably seen in his movies, through swift and speedy footwork.

Effective footwork can keep you at a safe distance from your opponent and can carry you into any particular range from which you want to attack. You can practice this drill for effective footwork: In a fighting, on-guard stance with feet wide, yet comfortably apart, shuffle forward and backward, side to side, changing direction at will, keeping in balance at all times. While shuffling, a relatively consistent distance between your feet should always be maintained. In shuffling forward, the rear foot should closely follow the front foot, constantly keeping the same distance; in shuffling backward, the front should closely follow the rear, also constantly maintaining the same distance. This is a shuffle . . . at no time should either foot be off the ground. The key is always to move on the balls of the feet, and to never cross your feet whenever you are fighting. Some exercises you can do to strengthen, as well as develop the agility of the legs include calf raises, hopping toe-to-toe, and skipping rope. Later on, when you can move forward and backward with ease, you can improve your speed and reaction time with a partner. Square off with your partner at a distance that is slightly out of his kicking range, so that for him to attack, he must make a step and lunge toward you. At this distance, which is actually your fighting measure, as your partner shuffles forward toward, or backward away, you must try to maintain the same distance from him. This simple drill will train you to always keep a specific distance from your opponent. And, no matter how fast or how powerful he is, no matter how effective his techniques are, if you can successfully maintain a specific distance from your opponent (so that he can never get to you), you can control the entire fight. When you have mastered the forward and backward shuffles, you can add lateral movement: have your partner move to the right, to the left or around you. Maintaining good mobility is a neglected skill in the martial arts, yet it can set apart JKD fighters from other practitioners.

BRIDGING THE GAP

In my previous column, "The JKD Shuffle," I stressed the importance of good mobility and footwork, one of the most neglected attributes of the martial arts, and that is separates JKD fighters from other fighters. I would like to now go into the concept of distance in jeet kune do. The fighting distance in JKD is defined as "the continually shifting relationship, depending on the speed, agility and control both fighters. It is a constant, rapid shifting of ground, seeking the slightest closing which will greatly increase the chances of hitting the opponent." With the concept of distance defined, Bruce Lee always maintained that the proper fighting distance has a definite decisive effect on the outcome of the fight. He made this evident in numerous demonstrations he gave at tournaments and other events during his early years of training.

Bruce could control a distance, and he could bridge a distance with great speed and agility. He could bridge a distance of several feet within a fraction of a second; before you knew it, he would be right in front of you, because he had developed, to such a high degree, those attributes which I discussed last time—footwork and mobility. Bruce could close a distance faster than anyone I have seen.

A frequent demonstration that he used to give was a finger jab (to the eyes) which he would launch on an opponent from several feet away. This several feet was actually further than the punching distance, and sometimes, even further than the kicking distance. He used to make this demonstration by inviting any black belt in a tournament or any able person from his audience to come out and try to block his finger jab. Time and time again, no one was ever able to do it, even when he began from several feet away.

To control the distance, one has to utilize good mobility and good footwork through quick shuffles, short shuffles, quick advance, short advance, quick lunges and changes in direct split second. To learn to control the distance, there are several exercises that can practice.

First, square off with a partner, and try to maintain your own fighting measure. Your fighting measure is the distance you must keep relative to your opponent, which should be far enough away that he cannot reach you (unless he lunges fully at you), but at the same time not so far that, with a short advance, you cannot close the distance and reach him with your attack.

With this measure established, we will go into an exercise called 'bridging the gap.' With your opponent standing at your fighting measure, you must try to reach him, first with a kick; this means you must lunge forward while throwing the kick. Then, you can practice bridging the gap with a punch; for this, you will probably have to slightly decrease your fighting measure. Once you are comfortable with bridging the gap for kicking and punching, you can make this exercise a little more difficult with your opponent moving. Once again, you must try to bridge the gap by kicking or punching, but this time while your partner is moving side to side or backing away. This requires precise distance judging. In throwing the kick or punch, you must anticipate your opponent's reaction and aim at where he will be when he realizes he is being attacked and not where he was prior to the attack. Also keep in mind that once the correct distance is attained, either for kicking or punching, the attack should be carried through with an instantaneous burst of speed and energy, so that your physical awareness captures your opponent by surprise.

Another exercise, which Bruce and I used to do, involved going through the kicking and punching exercises while one wore protective equipment and armor. The one wearing the protective equipment does not try to avoid being hit by moving completely away, but takes a glancing blow from the kick or punch. This trains the person not to back away too far during an attack so that he is out of range and cannot launch a counterattack. This exercise trains a fighter to step back just far enough so that he can immediately counterattack

In maintaining the distance when applied to a defensive opponent, your speed must be greater than his. Your opponent, being defensive, will always be moving away, and for you to keep up with him, and overtake him, you simply must be faster.

When you face an offensive opponent, you can actually allow him to bridge the distance for you. While your opponent is approaching you, you attack with quickness as soon as you are in range. You can take advantage of his movement or attack as long as you are faster.

Maintaining the proper fighting distance is important to the martial artist. If you can successfully control these distances, you can control the entire fight.

FULL CONTRACT SPARRING

In most traditional kung-fu systems, the instructor requires the student to stand in a horse stance for much of the first six months. Bruce had a dim view of this, noting that it was very good for strengthening the legs and for developing patience and self-discipline, but that it had very little to do with fighting. The phrase he used in reference to this less-than--practical exercise was that it was like "swimming on dry land."

He maintained that from the beginning, a student should learn to spare effectively so that he would be ready and equipped with the necessary skills of self-defense when suddenly confronted with life-threatening situations. In sparring in JKD, the student wears full protective equipment and goes all out; in this way, he can truly learn the correct timing and distance for punches and kick, and become immediately familiar with what it is like to fight under these conditions. It is a good idea to spar with all kinds of individuals – tall, short, fast and even clumsy. Clumsy fighters, at times would present trouble, especially to beginners; this type of person being awkward, fierce, and fighting in a broken rhythm – you don't know what he's going to do.

Sparring in JKD should be as close to actual combat as possible. It teaches one how to be calm and quick under pressure; the instance that an opening or opportunity occurs, the attack is already on its way. And, because of the simplicity of the JKD principles, the attack is also very direct and effective.

As mentioned in the last article, when sparring full contact, protective equipment is a must – equipment such as headgear, boxing gloves, training gloves, knee pads, shin guards, groin cup and mouthpiece. This allows you to get as much into the full contact as possible, and still protects you from injury.

In JKD, there are four ranges of fighting, And in JKD training, the student learns to fight within one range at a time. These ranges are: kicking, punching, trapping, and grappling. When starting to spar full contact, a beginner will begin at trapping range with finger gloves and mouthpiece for protection. Finger gloves are used instead of boxing gloves, because boxing gloves do not allow for enough sensitivity to the hands. In this range, the student learns to acquire a physical sense of the opponent's movements and to react almost simultaneously to them.

From here, the student usually goes into the grappling range, which includes the use of chokehold, arm bars, wrestling techniques, and even biting.

Next, we move into the punching (boxing) range, and the equipment used mainly will be boxing gloves, mouthpiece and headgear. Here, techniques are practiced one at a time, utilizing different types of offensive and defensive moves, such as parrying, weaving, bobbing, as well as the intercepting/stopping fist. First, the lead hand is mastered, then the rear hand is brought into play.

The fourth and last range is the kicking range; here, the equipment used are shin guards, groin cup, as well as knee pads. The knee is usually easy to attack. Therefore, when sparring, special attention must be paid to not kicking the knee. Most attacks are done with the lead foot, and most counters are done in coordination with the footwork – either advancing or retreating.

The final stage of full-contact sparring is the combination of hand and foot where the student learns to move in and out of the four ranges with ease, utilizing the appropriate techniques in each range. By this state, the student has examined every possible angle of entry and has trained in the simplest, most direct and most effective way of engaging in combat in each range. When training begins, we break down combat into separate and distinct ranges and separately perfect each technique; when training is at an end, we bring them all together so that the totality of combat is, once again, complete.

BRUCE LEE'S TRAINING EQUIPMENT

On the subject of jeet kune do, it would be incomplete without mentioning the training equipment used by Bruce Lee. The three people who helped Bruce make and modify equipment were James Lee, George Lee, and later in Los Angeles, Herb Jackson. Bruce wanted equipment with springlike qualities so they would react, absorb and strike back like a real opponent. This allowed the fighter to develop and improve not only power and speed, but timing and coordination as well. Bruce also wanted equipment that was good for training alone. Finally, he stressed the importance of full-body protective equipment to make it possible for fighters to spar full out and not allow them to get into the habit of pulling their punches, thereby testing the true effectiveness of their techniques. I will introduce some of the training equipment that Bruce implemented over the years:

Spring-action and other special devices
When Bruce started serious training in Oakland, he was impressed by James subsequently designed welding abilities; James subsequently designed and made equipment for Bruce which included a snap-back punching device, a wooden head for finger jabs and punches, a steel shin device for low kicks, and a mental dummy with springs. Some of these were later modified by Bruce to improve their precision.

Kicking shield
Bruce was one of the first innovators to use a football shield for kicking shield; these were the same shields linemen used to train. The first kicking shield was made by George, who put handles on the back. This was later modified by Herb Jackson with extra padding for added protection for the holder. These types of shields are now in common use in martial arts schools.

Focus mitt
The focus mitt was same used by boxer. Bruce put it to use for developing the lead hand and punch, and for speed and precision as well. Since it is worn by the trainer or partner who moves about, it is also good for maintaining the fighter's mobility. In addition, the focus mitt was helpful in developing accuracy of kicking.

Modified wing chun wooden dummy
The wing chun wooden dummy was modified by Herb Jackson, who

mounted-extra springs between the platform and the dummy to absorb the shock of greater impact. He also made it possible to change the hand positions so that it was employable for both left right stance.

Power rack
The power rack was a device used for isometric strengthening; this involved a part or parts of the body being held in a static position while a constant force is applied to it. This is useful for building forearm strength, which is, in turn, applicable in sticky hands and trapping. And, by pushing up against the rack with the shoulders, this equipment also developed springiness in the calves, thus increasing "take off" power in the legs.

Heavy bag
Bruce considered the heavy bag to be one of the most important and essential pieces of equipment to developing power and the proper placement of punching and kicking; in addition, it is excellent for conditioning (as when used in long workouts) and for training alone. Later, Bruce practiced on the giant heavy bag to develop more power in his kicks. However, it was so heavy that a special attachment was required and made by Herb Jackson to hand it in place.

Protective sparring equipment
Sparing in JKD requires the body to be adequately protected so that full contact is possible. Sparring without sufficient equipment would require the fighters to hold back, which runs the risk of developing into a bad habit when confronted with a real-life situation. For full contact, boxing gloves are used; finger boxing gloves (first used in other martial arts) were implemented and modified for grappling and trapping. Other protective gear used are Navy boxing headgear, body protector, hockey shin guards, groin cup and mouthpieces. An essential part of JKD is to spar full out and in full protective equipment to test the true effectiveness of techniques; otherwise, all technique (as Bruce used to say) is as ineffective as swimming on dry land.

Conclusion

It is encouraged that students who want to more fully understand JKD learn it in the way it was originally taught, and only until then does the student become proficient. He is then capable and mature enough (intellectually, physically and philosophically) to "absorb what is useful, reject what is useless, and add what is specifically his own." When a student is ready", I encourage him to alter or modify what I taught him as well as research other martial arts for stimulation and enrichment, not supplement.

In the many years I have been involved with the martial arts, I have kept a low profile. I have nothing to claim or prove. I have always had tremendous respect for the art of jeet kune do, and for those who practice it.

In closing, I ask that all JKD practitioners bind together for the sake of the future of jeet kune do and for the memory of Bruce Lee. We are only as strong as our weakest link. The key to group cohesion is communication, clarification, and understanding.

CASS MAGDA

WHEN IN DOUBT, STRAIGHT BLAST

The straight blast in jeet kune do is a devastatingly effective technique. It is the epitome of simplicity; in fact, it is so simple in execution that, at a casual glance, there doesn't seem to be much to it. However, as any JKD practitioner knows well, a casual glance seldom reveals what is really there.

I personally recall, in my training under Dan Inosanto, Dan telling me that in his observations of Bruce Lee in confrontations, the straight blast would inevitably come at some point, particularly if Bruce took his opponent seriously. In fact, this is the very technique Dan himself began with in his first few months of training under Bruce.

According to Inosanto, he first had his doubts about the usefulness of the technique because it seemed so simple and predictable. These doubts were soon dispelled when he got together with some fellow black belts for some friendly sparring. To his astonishment,

Inosanto found the straight blast worked so well nobody could stop it. Ted Wong used to mention how he found the straight blast extremely useful against such opponents as a boxer, who is not used to backing away quickly.

The Mechanics of the Straight Blast
The straight blast is derived from wing chun jung-fu's chung choi (repeating vertical fist), also known to wing chun exponents as the "battle punch," it consists of continuous vertical fist punching about nose height, along the centerline, one fist repeatedly taking the place of the other. In JKD, this has been modified to enable the practitioner to hit with a different flavor and angle, but the repeated piston-like action remains the same, and is considered the essence of the technique. The idea in JKD is to be able to use it without being bound to the structure, so that one can move from any structure one happens to find oneself in. This way, the ultimate advantage can be taken of any circumstance and opportunity.

Underlying Theory
The main idea behind the straight blast is to blast in when an opening appears and maintain a strong forward pressure on the opponent. This tends to keep the opponent on the defensive for the moment. It also acts as a structure that the opponent must attempt to counter, leaving the low line open, and also leaving many other options available, such as hand immobilization.
One can apply hand immobilization by trapping with the hits. One can also cut into the opponent's tools, this action acting like a simultaneous immobilization and hit.

Targets
The main targets of the straight blast are the face, the throat, even the chest, depending on what the ultimate goal is. One may want to sweep the opponent while he is defending against a hand attack. One may want to move the opponent on the retreat, which, in this case, would make the chest a better target, making it hard for the opponent to duck.

What Bruce Preferred to Do

I have been told my many first generation JKD students that Bruce always stressed, "When in doubt, straight blast." It was one way to handle a situation when the opponent is possibly superior in some way, such as strength or speed. The irony of the technique, once again, is that it looks ridiculously simple.

In fact, if you haven't personally experienced it, you won't believe how effective it can be. But then, that's what JKD is all about, isn't it?

HOW BRUCE LEE IS BEING MISINTERPRETED

"Absorb what is useful. Reject what is useless. Add what is specifically your own. Man, the creating individual is more important than any established style or system."
-Bruce Lee

The philosophy of jeet kune do has inspired many martial artists to a more investigative and open approach to learning and training, as well as inspiring the current wave of eclecticism in the martial arts. Everyone these days is "using what works." New eclectic styles preaching "totally" and "freedom of expression" are sprouting up everywhere.

Sadly, these new styles are nothing but a reaction; new packages of re-organized despair claiming similarity to JKD in their philosophy and application, but in fact by doing this they are missing the idea. My point here is not to argue over what is original (because nothing is really original), who had what first or who is borrowing form whom. These issues are unimportant. The philosophy of JKD is like any other philosophy, people can add or express their own interpretation of it. What Bruce Lee meant by the JKD philosophy in practical application is sometimes a far cry from those martial artists claiming to follow it. One of the most commonly misinterpreted phrases is the "Absorb what is useful," saying that opened this discussion.

The idea of absorbing what is useful does not mean choosing, collecting, compiling, accumulating or assembling techniques from different styles of martial arts thinking to yourself. "I'll take the best from all the styles and put it together to form a new style." To do this is to miss the point. We are not saying "collect what you like" or "put together the best" but absorb what is useful it is an individual investigation. To "absorb" means to "get into" the technique, training method and art you are interested in until you develop a "feel" for it. Until you experience "being" in it and becoming it you don't really understand it.

For example, looking at the Malaysian art of bersilat, trying out a few of their techniques, then saying to yourself, "I like their elbow technique. I think I'll add it to my style" is a step into the mud hole of self-delusion. To understand those techniques you need to go into the Malaysian art and train like they do, feel it, experience it for a while, both in the doing and the receiving, until you've got a grasp of it. You must become a bersilat main in order to truly understand bersilat techniques, attitudes, training methods, etc.

Once you have "absorbed it," that experience and knowledge gained is yours, not just something you've patrolled from another style. Only now can you start throwing away what doesn't suit you personally, so you can reject what is useless.

How do we know what is useless? What we think we see is sometimes not what we really see. For example, a karate man, kickboxer, kung-fu man and savate man were watching a Thai boxer throw a roundhouse kick against a heavy bag. They might immediately dismiss the idea that that kick had anything to offer them because they already feel they know that kick, but do they? If they investigated further, they might be in for a rude awakening. Anyone who has spent some time training in many Thai would realize that although it may look like the same kick, it is in fact not the same and it takes a great deal of training to perfect and maintain it.

"The idea of absorbing what is useful does not mean choosing, collecting, compiling, accumulating or assembling techniques from different styles of martial arts thinking to yourself, 'I'll take the best from all the styles, put it together and form a new style.'"

Not being able to perform a technique successfully is another reason for rejecting what you think is useful when it might not be. We should question ourselves why does that technique from that style work for them? Why doesn't it work sometimes? The important thing about rejecting what is useless is that you don't reject anything until you know why you are rejecting it. You could be throwing away a real jewel because of your own lack of understanding. Possibly your timing or distance is off, or your coordination needs improvement. Would you reject battling in baseball just because the times you tried it you struck out? Most of the time it's your own fault that the technique doesn't work, so before you reject anything make sure you've investigated why it doesn't work for you.

To "add what is specifically your own" doesn't mean to add anything for the sake of being different or to make yourself or style unique and different from everyone else. It is understanding the principle all the core that really counts. By knowing ourselves and understanding the root motions we can then modify to our personal preferences.

How do we know ourselves? We must experience a great deal before we can decide what our personal preferences are in technique. We must look at martial arts with eyes that can see what is functional from the perspective of structure of technique. To be able to discern what is functional requires understanding the principle in practical application coupled with experience. How many of us still drive the way we when taught in driving school? It is because of our experience in driving that we can add our personal modification or chest (as the case may be); like driving with one hand while operating the radio switch with the other, or turning the wheel by palming it instead of using both hands.

Man, the creating individual is more important than any established style or system. Does this mean you should create your own style? No, in order to understand this we must distinguish between style and "personal style." All boxers basically use the same methods and "style" but the personal style of Ali is quite different from Frazier. European boxers are different from American boxers. When we are creating our own style it is an investigation into what is the best way to get more power, more speed, more illusiveness for ourselves as individuals. Who created style, then? An individual or groups of individuals, did. So what becomes more important in this saying is about freedom, the freedom not to be bound by any method, style or philosophy "it limits our personal growth outside of that entity.

The key to all this boils down to the common denominator called experience. The JKD main activity seeks experience because only by experiencing can he arrive at any sort of self-knowledge, self-understanding, and self-realization. It is good to seek knowledge of techniques or training methods, but if you stop here you are merely an eclectic. You are creating a mosaic of methods and techniques instead of getting to the roots and essence of personal practical application. Knowledge has no understanding. Understanding comes from your own individual experiences with that knowledge.

I think Trevarian best sums it up by saying, "Do not fall into the error of the artisan who boasts of 20 years' experience in his craft while in fact he has had only one year of experience . . . 20 times."

JKD'S DISTANCE IN ATTACK

In The Tao of Jeet Kune Do, Bruce Lee lists the following principles of distance in attack. What follows is a more detailed, practical explanation of each.

"First principle is using the longest to get at the closest." This is to score the fastest hit when attacking from a distance to the nearest target. In kicking, JKD uses the lead shin/knee kick as the primary weapon. In punching, JKD uses the lead hand or finger jab to the eyes. In different ranges there will be an intuitive sense of which secondary tool to bring into play such as the elbow or the knee.

"Second principle is economical initiation(non-telegraphic). Apply latent motor training to intuition." What he means here is to acquire instinctive initiation. This is done by repetitively training the initiating technique until it becomes automatic. Hundreds of repetitions per day emphasizing explosive acceleration will develop this.

"Third principle is correct on-guard position to facilitate freedom of movement(ease). Use the small phasic bent-knee position." This means to keep the legs flexed and footwork slightly shifting, like a boxer or basketball player. Confidence comes from the ability to fire and return to the on-guard position ready for a counterattack. The correct on-guard position is important because the fighting distance you maintain and the confidence you have in it will depend on how well you cover yourself. The on-guard position becomes a safe haven to return to after a probe or attack sequence. Make it an unconscious habit and your mind will be free to think about tactics and strategy.

"Fourth principle is constant shifting footwork to secure the correct measure. Use broken rhythm to confuse the opponent's distance while controlling one's own." This means moving to keep a certain distance so your opponent has to step to get to you. You should be just out of reach but close enough to take advantage of his misstep. You can confuse him by feinting an attack when he takes this step. Footwork variations in your distance will also make it difficult for your opponent to time his attacks.

"Fifth principle is catching the opponent's moment of weakness. physically as well as psychologically." You can determine this by conscious use of fakes and harassing blows designed to intimidate and get respect. Lee student Bob Bremer says that Bruce would tell him that somehow he could tell when "you just weren't with him." That momentary lapse in concentration is the time to strike.

"The sixth principle is correct measure for explosive penetration." This means taking aim at the distance where the opponent will be when the attack is completed, not at the distance before the attack. The strike should have enough momentum and power to drive straight through the target and not fall short or push against it.

"The seventh principle is quick recovery or appropriate follow-ups." Study your balance after the attack and consider your defensive postures and covering moves. You may want to try to limit your opponent's ability to counterattack by cutting off or smothering some of his more dangerous options such as his foot position or his hand tools.

"The 'x' principle is courage and decision." In JKD we call this "x" because it is an unknown factor residing deep within each individuals psyche and the possibilities are unknown for any one particular situation. The confidence required for split-second decision-making ability and courage can be improved by careful progressive training

KEEP THE PRINCIPLE, NOT THE STYLE

Many popular stylized systems of martial arts originated from the success of a talented individual. That person's peculiarities may not be suitable for everyone in that style. Many styles also have lost much in the process of being passed down generation to generation resulting in ineffective but stylized knowledge. Accumulating stylized knowlegde and patterns without understanding the underlying principles leads one to become trapped by the style. The principle is always more important than the style.

In JKD, liberation from the stylized way of technique does not mean abandonment of the principle that makes that technique work. It may mean you have a different purpose. For example, the style may dictate that it is important to always cover the groin while kicking. This may be good for self defense, but if you are training for kickboxing and the groin kick is not allowed then it makes no sense to keep that as a habit and leave yourself unnecessarily exposed to the fury of your opponent. Your hand is better placed in the kickboxing on-guard rather than in front of the groin.

It is liberating to know we can change. The freedom to find another way to express the principle can mean to change the technique that originally illustrated the principle. For example the wing chun principle of dissolving arm to arm pressure by folding the arm at the elbow and coming back with a back-fist punch. The change of technique that illustrated the principle could be changed by pivoting at the waist to dissolve the pressure on the arm. The entire body turns, then comes back with a shoulder push, elbow smash, or even a leg-to-leg takedown. Same principle, different application.

We can learn much by researching other styles of martial arts. To understand the principles of their structures of defense, attack and counterattack rather then getting hung up on the stylized patterns of movement they use, will give you ideas you can modify and adapt to your own personal JKD structure. This allows you to change or modify your technique in the future because of a limitation such as age, injury, point of view or to solve a particular problem.

It opens up the need to see things differently and ask questions about the principles such as: Can it be found in other arts or different aspects of combat? Is it expressed the same way? Does it need to be? Is it important or not?

In JKD the five ways of attack consists of Simple Direct Attack (SDA), Attack by Combination (ABC), Attack by Drawing (ABD), Hard Immobilization Attack (HIA) and Progressive Indirect Attack (PIA). Most were derived originally from Western fencing, but Bruce Lee applied these attacking principles to his JKD using hands and feet. Bruce used the lead leg and hand like a fencer's sword. The principles guided the movement. If you can use ABD in boxing by exposing a target to get a counter hit , the same principle applies to leaving an opening for the grappler to attack that you counter with your own lock or hold.

Some principles to look at are: Superior positioning; Slipping (evasion); Centerline theory; Substitution principle; Retaining energy; Dissolving energy; Constant pressure; Longest weapon to hit nearest target; Correct on-guard positioning; Constantly shifting footwork; Leverage; Timing (Styles tend to favor a type of timing for counter attack.); Bamboo (yielding) principle; Economy of motion – (defense/offensive structure); Broken rhythm; Bridging the Gap; Five Ways of Attack

The idea is not to be limited to the stylized way but to use the principle with other aspects of fighting. Keep the principle, not the style.

ADAPTABILITY

Adaptability is the single most important trait a fighter can have. It is more important than power, speed, timing, balance, coordination, grace, fortitude, conditioning, aggressiveness, agility, precision, endurance, body feel, posture or form. To instantly respond to your adversary's every move and condition, and every fight environment, requires a flexible mind and a martial art suited to modification. Some say that conditioning is the number one trait, because if you lack stamina you won't be able to use your art after a few seconds, anyway. But I think adaptability is more important because if you're huffing and puffing and still have to fight, you've got to adapt to that lack of conditioning.
So what exactly is adaptability? The dictionary says it means "to make fit (as for a specific or new use or situation) often by modification." Adaptation also means "an adjustment to environmental conditions, or an adjustment of a sense organ to the intensity or quality of stimulation." A fighter's sense organs include his legs, feet, arms and hands for sensing his adversary's movements by feel. The senses also include the eyes, for marking changes in the timing of movement, and the ears for adjustment to verbal harassment. Of course, there is the sixth sense of intuition, which senses intangibles such as fear. Being able to adjust the senses means training them to know what to expect. Adaptability training should involve all your senses.
The fighter must modify his martial art system for fighting under various potential conditions. This means adapting to the quality or intensity of stimulation in a fight – stimulation such as a screaming, crazy-man swinging a crowbar in a bus, or a group of bikers yelling at you, or a guy foaming at the mouth, impervious to pain, determined to bite your ear off. Could you adapt your psyche and your martial art to deal with these?

Environmental conditions could be a parking lot or a packed men's room at a rock club. Are there obstacles like cars, or tables and chairs? Are other people in the way like at a rock concert? Can you adapt the current structure of your martial art to such environments – if you can't, you could find yourself in serious trouble.

If your style is primarily kicking, could you adapt it to work? Could you continue to fight if your arm or leg got hurt? What tactics do you know? What have you practiced? The Filipino and Indonesian arts excel at training in these situations.

What if you picked up a weapon like a stick or knife? Do you know how to use it? What if they were used against you? A champion kickboxer might face a sixteen-year-old girl trained in kali knife-fighting. The kickboxer must adapt to the sharp razor facing him, and it isn't going to be easy because she is trained! One cut in the wrong place could mean instant death. Can he adapt? Try to figure out how to adapt your fighting art to a boxing, muay Thai, wrestling, judo, kali stick, escrima knife, or taekwondo attack. How would you change what you know so you can use it?

If you can't modify your art, you've got to modify your thinking: 1) Learn to counter everything – physical and mental; 2) Develop adaptive knowledge under fighting conditions; 3) Practice environmental awareness in the places you frequent most; 4) Learn to use your art against other style's attacks – prepare for the unexpected; 5) Develop a philosophy of adaptability and make it the centerpiece of your training

CONSTANT FORWARD PRESSURE

In pentjak silat, constant forward pressure means attacking your opponent to keep him in a perpetual state of unbalance. Instead of being able to counter, your opponent becomes concerned with trying to regain his composure, footing, and equilibrium. As he's trying to escape or counter, he's already being countered. Because has no base from which to renew his attack, you can trample him with your counterattacks. Constant pressure is a martial arts water-hose blasting punches, kicks, elbows, body shoves, traps, leg sweeps and trips. It is hard, brutal, unrelenting, and unmerciful. There is no good way to counter – it's even hard to breathe! Constant forward pressure allows you to find or create openings, set-ups, various follow-ups or footwork placements. This concept can also be found in other arts such as JKD which uses the equivalent "straight blast."

Constant pressure doesn't mean trying to move your opponent straight backwards, but rather pressuring them in the direction of your technique (you might lose contact by pushing straight back). Instead, your attack must guide your opponent into your future hits, locks, sweeps, and takedowns. It's safer because you are not waiting for incoming blows, but instead actively overwhelming your opponent. Psychologically, this also puts you into a superior frame of mind.

You cannot apply this pressure intermittently. If you do, your opponent will push forward into the space you give him. In an encounter, an attacker will constantly probe you – pressing, hitting, and trying to get in and find a weak spot. If he senses you've let up, he will move in violently, without compassion.

Constant forward pressure is a fundamental tactic taught at the Magda Institute. It means total commitment. If the enemy is physically off-balance and struggling, he is also mentally off-balance and struggling – often he is desperate. When he attacks in a wild frenzy you must not give in. Cracking under emotional pressure is the worse thing you can do because you'll end up covering-up, helpless, praying the attack will end. The emotional pressure to quit can be kept at bay by pressing forward; otherwise, when a opportunity comes to counterattack, you will have no emotional reserves left and will be unable to take advantage of the opening. Proper training and discipline will insure this never happens to you.

There are also enemies in life pressing you and looking for a weak spot. These enemies are indifference and procrastination. Take your health, for example. Those two enemies are always there, waiting for you to take it easy so illness can take over and destroy you and your happiness. This process doesn't happen all at once, it's subtle. It's not like a punch in the face, but it does hurt because before you know it, the days, weeks, and months will quickly go by. Five years later you'll be depressed and angry, wondering why you are overweight, sick, and unhappy with yourself. It's because you stopped pushing, let things slide, and procrastination pushed itself in and cunningly stole your health and happiness. You've got to push to keep the pressure on indifference and procrastination so they can never take control. They are so dangerous because they are so deceptive. According to an old silat saying there are two enemies – the one on the outside and the one on the inside. Keep "constant pressure" on both!

THE CORNERSTONES OF JEET KUNE DO

In JKD we always search for ways to make ourselves more functional in combat. This can be done by researching other arts, fitting what is useful into our structure, putting what we learn through the rigorous test of full contact sparring, and then eliminating what doesn't work or modifying it so it does. In this research we use the criteria and theory of JKD as a method of study. JKD is our way to study other things to decide if they're functional or not. Dan Inosanto once told me that one of the most important things that Bruce Lee taught him was the ability to decide what was functional and what was not. He called it, "The Functional Eye."
"Simple, direct, and non-classical," is a phrase which describes the three cornerstones of JKD. These cornerstones are the criteria for our method of study and analysis of what is functional and what isn't. They are used when analyzing other martial arts techniques or when trying to improve within our own system of JKD.
The first cornerstone is "simplicity." If a technique sequence against an attack takes six moves then the chances of it being used successfully in reality are slim. It's a simple fact that the more moves one has to make,

the more chances there are of something going terribly wrong. So part of using simplicity as a criteria is to ask, "How can that six-move sequence be shortened to three moves? Can those three moves be shortened to two?" Ultimately, modifying and changing a six-move sequence to one or two moves and getting the same end result is a JKD way of thinking and studying.

The last cornerstone is "non-classical." This is the freedom to go outside the established classical system and break the rules of the techniques or theory. The classical system says there is only one way to do something. "Non-classical" in JKD means personalization. When we are being non--classical, we have the freedom to change things for our needs. We may absorb a theory or technique from another source but accomplish it in quite a different way. A lot of the time, as a result of these modifications, the finished motion may end up only faintly resembling or looking nothing like the original source. The modifications change the technique, principle, or training method into something unrecognizable from the style of origin, hence it becomes non-classical. It may also mean that we don't go outside our system to absorb from another source but instead modify what we already have or even create something new to solve the problem.

Just as a three-legged stool provides a steadier base than a four-legged chair, the three cornerstones of JKD can be used to improve the martial arts skill of any style by providing a steady base for using what works.

MASTERY IS A MOVING TARGET

The wrong questions to ask are: What is the meaning of my life and training once I become a master? When will I get 'it'?
A martial artist's frustration in training is about the lack of an answer to those questions. Instead ask: What's the meaning of my life and training today, NOW, before you get the skills and knowledge and become a master. Here are five things to think about.

1. You Get The Elusive 'It' Before The Mastery

It requires a new mind set. You don't have the skill yet but you are on the path working for it. You get the spirit first then the skill and knowledge. Focus on what you love about training and learning. You have no competition, you are the only player. There's no one to beat in a game of solitaire. As you move along, the spiritual-philosophical path opens up to you and you get a taste of the power of your invisible self. You discover learning martial arts is a game that you play with yourself.

2. Trust Yourself, For You Are The Only Guru

If you meet Buddha in the martial arts dojo, kill him! Why? Because you are the only guru you will ever need. No outside authority can give you meaning. Of course teachers light the way for us and we need to be respectful to the martial arts traditions. But we need to keep hold of our own minds and trust our own intuition in this process. Systems and styles help only up to a point before the individual finds out enough about himself to know what is best.

We need to echo the Buddha – "Believe in nothing, no matter where you read it or who has said it, not even if I have said it, unless it agrees with your own reason and common sense."

3. Make Peace With Your Inner Enemies!

Kahil Gibran in his book 'The Prophet" said: "Bless the darkness as you bless the light." Embrace your martial art difficulties as you would your successes. You are always going to have problems on the path. Accept that! Face them, stop blaming and "get over it"! 19th century philosopher James Allen said "circumstances do not make a man, they reveal him" Your problems will be your greatest teachers.

4. Being A Master Is Nothing Special.

Zen masters remind us that enlightenment is "nothing special" and neither is the mastery of the martial arts. To paraphrase the ancient Zen masters "Before you become a martial arts master, you chop wood, carry water. After you are a martial arts master, you chop wood, carry water". Most martial art masters live normal lives without flaunting their skill and live with a strong sense of responsibility in service to the world around them. They are surprisingly very ordinary. Being a master is "nothing special."

5. The Martial Art Master "Just Is"
The ancient masters always regard themselves as beginners, with minds open to the experience, the momentary adventures of life, new things to learn and enjoy. In his book "Mastery" George Leonard writes: "Mastery is not perfection but rather a journey and the true master must be willing to try and fail and try again" Learning itself becomes an art.
The martial arts life is a moving target. Just when you think you've mastered it, it moves again. The beginners mind is the only "technology" you'll ever need in finding solutions to the martial art's never ending stream of challenges.
So ask yourself the right question: What is the meaning of my life training today right now?

DARE TO BE INCONCLUSIVE

Today's martial artists are knocking on the door for the personal experience of "something more" which is the heart of the essence of what it is to be a martial artist – a fighter. They want more of "it."
Many fighters have had this peak experience of finding flow, perfect harmony, the feeling of complete perfection and invulnerability that seems to lift them right out of themselves. Such experiences and personal development along these lines has to be disciplined and discovered anew, in a personal way. Such an experience cannot be taught or even described in a way that is easily understood. What can be taught is how to discover! The traditional way of teaching such discovery is through the use of repetition and progressive approximations to all-out fighting. These types

of approximations include various levels of sparring and two-man drills that nudge one closer and closer to the truth until a discovery is made.

Any great style provides these levels of progression, different levels of understanding, and a spiritual experience of training and fighting. There is something useful for everyone and a further opportunity to rediscover new meaning and greater realization again and again. That's why it has survived – why it is cherished as a great system. This way is open-ended and inconclusive.

The "how-to-discover" requires one to be ready to abandon any fixed notion so that a new, more comprehensive view – a deeper experience of realization – can take its place. With all the various systems of martial arts comes the perplexity of choice, of alignment and partisanship as to theories and assumptions, even political and prejudicial beliefs. Many assume the beliefs of their instructor without thinking twice. Taken literally these various "truths" incorporated into a style become dogma. Dogma says, "Here is the only way to do it." Dogma is final, not inconclusive.

A martial artist trapped by such dogma will say that anything new has to be accounted for in terms of his own theories that are familiar and acceptable. If they don't fit then they are unacceptable. It is like a drunk looking for his keys under the light of a streetlight because that's where the light is – rather than where he lost them in the dark!

This leads to the peculiar attitude of martial artists being able to deny their own observations and experiences more easily, rather than deny the pet theories of their style. I once had a college friend show me how he blocked a stick attack with his tonfa. He said the theory was that the energy of his block was so hard that it would allow him to counter without worrying about a possible re-counter or combination attack. When we tried it and my stick combination was not stopped on repeated attempts he refused to believe his theory wasn't true!

There are always some facts left out of any system, anomalies that do not fit into the framework of accepted explanations. The alternative to this is to be personally courageous and experiment and explore in a way that is open-ended. If you keep your program open-ended then that attracts new experiences and new ideas about them. Good teachers and good training partners certainly help too!

Inconclusive doesn't mean to be unsure, undecided or gullible about your style. It just means never to form a final judgement – to remain open and reaching for new experiences, ideas, and meaning. Spiritual experience realization and know-how are there to be discovered. In order to discover more of that "something more" try to be experimental and inconclusive.

POLITICS IN MARTIAL ARTS

We hear again and again that martial artists are turned off by politics. Frustrated, they cry "I hate politics, I just want to work out," or "He got that (rank, position, award) by brown-nosing," or "All we do is waste time in these meetings." Pleeeease!! The fact is, nothing from running a school to organizing a tournament can be done individually.

Politics is life. It is the basis for getting things done as opposed to the fantasy brought to you by "strong leaders." Every relationship with instructors, training partners, friends, or spouses is political and depends on lots of give, a little take, and the acknowledgment of assumptions. Of course, splits regularly occur between instructors, students, people, and organizations – but the fact is that most such failures are caused by the failure "to invest" sufficiently in the relationship. Investing means paying the price of frequent compromise and, above all, spending time. I like to call that "hang time."

Attending meetings and spending time together isn't always about getting things done. Under this veneer they're also about understanding how so-and-so is feeling – which inches toward an eventual consensus about a future issue.

Some martial artists quit and move to small schools or garage groups to avoid politics. Nice try. The only place to avoid politics is in a cave by yourself. These small groups are more informal, so rank, rules, and procedures tend to be not so important. Everyone knows their place. That's an example of acknowledgment of assumptions. But assumptions must be constantly nourished and maintained. Even groups of three or more people have cliques. Some will feel that they are being ganged-up on or overlooked. Some people will use jealousy, back stabbing, character assassination, and hogging the limelight to get their way. Hey, it's called reality. But in my experience these people eventually get theirs. When the time comes for a special rank promotion, demonstration team opening, or other special recognition, the jerks are usually left out. They then inevitably run around screaming "I'm a victim…I hate politics!"

The fact is, no successful instructor or martial artist is unsullied by politics. Effective human beings are compromising human beings. In his book, Leadership, author James MacGregor Burns discusses the fact that inspiring leaders such as Ghandi and Martin Luther King spent a huge amount of time in a transformational leadership style, talking with their followers, especially their inner circles, mending bruised egos, soothing slights, meeting, talking, meeting and talking, and meeting and talking… you get the idea. These leaders invested in relationships and became experts at reading people – they were super-compromisers. They bent, wiggled, twisted, turned over, and gave in – all to get things done.

To "hate" politics is naive. Without politics how could rank be bestowed, tournaments be run, schools exist, knowledge be spread, seminars be created, or higher standards be set? Politics is the art of getting things done with people. It's as simple and complicated as that.

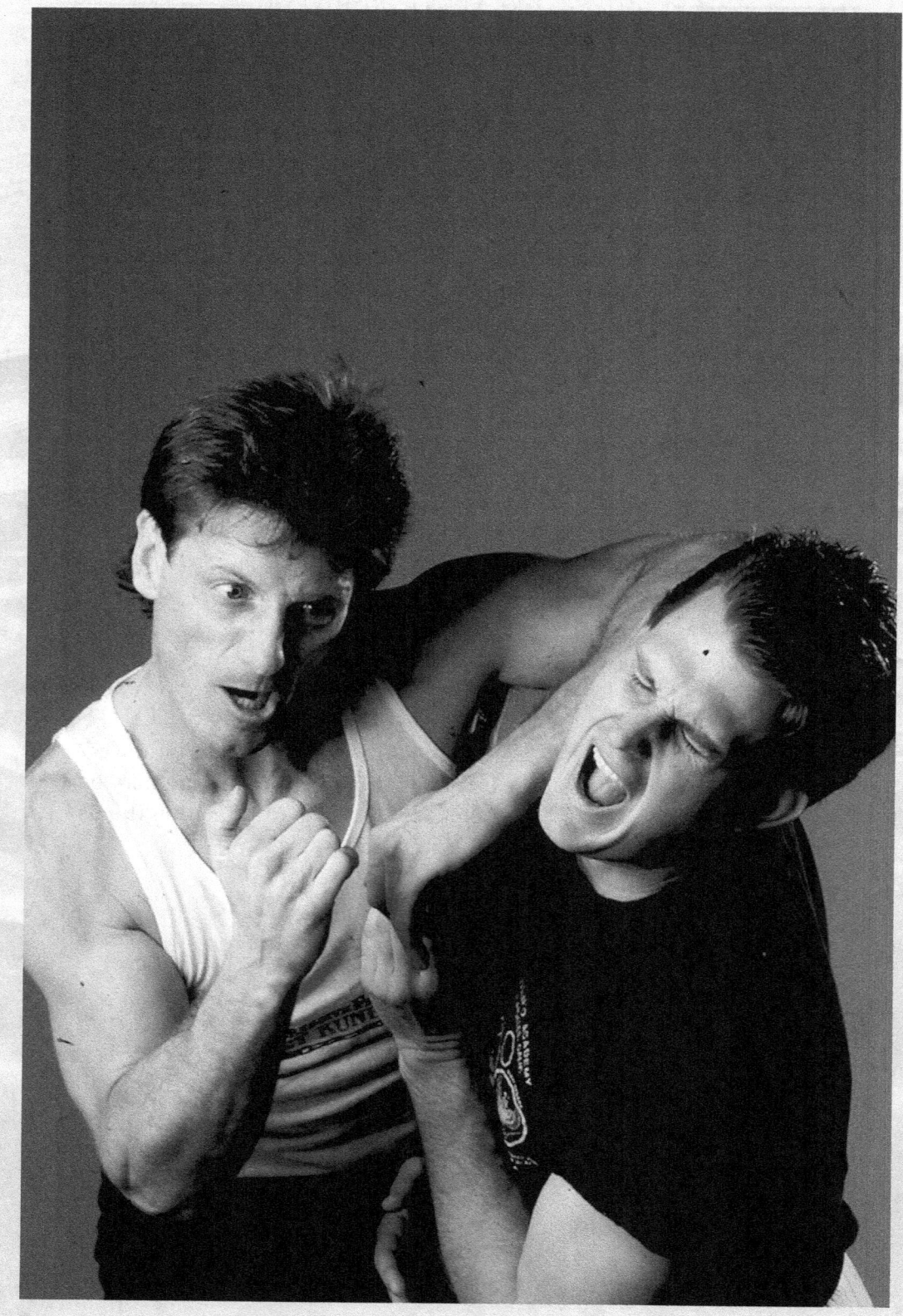

PAUL VUNAK

JEET KUNE DO CONCEPTS

"I'M SO GREAT As I travel around the world, I have the ongoing opportunity to interact with many different martial artists from all walks of life. I see how they learn, train and polish their skills. I am also an avid sports fan, so I am intimately familiar with the training habits and mentalities of world class athletes in other fields. The primary difference between the training mentalities of the athlete and the martial artists is not some secret technique, but a training attitude that has no room for complacency.
Most "martial artists" I have met have an unwarranted and untested confidence in themselves and their abilities. This leads to an artificially inflated senses of self-worth. I simply cannot tolerate any conceit in myself or my students, so it is difficult for me to swallow this attitude from "classroom warriors."
I am truly incredulous that anyone truly interested in streetfighting could be conceited. There are just too many variables and too

many scenarios when even the most talented fighter can find himself in a vulnerable position (i.e., mass attack, sucker punches, beer bottles over the head, just plain dumb luck, etc.) The simple fact is that most martial artists never put themselves in a position to test their mettle.

This is not an insurmountable task. I've got a few suggestions, provided you follow them that will keep that artificial sense of self-worth out of your training and, hopefully, cut of your life. First, in a street-fight, there are four basic ranges: kicking, punching, trapping and grappling. If you think you're a deft kicker, get in the ring with a Thai boxer (make sure he's a real Thai boxer, not just some Joe off the street with his hands up and a bouncing knee). If you're good with your hands, get in the ring with a boxer and you'll see how good your hands really are.

Tapping your game? Tie up with Inosanto and see how well your traps work. Grappling, you say? I've got news, my friend. Any one of the Gracie Brothers will give you a very serious reality check.

The principle is to find the top people available to you in each range and play the game with them. This is the best method I've ever seen for improving your skills and bringing yourself down to earth.

In short, "He who knows not and knows that he knows not is asleep… awaken him!"

ISOLATION TRAINING (HONING YOUR SKILLS)

The process of isolation training is to pick a specific motion, then isolate and train that same motion. Isolation training is useful in any art for improving the effectiveness of that particular art and its tools.

I have found that to fully take advantage of this training method, one should first identify the weapon (hand, foot, knee, head, elbows, etc.) then choose the most effective art and the appropriate range from which to launch it. Remember to choose the proper range for the weapon; i.e., kicking range for the feet, boxing range for the hands, trapping range for the head butts, knees and elbows, grappling range for locking, breaking, choking, pinching and biting. Then identify the art which is best suited to your own preferences (savate, wing chun, kali, etc.)

Understanding that we have only a limited number of "tools" on our bodies that can be used to inflict damage on an opponent, isolation training allows full development of those tools.

Let's take the lead jab as an example. Choose an effective art (Western boxing), then, as Bruce Lee always said, "Use no way as way." Borrow a weight training mentality and apply this to achieve your goal, which is to increase the effectiveness of your weapon or technique.

Now we'll example the weight training reference in the previous paragraph. First, a weight trainer identifies and examines a specific group of muscles. For example, he or she will do curls for biceps, flyes for pectorals, etc. He or she will then perform a specific number of repetitions of that particular exercise for a specific number of sets.

Using this mentality on our lead jab, we work five sets of five jabs, increasing the intensity with each jab and alternating sets between the right and left hands. Then we move to another weapon, such as the thigh kick, and repeat the process.

Finally, make sure you don't just go through the motions. Inject full intensity and use the full range of emotional volume. Use your imagination and picture a real opponent in front of you on the heavy bag. Pick different targets and fire your guns!

Good hunting!

THE EYE JAB

Is it possible to give the eye jab too much credit? I don't think so. The eyes are the most valuable sensory organ. As a result, nature has provided us with a tremendous protective instinct and very low pain threshold in the eyes. In other words, nothing shuts the body down quicker than a good shot to the eyes.

I recently viewed a videotape featuring some of the greatest moves in

NFL history. In one scene, a 230-pound linebacker, full of adrenaline, is about to slam a half-back into the next county. At that moment, a referee sees a clip on the other end of the field and immediately throws his flag. Instead of landing on the ground, the flag catches the fullback in the eye. Never have 40,000 lane witnessed anyone drop to his knees faster.

Have you ever had one of your eyelashes brush against the surface of your eye? It becomes almost impossible to concentrate on anything else until you get that lash out of there. Once it is removed, the sensation lingers for several minutes.

In a streetfight, one must always seek to make the adversary more concerned about his own welfare his reasons for fighting in the first place. Needless to say, a shot to the eyes can do much to accomplish this.

However, a shot to the eyes is not a "magic button" to end any encounter. Has anyone ever thrown anything at you unexpectedly? Did you notice how one hand immediately shot up to cover your eyes? When was the last time you heard a loud bang? Did you notice how your eyes closed reflexively? In other words, there is probably not a person living who does not instinctively and reflexively protect his/her eyes. Of course, a trained martial artist can take advantage of this, with enough practice, in that a feint to the eyes will instantly distract all of the defender's attention to that area, thus leaving other areas open for attack.

One great drill is to have one person wear boxing gloves. This person can punch and kick. But there is one catch; this person must wear swimming goggles.

The other fighter has no gloves and must keep his hands open. Both fighters then spar. The partner without the gloves is trying to take his opponent out by going for the eyes. This is usually accomplished by a "bil gee" (finger jab) or taking the opponent to the ground and applying a mount position.

Remember, the opponent with the gloves can still punch kick. This combination of stipulations generally proves very realistic and is highly functional.

USING THE ELBOW

When we think of an elbow strike, we tend to picture a rather gross, demonstrative motion. It is easy to summon up images of some kata containing graphic elbow strikes followed by a loud kiai, or perhaps a Thai boxer winding up from Cleveland, then breaking through kicking and boxing range to finally land that bomb. (For the record, this sort of telegraphing is not common among really good Thai boxer.)
However, there are some who truly understand the versatility of the elbow strike. Simply because it is a clublike, short-range weapon doesn't negate subtle movement.
It is very important that people do not assume that one is bound to John L. Sullivan moves. There can still be finesse, subtlety, and pinpoint accuracy. How well one uses the elbow is largely dependent upon one's mentality.
First, we must understand that the elbow is not a "smashing" motion, like a head-butt. It is a cutting tool that rakes through the head and face. One of the elbow's fortes is its propensity for causing sudden pain and immense bleeding, as contrasted to, say, a groin shot where the pain tends to creep up on you.
It is important to note that the actual surface area that one strikes with is just the very tip, perhaps the size of a quarter. If one is trained properly, the elbow can be a wonderfully barbaric tool with a high degree of versatility. At this point, I would like to offer some training tips to hopefully facilitate a new attitude concerning the elbow.

1 - Shadow box with your elbows as you would with your hands. (Cover the basic jab, cross, hook, uppercut and over-hand motion.)

2 - Practice "grazing" blows on the heavy bag instead of smashing the entire forearm into the bag. (Most people strike with far too much surface area. This severely compromises the damage that one will do to the opponent.)

THE WOODEN DUMMY - DO YOU REALLY NEED IT?

You bet your lop sao you do! A very common question I get regarding trapping is, "Do I need a wooden dummy?" my answer is always a firm affirmative. It's possible to learn trapping without a wooden dummy, but that's analogous to learning boxing without a heavy bag.

If one wants to excel to one's fullest, one needs a method in which one can train solo, repeating motions until they become second nature. To fully internalize a technique, you've got to make it a part of your subconscious mind so it becomes a programmed reflex.

The wooden dummy affords a student the opportunity to not only train, but to repeat motions thousands of time on Superman. When you think about it, that's what the wooden dummy is – Superman. I've never met anyone stronger or more invulnerable than my wooden dummy. And any wooden dummy, if properly made maintain perfect form. After performing multiple traps literally thousands of times against Superman with perfect form, when one goes up against a human, regardless of size and strength, one "feels" like one can go through the "mere mortal" like a hot knife through butler.

I firmly believe the key to effective wooden dummy training is "repetition." The only way to make the training work is by putting in the hours. I remember my instructor. Dan Inosanto, relating a Bruce Lee story to me once upon a time. One day he stepped into the gym and saw Bruce all sweaty in the corner, practicing his bon sao on the wooden dummy. He looked quite intense, so Dan didn't bother him for over an hour. At that point, Dan suggested that Bruce join him, along with Linda and the kids, for some Chinese food. Bruce told Dan to go ahead and he'd catch up later on.

Linda, Bruce's kids and Dan ended up eating without Bruce. After Dan returned from lunch to drop off Bruce over in the corner, still doing his bong sao, saying he only had a couple more hours to go before he switched to his left hand.

LEARNING TO TRAP QUICKLY

We a martial artist thinks of "trapping," images of a blindfolded Bruce Lee performing Chi Sao with a partner quickly spring to mind. Or, perhaps we picture students lined-up doing elaborate energy drills. Whatever the image, it I s very easy to picture yourself spending many, many years achieving proficiency in trapping.
In the style of Wing Chun, an art known for trapping, I have seen students who have spent five to ten years practicing their style and who have yet to learn how to trap. I personally feel this is because of the progression of instruction, which has led to the common belief that, before you can trap while sparring, you must go through several stages of drilling. Most subsets of Wing Chun will have you learning Sil Lum Tao, then, after some months, progress to Don Chi, then, ultimately, Chi Sao. By now you've put in a number of years, and you're just beginning to understand traps.
Bruce Lee's belief was that one could go directly to Chi Sao and, after a reasonable amount of time practicing, segue into trapping while sparring. Based on questions I got from people in my seminars, literally all over the world, and based on watching students spar, I feel that most people are emphasizing the wrong things when they train.
Instead of worrying about which way the toes are pointed during Don Chi, or correcting the "pinky" on a Taun Sao, one should be more concerned with how many boxers will be sticking a jab in one's face. Attributes such as footwork and timing are directly related to one's ability to enter and trap.
Imagine spending 20 years on all of the intricacies and nuances of trapping drills, then having a YMCA-trained boxer pummel your face to a pulp when you try and enter. I have seen this happen to so-called Masters! If you train in a static posture, rigidly thrusting out straight punches and fastidiously worrying about inconsequential things, when you get in a fight with a street fighter who emphasizing knocking your block off, you will lose!

Therefore, I'd like to share with you all a basic drill which will hopefully shift your priorities more toward functionalism. Partner A puts on boxing gloves and a motorcycle helmet. Partner B uses a trap he/she wants. The intention is that B is to enter with a straight blast until A blocks one of the strikes. At this time, B performs a trap. Perform this drill at half speed, and repeat the process every single time you wish to practice the trap. This way, you can practice movement against a partner really out to hit, and take a step toward reality.

MAINTENANCE

This month's subject deals with maintaining the quality of one's fighting ability. As we have discussed before, one's fighting ability depends on the quality of one's attribute, such as speed, power, coordination, footwork, etc. The major point I would like to project here is that each attribute requires a different time frame to maintain.

The second point worthy of discussion deals with range. Each range requires different attributes. First, I would like to break down each range and its respective attributes. Of the four possible ranges one human being can fight another in, long range or kicking range seems to require the most attributes – attributes that tend to deteriorate quickly.

Wrestling range is a close second, with an emphasis on power, strength, size, endurance, etc. Boxing range is a third place on the Vunak attributes requirements list. Finally, we have trapping range, the range close enough to feel the opponent's intentions and respond with minimal energy and maximum effectiveness; i.e., head-butts, elbows, and knees (all looks that do not take a Bruce Jenner to use.)

Now let's list and delineate each attribute and establish an idea of the degree of maintenance required of each:

APPROXIMATE MAINTENANCE TIME

1 - Awareness one couldn't lose if he tried.
2 - Sensitivity is also like riding a bike, you never seem to lose it.
3 - Proper mental attitude usually stays with one throughout old age.
4 - Body mechanics needs by 10 minutes a day to maintain.
5 - Strength usually leaves us relatively quickly; however, if you perform one repetition per week of your maximum weight you will maintain that weight.
6 - Footwork will last a lifetime provided there are soft type movements added.
7 - Speed starts to decrease around 40; however, 10-20 minutes per day of work one can maintain 80-90% of speed well into the 60s.
8 - Power is a combination of speed, strength, and body mechanics. Most of those three stay with us very long.
9 - Timing gets rusty but never goes away forever. It also comes back very soon.
10 - Coordination takes minimal effort to maintain.
11 - Balance also takes minimal effort (10/15 min. daily).
12 - Spatial relationship stays with you.
13 - Agility is lost when limberness gets lost.
14 - Stamina is lost extremely fast.
15 - Conditioning needs minimal effort to maintain.
16 - Limberness is lost perhaps the fastest and comes back perhaps the slowest.
17 - Rhythm usually stays with the young-minded person well into the 60s.
18 - Precision takes perhaps 20 minutes a week to maintain.
19 - Explosiveness is usually replaced with precision around 60.
20 - Flow is made up of the two attributes we never lose; therefore, we never lose the ability to flow. *

* This list is not to be taken too seriously. There are other factors we have not considered like genetics, mindset, etc.

THE WATCHER

We have briefly discussed in previous articles what so many Eastern philosophers refer to the "Watcher" or, the "Observer." If you really thing about it, there is something inside each of us that is continually aware of every little nuance of our existence. Once this "Watcher" is acknowledged, the second (and far from last) step is to cultivate it. "It" (for lack of a better word) serves as a vehicle in which all personal growth (or what Carlos Castaneda refers to as personal power is derived. Unfortunately, the beginning stages are extremely difficult. The largest single hurdle is simply to believe in, or understand the concept. Once belief is achieved, what once was just a concept will become your best friend. All other problems in life are simply hurdles which your "watcher" converts into personal power. Thus we have, as Bruce Lee would say, a circle with no circumstance.

The reason that I haven't gone into this topic previously is because its nature is extremely esoteric. My previous training in JKD doesn't exactly promote this kind of mentality. Yet, I am still growing and trying to achieve an obscure, yet important, goal that Bruce had somehow grasped.

Bruce Lee had a very direct and honest way of both fighting and living. He developed his "watcher" in such a way that it continually tapped his personal power. Obviously the major source was his martial arts. The "watcher" has no limits. Bruce's mind-set rubbed off on his students. For examples, when I watch Dan Inosanto move, his speed, his intensity, his power just never dull. He is quicker now than 11 years ago! However, to this day, Dan remains in awe at the abilities of John LaCoste. Dan confesses that he still cannot emulate LaCoste's footwork . . . and John was 89!

I don't pretend for a moment to have mastered this level; however, here are some tips that I have used to develop my "watcher".

1 - Perform each movement as if it were your last. This assumes that our

common denominator is martial arts, regardless of the style.

2 - Never "think" while you train. Internal mind chatter is the antithesis of the "watcher". The consciousness of the self is the greatest hindrance to mankind." – Bruce Lee

3 - The "watcher" never judges. It just simply acknowledges and registers.

4 - Always be as intense as possible, and then square it! This is very important no matter whatever you do, or how you accomplish it. Intensity is the opposite of sub-vocalization. If you say you're intense, usually you are not. If you think you are, you NEVER are.

5 - Take time to be alone. Take time for both introspection and abandon . . . with as little outside stimulus as possible. If you have truly achieved an intensity, then you can now calmly meditate, without hypocrisy.

VISUAL AWARENESS

Anatomically speaking, the spot one chooses to look at on his opponent (during training, sparring and fighting) can be a very important. There are definite benefits in staring at certain areas over others. This is a controversial issue among different styles. Some arts will have you stare into "the window of the soul," the eyes. Certain arts believe it is better to look at the forehead, between the eyes. Some say look at the hips (the center of the person) because nothing moves before the hips. Other arts simply ignore the issue altogether, where the eyes of the student do what comes naturally, stare at the hands and feet. Let's discuss the various areas in more detail, and explore why Bruce Lee was not in favor of any of them.

The Eyes
Staring into the eyes carries an air of mystery, and there is a myth of instant omnipotence the moment one looks into their opponent's eyes. The fact is, the eyes are not used to attack. Looking at the eyes give you no more information than looking at the ears.

The Hips
Unless your opponent is so tall he literally lowers above you, staring at the hip draw your attention too low, where vision is better below the point of focus than above. So, short of an opponent with hips close to eye level, the field of vision is narrower the lower one looks, decreasing the peripheral vision.

The Arms and Legs
If one chooses to stare at the limbs, one should limit it to the limbs, because staring at the hands and feet is extremely unwise. Picture staring at the last six inches of a whip, it cracks. The hands and feet are far too deceptive and quick. I fear you'll end up feeling the strike before you ever see it.

Why Bruce Lee Felt the Chest is Best
Bruce Lee felt the chest offers the best signs of the opponent's attack. One should gaze into the chest without fixing the eyes. "You should know the color shirt your opponent is wearing without reading the fine print."
- Dan Inosanto

The eyes pick up information by rapid tiny movements (30-60 per second) called scanning. When the eye becomes heavily focused on a point, the process of scanning is restricted and the information is lost. The more specific the point of focus, the less information we receive. This "tunnel vision" suffocates the ability to respond to the many and varied possibilities that occur in combat.
Staring at the chest area without fixing your eyes allows you to see the entire field of vision. It also allows you the best chance to know with

which angle the opponent is attacking. As the chest is the early-warning sign of a punch or kick, this type of focus could be just the edge you need!

ECLECTIC MY...

Although I'm sure the readers get tired of always hearing what JKD is or isn't. I personally don't believe there should ever be a cessation of people's interpretations of JKD. Just as so many, for so many years, have given their subjective opinions of the works of Nostradamus or the quatrains, this functions to keep us from taking the accomplishments of certain people for granted.

My only objection is when people with absolutely no functional or practical background take liberty with their personal opinions. This leads me to my "favorite" phrase, and the topic of this column, "Like Bruce Lee, I teach eclectic martial arts."

First and foremost, once and for all, JKD is not eclectic. Eclectic means to pick and choose form different systems or doctrines. Bruce Lee never picked anything! He discovered common flaws and hacked away at the unessential until his truth remained. If one particular truth was found in, say, Thai boxing or wing chun, he would simply note the elements he saw in that style that came closest to his truth.

In my opinion, the single worst thing ever discussed or written about JKD is that it is a conglomeration or arts, and thus eclectic. While JKD does have principles that one may interpret as rules or precursors (i.e. maintain centerline, learning to fight at all four ranges, etc.) none of the aforementioned characteristics detract from one's individualism. If, for example, one is asked to get from one end of the swimming pool to the other, he can Australian crawl, dog paddle, or float on his back. However, he wouldn't breathe underwater, or swan dive into the shallow end. JKD is a synthesis of one's personal power by the continuing improvement of one's own efficiency, and the continuing educational process.

Eclecticism on the other hand is, to randomly accumulate styles and techniques. Since most styles take a lifetime to accommodate, the eclectic martial artist is generally forever trapped in the role of beginner. While many eclecticists are quite proficient verbally, and many more shamelessly plagiarize the early writings of Bruce Lee, they create a very real danger in that, when given a forum to sound off, there will invariably be some "seekers" who will take them seriously. While these people speak from ignorance with an air of authority, the JKD practitioner has admitted his or her ignorance, and is on a continuous quest to discover the cause of his or her ignorance.

If you are studying several styles, please do not take this as a put-down. Eventually, common sense and a propensity for functionality will lead you to the truth. Just remember, the process is always more important than the product.

THE DIFFERENCE BETWEEN KNOWLEDGE AND WISDOM

Knowledge and wisdom are by no means synonymous. Knowledge in the martial arts has to do with the amount of information one has acquired over the years. One goes to college to "learn" and area of knowledge. Once this person has his degree and begins practical application on the job, or in the field, then he acquires wisdom. The problem with a large percentage of instructors is that they don't see it as a "stage" or a means to an end, but rather an end in itself. One who knows but cannot apply, we call "intellectually bound." This is why we continually see "techniques" in books and magazines, or seminars that are absolutely ridiculous. They were concocted in the "lab" and obviously never tested. One must absorb what is useful and reject what is useless. How does one reject what is ultimately useless without applying it over and over again to find out its merits and faults? This must be done against different styles, streetfighters, boxers, etc. repeatedly. If the instructor has gone through those rigors, then we can say that person has acquired wisdom.

There are four stages in acquiring wisdom:

1 - You learn a technique;
2 - You practice it (this is the testing ground);
3 - You master it (mainly referring to form);
4 - And finally you functionalize it. This last stage, or functionalization is wisdom.

When you have instructors who jump from stage one and assume stage four, their students are being taken for a ride (and usually an expensive one). For example, when Bruce Lee and Dan Inosanto were developing JKD after Bruce discovered that straight wing chun had certain limitations, both investigated every art they could get their hands on over a nine-year period. These arts also had to easily integrate into the synthesis of JKD meeting one criterion – "street fighting". These arts were tested full contact over and over again, discarding what was not functional and integrating what was useful (this was well before there ever was full contact). The result of nine years of this type of training develops a certain way of moving.

THE BODY TALKS. A good baskeball player can spot another good player just by watching the person dribble and move for five seconds, or by watching one shot. In any sport, the way a person moves is a dead giveaway as to his level (or lack) of prowess. A good example is the countless number of instructors attempting to imitate Bruce's development of JKD by combining styles (the eclectic movement). First of all, one doesn't just arbitrarily pick styles and put them together. Secondly, they must be tested full contact for several years against various opponents. And, finally, there must be a way to develop the attributes necessary to make the techniques work. When all of this has happened, that person has converted knowledge into functional use, and this end result is wisdom.

Knowledge: The accumulation of Information

Wisdom: The ability to use information one has.
My advice to all students inquiring as to which art or arts to study is watch your potential instructor, but don't listen to his mouth, listen to his body.

THE IMPORTANCE OF COORDINATION

Remember during your high school days, while playing sports, one guy always seemed to just cruise along doing everything right. In basketball, he was the playmaker, in football, the quarterback, in baseball, probably the pitcher and team captain. While everyone else worked hard, and still made natural mistakes, this guy never made mistakes.
Some players could be observed, and it was quite obvious why they excelled. They were strong, fast, could jump high, etc. This "other guy" just looked average. There was nothing you could put your finger on to give you a clue as to why he was so much better than you. He was just good, REAL GOOD!
The attribute this fellow possessed, to a very high level, was coordination. The work "coordination" literally means "the harmonious functioning of interrelated muscles, organs, bones and nerves." Coordination simply comes genetically to some people, but it can be taught to all people. The key to developing coordination in a martial artist is weapons training. This is why Filipino arts begin training with weapons.
The level of coordination that it takes to work with sticks, knives, swords, short sticks, double sticks, etc. is five times greater than the level of coordination required for anything empty-handed. Thus, since coordination is universal, when a weapons trained individual returns back to empty hands, he/she is five times more coordinated.
Now, let's talk about what effect coordination has on martial arts. Through the eyes of JKD man, I can tell you that coordination on a rudimentary level helps everything we do. On a more functional level, it gives one the ability to apply much more pressure on an opponent, due to the

fact that the opponent is being assaulted by both hands and feet, elbows, head butts, eye jabs, arm wrenches, etc., in an unpredictable flurry. All of these weapons are coordinated through body control. The brain/nerve/muscle response of a well-coordinated person allows that person to hit and fade wherever and whenever he/she wants to. And, therefore, such a person can make the all-important transition of freeing the mind from the thought process and letting the subconscious take over.

Here are some major ways you can improve your coordination:

1 - Implement weapons training into your program
2 - Rhythm and coordination go hand in hand. Start fiddling around with bongos or chums. Learn to use both hands and feet simultaneously.
3 - All sports require a degree of coordination; however, some require more than others. Handball, for example, requires a great degree of hand-eye coordination.
4 - Speed bag drills improve hand coordination dramatically.
5 - Skipping rope is invaluable for developing coordination in the feet.
6 - Perform any desired movement blindfolded. This enhances the visualization process necessary for brain-nerve coordination.

THE PURPOSE OF SEMINARS

The word "seminar" refers to a group of students participating in research or intensive study. There are many purposes served by instructors traveling around the country from school to school. Thirty-five years ago the idea of one instructor flying to a different school (actually teaching their students) was unheard of. Bruce Lee popularized the idea that no one art has it all and instructors all over the country became more open minded to this concept. Now we have a great deal more instructors accepting the nation that there are, indeed, certain individuals who can spend a weekend with their students and integrate (not indoctrinate)

certain principles to both enhance their art and serve as a sort of shot in the arm to increase their school's enthusiasm and enrollment, if brought back on a regular basis.

The instructors who are continually hopping on a plane giving a seminar in a different city every weekend each have their own distinctive approaches. For example, Bill Wallace has a "way" of fighting that is both different and functional. Fumio Demura has his concepts and techniques that obviously work within his realm. Francis Fong and Chai Sirisute have a great deal to offer any school. There are a few individuals giving JKD seminars, such as Larry Hartsell, Chris Kent, Ted Lucaylucay, myself, and a few others. We all have one common motivation in doing seminars. We all would like to educate the public, and ultimately keep Bruce's philosophy alive. I (as well as my JKD brothers) have but one way to repay Dan Inosanto for sharing with us the art that he and Bruce developed. KEEP IT ALIVE!

One must understand that a seminar serves as a vehicle for personal growth, and not a teaching credential. What one gets out of a seminar is dictated purely by their existing level, attitude (having an empty cup), rate of understanding and absorption, training intensity, etc. There should never be such a thing as an instructorship seminar, in which graduating from a two-day (or week-long) seminar entitles the participant to teach that art. Going to one seminar gives you about as much chance to become a valid instructor as you have of learning the Chinese language a week. Now move to Hong Kong? Good Luck! If seminars are used, and not abused, all of us have a wonderful vehicle for personal growth and sharing out art.

THE FINE ART OF BITING

Anyone can bite, right? That's like saying "Anyone can punch." In theory, anyone can double up a fist and strike you, but how many people can knock you out with a blow from either hand? The same attitude could be applied to biting.

In Filipino kali, the art of biting is referred to as keenamutal, it actually consists of using the teeth to rip and tear the tissue of an opponent. To render the type of damage necessary, one must have understanding of not only how to bite, but where to bite. One must also have the sensitivity and grip strength to prevent a counter.

If you are engaged in a ground fight and a limb or an appendage is bitten, your natural response is to pull away. If the bite is to the torso, the automatic response is to push the biter's head away from your body. A person versed in keenamutal understands this well. Much of keenamutal is based on this process – developing the ability to grab a limb and to have the grip strength to prevent it from escaping.

Certain areas are more conducive to "containment." Also, there are ways of holding onto the torso to present the opponent from pushing the head away. The bottom line is to look more like a rabid monkey than a human being. Picture yourself clutching an arm and biting, tearing and twisting while a frantic opponent is trying to pull that arm away!

Those readers unfortunate enough to have suffered a dog bite know where I'm coming from. Did the dog simply reach out and chomp down on your calf, or did he shoot out at you and, before you could react, sink his teeth into your flesh with maximum force. This is generally followed by locking the teeth and jaws and twisting while pulling back. If you tried to push the dog away, you only assisted his pulling motion and helped him rip your flesh. Observing animals biting is one way to learn total commitment to the bite as an animal can't stand on its hind legs and punch you out. The teeth are the animal's only means of defense. However, we don't recommend running out and antagonizing a pitbull to become more versed at keenamutal.

In other words, the notion that anyone can bite and there's "nothin' to it" is ludicrous. As a matter of fact, it would be indiscreet for me to publish sample drills here, as biting, even in practice, is very dangerous. There is the risk of damaging the teeth and gums, disease transmission, and serious injury. Therefore, all I can state is that biting is such a refined art, it can only be learned from an experienced and careful instructor.

MY JKD IS BETTER THAN YOUR JKD

You know, I really feel sorry for the potential JKD students of the world. For that matter, I pity anyone who has an honest curiosity about Bruce Lee, and what he was all about. I've personally been involved in the study of JKD for 16 years, and I've pursued this learning with the gusto of a madman because, to truly appreciate the nuances of the concepts Bruce and Dan gave us, there is no other way.

The bottom line is one must truly commit to living the way of JKD. This involves some fundamental principles such as relaxation, instinct, awareness, evasiveness, interception, emotional control, dissolving the ego, etc. And, you know, after all this time, I thought I might actually have a handles on some of these concepts. But I guess I was wrong.

You see, dear reader, although I thought I had at least a partial understanding of JKD and what it's all about, I'm thoroughly confused by what I see, hear, and, most of all, read these days. Here we are, nearly 19 years after the death of Bruce Lee, and as far as I see it we now have some 30-plus "styles" of jeet kune do. Each, of course, is better than the other.

Let's see, we have old JKD, new JKD, traditional JKD, modified JKD, redactive JKD, JKD concepts, and my new personal favorite, ORIGINAL JKD.

Hmm, how does it work? Maybe in original JKD they don't teach the concepts? No, wait a minute... maybe in JKD concepts they don't teach the original... or maybe...

Let's try to look at it another way. Let's try sports. I think that Jerry West was an "original" basketball player. But now there's Michael Jordan. I guess he's just basketball concepts.

You know guys, in 100 years we're all going to be worm food. We might have some seventy or eighty years, that's some 23,000 days on this earth. Twenty-three thousand chances to "seize the day." How long are we going to waste our time on semantics. Why don't we just be thankful for what we've been given?

Oh, yeah. You might recognize this little saying some guy who left us

almost two decades back gave us:
"Jeet kune do is only a name. Please don't fuss over it."

THE ARM WRENCH

There are many weapons one may use in an all-out streetfight. One may punch or kick, head-butt, knee, elbow, lock, flip, throw, bite, etc. Each and every tool has its own relatives risk to reward ratio. Any time one punches, for example, he runs the risk of being blocked and locked or counterpunched. Any time one kicks, especially with a high kick, he runs the risk of having his leg grabbed. Any time one tries a joint lock or a flip, he risks the opponent catching his rhythm or stumbling.

In any case, my point is that one must constantly evaluate the best way to inflict damage on an opponent with the least amount of risk to oneself. With this in mind, I would like to get on to the subject of this month's column, the arm wrench.

One definition of an arm wrench is to suddenly apply pressure (a violent sudden pressure) against the elbow joint. This usually occurs when the opponent has extended or locked his arm. Since most martial artists do not fight in trapping range, the arm wrench is seldom ever attempted. My point is that the elbow is a target which presents itself for a wrench very, very frequently, and should not be overlooked. If applied brutally, with accurate timing, the "reward" is far greater than the risk of a punch. When the elbow is jerked past the 180-degrees mark, one goes into instant shock. All of the physiological ramifications of "shock" occur. We're not talking about a broken nose here. The body "shuts down" emotionally, mentally and physically. However, as with any other tool one wishes to hone and sharpen, the arm wrench needs a training method. If there is no realistic way to perfect it, it will become just another techniques we take with us to our grave.

Allow me to recommend a training method to assist us in perfecting the arm wrench. Side A has a set of boxing gloves and a motorcycle helmet (his elbows are taped and tied in such a way as to prevent hyperextension while still allowing him the ability to punch). Side B has no protective equipment on whatsoever.

Both sides spar starting very slowly, say at 10 percent speed. Side B consistently enters with an appropriate tool and immediately goes into the wing chun battle punch. After side A gets his helmet hit several times, his visceral response will be to extend his arm or both arms to prevent the further onslaught of the punches. This enables side B to practice and apply the arm wrench. This procedure is gradually accelerated and the amount of tools are proportionally increased until both participants are engaging in full contact. This is of course, the "Readers Digest" condensed version of the drill.

THE FINE ART OF FAKING

Between two people of equal talent, the person who fakes better in a street-fight will be victorious. Throwing a fake may appear relatively unimportant when compared to the more graphic attributes such as size, strength, speed and so on; however, nothing could be further from the truth! The fake is a common denominator among every great boxer. Faking is indicative of an evolved fighter.

Someone who has fought many skilled adversaries and experienced the "rigid rod of reality" knows that a good fighter is always moving. This being the case, the Single Direct Attack doesn't always work. When dealing with a foe who consistently bobs, weaves and slips, we must segue into another mode of attack.

Our opponent must believe one variety of strike or attack is coming, when actually another is. An example of this would be faking a straight jab and shooting out a low round kick. This is the only way to overcome an adversary of superior attributes.

The particular mode of attack is called a "Progressive Indirect Attack." It is progressive in that it takes up distance, and indirect in that it takes up time. It is important to note here that if one retracts the strike after the fake, the attack is no longer progressive and we lose the desired results. One must fill both criteria.

The Progressive Indirect Attack not only enables one to hit a considerably higher level of opponent, but it usually will allow the blows to land by surprise. Understanding PIA triples your odds of knocking out your enemy. How often have you seen a kickboxing match where an opponent absorbs a tremendous amount of punishment but just doesn't go down? I have seen many!

Blows which flail from the ground up give the opponent's subconscious the time to adjust neurologically and physiologically, tensing the appropriate muscle groups, thus preventing a knock out.

Conversely, how often have you witnessed a match where a subtle (and not-very-powerful) hook comes out of nowhere and kayo's the fighter? Our first reaction is to feel that the fight is "fixed," but upon closer observation we see that the reason the person was knocked down had to do with one major point: THE BLOW CAUGHT HIM BY SURPRISE! This is the core advantage of Progressive indirect Attack.

People proficient in the very lethal range of trapping, where one must enter into close range, find that the most efficient way to enter into this range is with PIA. Since the opponent is caught by surprise, one's chances of running into a punch or kick while simultaneously looking for an opening for the "finishing" assault of headbutts, knees or elbows.

In short, the fake may not be an end, but it's a very effective means.

KINESTHETIC PERCEPTION

Bruce Lee used to talk about the importance of "feeling" one's muscles throughout the range of motion, or to perceive whether or not they are tense or loose. Once the ability to monitor personal muscular contraction is accomplished, one can then make the proper neurological adjustments.

By "adjustments," I mean that we can regulate the amount of tension in specific muscles. When throwing a blow, there are always two muscle groups interacting simultaneously; the prime movers and the antagonistics.

The prime movers are responsible for the desired motion, while the antagonistics are the muscles on the other side of the bone that actually hinder the very movement (not unlike putting one's foot on the accelerator and the brake at the same time). The degree of tension/contraction in the individual muscle, and the balance between the activities of the different muscle groups is what Bruce called "kinesthetic perception."

This perception is balanced by our central nervous system. As our kinesthetic perception improves, we not only learn to feel the state of our muscles, we can actually change that state. We can learn to reduce the tension of our antagonistic muscles (letting off the brakes), while, at the same time, increasing the intensity of the prime movers (stepping on the gas).

Let's pause for a moment and discuss how we can improve our kinesthetic perception. One way is to perform an isometric contraction. One is then forced to regulate the degree of tension on the muscle and joint. This provides us with a sort of barometer in gauging just how tense our muscles are, and the degree of contraction in those muscles. Therefore, in short, isometrics serve as a vehicle for both improving tendon strength and kinesthetic perception in the process.

Good luck. And always remember, during isometrics, keep breathing.

GENETICS: THEIR ROLE IN OUR POTENTIAL PEAK LEVEL

Obviously, genetics play a major role in the (eventual) peak levels one can reach. Not only physically, but mentally and emotionally. Or do they? In my opinion, blaming one's heredity for one's lack of prowess has no place in the psychology of a warrior. This mentality is fostered by observing patterns in life that substantiate it. For example, intelligent parents usually breed intelligent offspring, etc.

However, a notion that is common among many Eastern religions was popularized by Albert Einstein, and substantiated now beyond anyone's doubt: Learning, psychologically as well as physically, does not create new pathways. Instead, learning alters the sensitivity of existing pathways. In other words, leaning is self-discovery through a continuous process of hacking away at that which prevents us from achieving the level that already exists within each of us. This "hacking away" can be defined as discovering the cause of one's ignorance, getting rid of psychic hindrances, dissolving the ego, etc. The single most important aspect in the internalization of this revelation lies in the belief system. The degree of one's beliefs is directly proportional to the eventual manifestation of it in life. All of us possess the skills of Carl Lewis; all of us have the ability to memorize a phone book. The body's mental, physical, and emotional potential is staggering. For men to duplicate what the average brain could accomplish would require a computer the size of the Empire State Building, and another building just as large for a cooling system. Any mother can lift a car if her child is underneath it. Under particular circumstances (e.g. hypnosis), people have done things that would boggle the mind. We unfortunately use only 5 percent of our brain.

Now we come to what apparently is a dichotomy. Genetically gifted people usually excel in whatever endeavor they attempt. However, it is a fact that we all have the ability (which usually lies dormant in most of us) to far surpass a Carl Lewis, and make most nuclear physicists look relatively stupid. Why then are these not common events? We see genetically gifted people excel regularly. Why do we not see an average person breaking records or winning Pulitzer prizes? Man needs the past to ensure his beliefs and security. Before Roger Bannister broke the 4-minute mile, it was "thought" to be a physical impossibility. One year later, several others followed him. Tapping one's potential is by no means a tangible or even attainable goal for most. I am by no means implying that I have discovered the many truths needed in attaining such a rare level. Bruce Lee considered his ability to tap into this vast reservoir perhaps his greatest accomplishment. I feel once this accomplishment is achieved, the door to enlightenment is at least within reach.

In terms of the work "enlightenment," the martial arts are only one path we may choose to follow. Destructive head-butt, knee, and elbow attacks may seem a dubious path toward inner peace. Someone able to tap the inner reservoir has to understand violence at an uncommon level. Conversely, their internalization of inner peace must, of necessity, be proportionate. The one man I know who has come closer to this quest than most will ever know ironically would never disclose it openly. When the ego is dissolved there is no need to impress your fellow man.

PAIN TOLERANCE

The victor of an all-out street fight will be the man with the superior mix of attributes (some 25 or more). This discussion refers to a fight, not an altercation (which involves the average man on the street). Contact with a 70-pound, 6'6" man on PCP is a fight.

When two fighters are locked in combat, bent on each other's destruction, both will be receiving numerous signals of pain. Pan tolerance is the main attribute that will determine which fighter breaks down and "covers," blocking his head (or groin, limbs, etc.) from further punishment. This allows the man delivering the blows a free ticket to attack where he wishes. The man who covers (usually is the man who loses.

No matter what one's interest within the martial arts, whether it is point tournaments, breaking, or self-defense (street fighting), pain tolerance is necessary in training. The most efficient way of accomplishing this through experience. Get used to hitting someone hard, as well as taking a punch. Both can cause pain. Full-contact training should be supervised by a competent instructor.

There are many types of pain tolerance. For example, I regard Thai boxers as "real" because their hardcore full-contact training results in certain types of pain. However, many Thai boxers have trouble with pain caused by joint manipulations or pinching/biting attacks.

Outside the martial arts, pain tolerance plays a role in other sports, like football. We work with the Dallas Cowboys to improve certain attributes. Now one would expect a Randy White or Ed Jones to have a pretty high pain tolerance, and believe me in the realm of football they do! However, when attacked with nerve strikes (hitting certain meridian points in the arms or legs), even Randy or Ed can fully appreciate the painful merits of these strikes. I've watched them hopping around on one leg squealing after a knee to the thigh.

Pain in a streetfight can create an emotional trauma resulting in covering (and possibly losing the fight). There are many different types of pain. One is less likely to tolerate pain when it has never been experienced. The best way to train pain tolerance is by full-contact sparring. Whatever you do, train full contact!

DAN INOSANTO'S CONTRIBUTIONS TO JEET KUNE DO

Recently there has been a surge of conjecture regarding the evolution of jeet kune do. This column is not intended to define JKD, but rather charity an absurd misconception regarding kali's role in JKD's evolution. Bruce Lee's original art was wing chun. After seeing certain limitations in wing chun (or any one art), the next obvious step was to investigate the principles, concepts, and techniques of various different arts. The process of this investigation is the very essence of JKD.

In 1964, Dan Inosanto first met Bruce Lee. At that time, Mr. Inosanto already held black belts in several other arts, and was a world-class martial artist in his own right. Dan's athletic ability was and is at an uncommon level. At 145 pounds, and standing 5'6" Dan was the leading ground-gainer at Whitworth College, running the 100-yard dash in near-world record time . . . 9.4 seconds. These points all became most after sparring with Bruce for just a few seconds!

截拳道

Immediately after their first encounter, Dan became Bruce Lee's student. Over the next nine years, both Bruce and Dan literally dissected and synthesized every martial art and philosophy salient to the concept of JKD . . . street fighting! They absorbed what was useful, rejected what was useless, and added what was specifically their own.

Over the next nine-year period, Dan Inosanto remained, with Bruce, the integral catalyst behind the mutual development of the style/concept that is now known as jeet kune do. This procedure began by blending such popular sports such as Western boxing, to the more sublime, less--known styles such as drunken monkey, chin na, and bak mei pai. There were approximately twenty-six different styles which lent themselves to the overall synthesis of JKD.

Of the many highly skilled students that Bruce Lee taught during his lifetime, only three ever qualified to teach jeet kune do – James Lee (deceased). Ted Wong and Dan Inosanto. Taky Kimura is senior to all three; however, he trained with Bruce prior to the development of JKD. The unspoken and intrinsic credential of Dan Inosanto is simply the fact that after Bruce's departure into the world of film, he was conferred the responsibility of maintaining the true authenticity of JKD.

After Bruce Lee's death in 1973, Mr. Inosanto. Bruce's protégé, continued to cultivate and refine the original process by which he and Bruce developed jeet kune do. This process is not static, it is dynamic in nature and continues to evolve, as was Bruce's intention. The notion that Dan's integration of kali (the 27th art) in any way, shape, or form is diluting the essence of the JKD is absurd! Could anyone be so naïve in their thinking as to assume that the addition of another aspect of a functional art makes JKD any less effective? Did art number 13 dilute the art number 12? Did art number 25 dilute art number 4? The answer is obvious.

Where is all this leading? Very simple. Why are a few individuals insinuating that Dan's Filipino kali is detracting or watering-down true JKD? Could initiated egos and the prospects of initiated bank accounts be the reason? What are the ulterior motives behind this sudden attack on Dan Inosanto, the man Bruce Lee personally chose to carry on his legacy? Some have insinuated that a prerequisite for authenticity in teaching the true style of JKD (using "no way as way"), one must have been born in a certain country or have a certain ancestral background. It was asked of Bruce, in a taped conversation . . . "Why leave the mantle of JKD to a Filipino?" Again, a simple answer, as was Bruce's style. He said that "There is no place for nationalism in jeet kune do."

DON'T LET LIBERATION BECOME A PRISON

What can be gained from yet another individual's interpretation of JKD? After all, haven't we read literally hundreds of them over the years? And, whereas man of them have been accurate and qualified opinions and explanations, haven't the bulk of them been B.S. from people who merely wanted to be associated with the Bruce Lee name but didn't know what they were talking about, or pure speculation on the part of well-meaning but ignorant individuals? Although this has done a lot to keep the name of Bruce Lee and his concepts in the public eye, it has also made it nearly impossible to figure out which book, video, article or column is accurate. Does studying with Dan Inosanto for several years, or even with Bruce Lee for several months, guarantee authenticity? Will reading all available literature and studying (redacting) the numerous resources available to us ensure a well-rounded and knowledgeable perspective?
What happens when so-called "authentic" JKD concepts instructors contradict one another? Whose map is the most accurate and drawn from the actual experience of traveling: whose experience is limited to the classroom; whose background is based on "diving right of succession" ("I trained with Bruce himself for one year, therefore, I know infinitely more than those who never knew him, but have been training with Dan Inosanto for 12 years"), and so on?
Perhaps the only criteria of an "authentic" JKD spokesperson rests with his fighting skills, technical prowess, or duration of study. It is, however, important to measure duration of study in terms of hours, not years. Ten years of study at one hour daily can yield the same result as five years of

study at two hours daily. Furthermore, a person who has trained on-and-off over a five-year period can claim to have trained for five years, but in terms of hours, the individual's training may be minimal.

Maybe the final word rests upon an organization of various individuals with varied levels of JKD exposure who can formulate a "Way." But this endangers the JKD concepts of "freedom" and individual expression, and is fertile soil for dictatorial practices. I myself have been questioned for going in my own direction and creating Progressive Fighting Systems. Is it valid for one group to prescribe the "right Way" and then deem all other "Ways" as wrong?

However, if there is no prescribed "Way," what about all of the valid cases of abuse? What about the unsuspecting student in middle America ready to shell out his hard-earned cash for a seminar from a supposed JKD authority, who can't even explain the most remedial aspects of the concepts?

Bruce Lee evolved to an uncommon level of skill in both martial arts and life. His ideas were a result of accommodating (not accumulating) all Ways, hence being bound by no Way. However, he had a foundation for what he did. Just as one learns to crawl before one can walk, one must learn specific ways and means of doing things before one can liberate oneself from them. One cannot spontaneously make oneself a JKD expert based on one's personal idea of being "liberated." There is a curriculum in JKD concepts. There are specific "Ways" of doing things which must be learned from a competent instructor. Bruce Lee spent countless hours formulating what he felt were the most effective and streamlined methodologies of delivering and implementing martial strategies. Yet, once his concepts are learned, the real learning has only begun.

Every time we compare "this JKD man" to "that JKD man" or this school to that school or this article to that article, etc. we are blindly searching for "the one Way," which defeats the whole purpose. We have to free ourselves from the priorities of "best and worst" and "right and wrong." When a finger is pointing at the moon, the fool sees only the finger.

BROKEN RHYTHM

Rhythm is an attribute/quality no less important than speed, power, timing, etc. However, one can visualize qualities like speed by observing a cat, and power by watching Mike Tyson, making these concepts easier to grasp. Rhythm, on the other hand, is a bit more ambiguous. Where broken rhythm is presented, the concept becomes even more distorted. Webster's dictionary doesn't shed any further light for us either: "Movement and fluctuations marked by the regular recurrence of related elements."
To put it simply, rhythm is the consistency between elements (+ movements) over time, the consistent lapse of time from one technique to the next, or the "in-between" time when no blows are thrown. Broken rhythm changes this consistent pattern by the insertion of movements in between the "beats" of the established rhythm. It can play an important role in a fighter's offensive and defensive success. Development of broken rhythm can take place in the following ways:

1 - Learn – In order to break an opponent's rhythm, you must first learn to match his rhythm. Therefore, work drills in rhythms of three with pause in between sets (jab/catch-jab/catch-jab/catch or punch-block--punch).

2 - Memorize / Master – Study and practice ways to change rhythms and observe, and develop skills of broken rhythm of boxers, fencers, broken rhythm styles (i.e.: drunken monkey), etc. Apply these to your regular training routine.

3 - Functionalize – When you spar, try to hit your opponent with half speed, then quarter speed, then double speed. See if you can hit your opponent in between his jab-cross rhythm combination.
Establish the rhythm, then break it in different ways. This will "motor--set" your opponent first and make it more difficult to respond to your

broken rhythm attacks.

When a fighter always uses the same rhythm, he establishes "routine" which is a type of telegraphing and leaves him more susceptible to his opponent's counters, stop-hits, and broken rhythms. He leaves himself open to be read, like so many pages in a book. When one cannot break the rhythm, he becomes "motor-set" and not "responsive." To learn the patterns of fighting (& life), then break them, is to become free of conditioned routines is to be responsive to your opponent (and world or nature).

"My technique is a result of your technique, my movement is a result of our movement."
Bruce Lee

THE PERIPHERAL OPPONENT

Regardless of the endeavor undertaken in life, training is the single most important aspect in developing one's fullest potential. In the martial arts, the more efficiently one trains, the more "intense" they become. Think about the intensity of other athletes' training required to achieve their level of proficiency. Imagine sitting in on a Pittsburgh Steelers practice during mid-season, or being ringside with sugar Ray Leonard in training camp a few weeks before stepping in the ring with Marvin Hagler, or perhaps watching Mikhail Barishnikov during a typical eight-hour practice day before a major performance. It's not likely that you are picturing these athletes having a tough time keeping their minds on training. Imagine them now as martial artists. Would they drop what they are doing to answer the phone or console a neighbor who's whining about the noise form a few rounds on the speed bag, or let little lodine show them his He-Man Monster Pak? It's doubtful that any of these things would stop those athletes in the middle of a full-effort roundhouse kicking session on the heavy bag.

These distractions are only a few that do affect many martial artists. I call these physical (external) interruptions the Peripheral Opponent (P.O.): but this is only one side of the same coin. The other is within ourselves when we train. The emotional (internal) Peripheral Opponent is the "little voice inside" that never shuts up: are you going to get that raise at work? Will that big real estate deal come through? Where was the place that you stuck the set of keys you lost yesterday? Whether the distraction comes from within yourself or someone else, the common denominator of virtually everyone who has attained an uncommon level of proficiency is victory over one of the toughest opponents, the Peripheral Opponent. Everyone has an exclusive P.O. a monkey that most people don't even know is on their back. What could they accomplish if their monkey stayed in the zoo! Getting rid of the physical P.O. is much easier to accomplish than the emotional P.O.

Physical distractions can be reduced by altering the time one trains (early morning or late night) and where one trains (a private area without a phone). It should also be common knowledge to friends, relatives, wife, kids, and your family pet, that when you enter your "space" to train, you should not be disturbed, whether you train at your school, in a converted room, garage, or on the roof. Be patient, however. It may take a while to effectively "train" your circle of influence, but the effort will be most worthwhile to your over time.

Now we must contend with the toughest opponent of them all – you. Halfway through a great session o the heavy bag, that little voice in your head starts asking if you can make this month's house payment and still get the new tires your car needs so much. You create an emotional opponent by even thinking about the way you are punching and kicking. Bruce Lee said that this kind of distraction or "consciousness of the self is the greatest hindrance to mankind." So, to put it in a nutshell, the martial artist who can cut off any internal dialogue is getting more out of one year of training than he would in ten y ears with his P.O. This is because the information we get from the senses (stimulus) is "purely" interpreted by our brain and acted upon more efficiently by the firing of nerves in the correct muscles (response). Distractions radically decrease the entire stimulus/response process by giving a conflicting signal. This was one of Bruce's biggest revelations, and had a lot to do with why, at an early age (early 30's) he attained such a high level. Bruce used to say, "I'm taking the elevator while others are still using the stairs."

It's 10:00 p.m. and you've been home from work four hours (plenty of time to wind down). You enter your "training space" and now it's your time (not Miller time). Lie on the ground, relaxing all parts of the body, eliminating internal dialogue. You will find that if you stop thinking, stop questioning and stop listening to that little voice, you can begin your training without your Peripheral Opponents. This is an advantage to you in emptying yourself to train as intensely as possible for the duration of the workout. This may take some practice to perfect, but worth the effort. It is sort of like waiting for the elevator because once you catch it, you end up getting there much faster than walking up those stairs. Good luck!

LINE FAMILIARIZATION

Of the vast amount of qualities that fighter's possess, or choose to develop, line familiarization is relatively unimportant to most. With so much emphasis on speed, power or limberness, it simply takes a back seat. However, as one increases the awareness as to just what line familiarization is, so too will he allocate the amount of necessary time to develop it. When we use the word "line," we are actually saying angle of attack. The word "familiarization" is self-explanatory. Hence, line familiarization means to be familiar with the angle of attack that the opponent launches. There is only one way to become familiar with anything. You must practice, or as we say, put in the "fight-time." There are NO free rides. A heavyweight professional boxer, for example, may spend 15 years boxing and get into an altercation with a white-belt. Catching a front kick in the groin, he will LOSE! The boxer lost for one reason. He wasn't "familiar" with that line of attack.

Another scenario, perhaps more likely, would be that of a black-belt of 20 years, being used to sparring within the confines of his own style ONLY, being taken to the ground by a high school wrestler and beaten. Obviously, no matter the style of the black belt, if he had incorporated the liens of attack familiar to the wrestler, he would have, in theory, had an appropriate counter.

Now we come to the Catch-22 – the word "theory". The aforementioned explanation of line familiarization is on the most rudimentary level.

Now that we have a basic understanding, let's take it a step further and dissect the work familiarization. A JKD man strives to divorce the word "theory" from his arsenal. This, again, is done by implementing good old-fashioned fight-time. Therefore, to those of us who study JKD, familiarization does NOT consist of generically theorizing something, putting on paper the number of styles your art has incorporated and PRESTO, we have an armchair "eclectic" JKD man! To truly get familiar with the heat you have to get into the kitchen.

The longer, and more intensity one trains in different arenas (i.e. boxers, wrestlers, savate men, Thai boxers, etc.), the more equipped one is like absorb what is useful, reject what is useless, and add what is specifically one's own.

When this occurs, the attribute of line familiarization segues into one of the most important attributes one could ever possess – AWARENESS. With awareness, we now can "intercept" and enter the path of becoming truly JKD!

THE MOMENT OF TRUTH

Jeet kune do offers many of us an ideal vehicle for personal growth. Often it begins as a fancy. To be like Bruce Lee, to defend one's self, to keep the body fit, etc. However, the scope of JKD's is not a style, but is art. Actually, it is the artistic process of more fully realizing our potential and expressing. A WAY OF LIFE. It deals not only with punching and kicking, but also with eating and sleeping. The battles one continuously fights in everyday life far outweigh those rare battles of actual combat. However, if one can effectively deal with "real" fighting (two opponents bent on each other's destruction), then the battles of life become more easily manageable. The process of fighting, like the process of living, is the art. A search for truth.

The way of JKD is motion through life. It is the doing and not what is done, the journey and not the destination, and the experience and not the outcome. When one lives within the process and not for the product, each moment can be mounted and action in life becomes direct, immediate, and "free." Awareness becomes "unconsciously conscious."

What are the limits of our potential if we could focus all our energy into each moment? How much more could we see if seeing was uncolored by past experiences and preferences? How much could we create if nothing had been created before?

"To express yourself in freedom,
you must die of everything yesterday.
From the old, you derive security;
from the new, you gain the flow."
Bruce Lee

Living in the past halts creativity and the artistic process. Living in the future dilutes the present. The here-and-now is reality, and the past and future are illusion. "What is" is and not what "it" was or will be. "What is" is constantly moving and changing, evolving. It is the truth, totality, and freedom. It is the realization of what lies in our innermost selves. It is JKD!

THE IMPORTANCE OF GRAPPLING

The words had been exchanged, and both young men had decided to settle it outside. Joe had a reputation around the school for being one of the toughest members of the varsity wrestling team. Bill wasn't afraid. After all, he was a black belt.

The two combination squared off. Bill dropped into a cat stance, Joe simply put his head down and charged. Bill's front kick knocked Joe back but, surprisingly, did not take the fight out of him. He rushed in, grabbed Bill around the waist, and took him to the ground.

Joe tied Bill up like a pretzel. Every limb was restricted as Joe struck Bill repeatedly in the face with his free hand. As Joe pushed Bill's head back into the pavement, everything went black.

To say that most martial artists would be in for a rude awakening if met by someone skilled in grappling is one hell of an understatement. It is quite comforting to assume a wrestler would not get past one's "deadly" punches and kicks; however, the wicked rod of reality will soon strike with the sudden realization that man does not always drop with one punch or kick.

Indeed, most people are conditioned by too many John Wayne movies. Wayne would simply draw back his massive hand and strike, and his hapless opponent would be lifted up and hurled across the room, landing dazed and unconscious. In the real world, most people can take strikes.

Have you ever had the experience of being extremely angry? You could be hurt or even seriously injured, yet all you could think about was your anger. There are documented cases on record of people being shot and living long enough to kill their attackers. Most real fights end up on the ground.

This makes it hard to understand why ground fighting is one of the most neglected aspects of the martial arts. Very few martial artists appreciate how dangerous a wrestler can be, yet most of the experts unanimously consider Gene LeBell the toughest man alive.

Recently, there has been some nonsense written about overcoming grapplers written by, I suspect, individuals with little or no "real world" fighting experience. Ground fighting is an extremely intricate form of combat, which requires experience and understanding. If a wrestler were to be able to get the average martial artist, with no grappling experience, on the ground, he would be able to do anything he wanted.

When evaluating which style of grappling is the most effective, one must take into consideration that each style has its own strategy and approach to combat. There are numerous types of wrestling, such as collegiate, freestyle, Greco-Roman, dumog, kinimutal, sumo, jujutsu, sambo, etc.

One of the most intriguing forms of ground fighting I have encountered comes from Brazil and is known as Gracie Jujutsu (see last month's cover story). This art was developed by the Gracie family in Brazil, after having learned traditional jujutsu form a Japanese immigrant. The ground techniques include takedowns, locks, flips throws, and one of their fortes – chokes. However, the intricate methods employed to gain superior control are highly sophisticated.

Regardless of the specific school of grappling, this type of training is well worth the effort. A man with 20 years of martial arts experience can be easily beaten by a person with as little as a year of grappling training if (or when) the fight goes to the ground.

SO HIT THAT MAT, AND GOOD LUCK!

DISSECTING THE CORPSE

In any avenue of life, whether it be work, education, sport, military, martial arts, etc. the way you train will specifically affect your level (or potential level). Accordingly, we must assume that if one's martial arts training is unrealistic, the way they approach (and the effectiveness they have in) a street-fight will inevitably be unrealistic. This, ultimately, is the reason behind many of the questions I get from people at the seminars I give, regardless of the state (or country), the school, or the style. Both students and instructors alike comment, "I got into this fight and none of my techniques worked, then we ended up on the ground – wrestling or struggling. Why?

When one practices techniques in a certain way, there is an imprint created in the brain that produces that same reflex or response again and again. This conditioning relies on the same stimulus to create the same imprinted response. If a new stimulus is introduced, the brain's imprint is unable to produce an appropriate new response. So all training involved in creating the imprint becomes inappropriate in dealing with different situations.

One is likely to awaken in a hospital bed with the painful realization that blocking punches that swing through wildly or strikes that retract quickly in combination is a far cry from the locked-out punches one has been training against for months or years. Although a block and/or barrage of strikes against a static partner maintain the same locked-out "pose" may be aesthetically dramatic, it has as much to do with a realistic street-fight as swimming strokes on dry land. The impression made by a snapping gi, a powerful block, a loud kiai and demonstrative strikes can be awesome. Unfortunately, combat isn't a show! A fight may occur while you are wearing a suit, nursing a sore throat, holding two sacks of groceries, and finding an uncooperative opponent who knows how to swim in the water.

This is the answer to many of those "Why?" questions, and the reason I have said over the years: "If any style would equate themselves to (e.g.) boxing and not assume that an opponent will attack with that one particular art they study, they would be more prepared with the realities of combat," By no means am I saying boxing is totally the answer. However, developing "basics" through boxing or another similarly functional method has the advantages of full-combat, unpredictable movement not stopping after a point is scored, and teaching footwork, timing, distancing, pain tolerance, etc. Most importantly, boxing involves understanding the way 99 percent of people strike, with wild swings or retracting jabs – not a locked out blow!

If you really want to swim, you have to get wet, or you might be asking why you sank when you fell into the water.

PLACING IMAGE OVER ABILITY

When I first agreed to do a column with this magazine, the editor told me that, within acceptable limits, I had an open floor to talk about anything. In my opinion, you, the reader, buy this magazine to learn, and couldn't care less about opinion and politics. That is why I have tried to limit my comments to things of interest, and not take shots at anybody. Occasionally someone steps so far over the line that somebody has to stand up and say, "Hey, this is wrong!" Such is the case with a letter to the editor, which was published in a recent issue of another magazine.

I was extremely disappointed because the author of the letter is a person with whom I have always gotten along and who was, for a very brief period, my student. Unfortunately, it appears that some of us were taught a different set of ethics than others.

The letter itself is a very lengthy rebuttal to comments someone had made about the letter writer. However, instead of simply telling another side of the story, the writer relied on an old lawyer's trick – attack the accuser. One of the people attacked in the letter was my own instructor. Dan Inosanto, who not only did not make the comments, he was unaware that they had even been made!

I'm not going to bother refuting the statements made in the letter. Dan Inosanto has a reputation for being forgiving to a fault. If an instructor on the level of Dan didn't think much of my skills, this is not a fact I would broadcast to the world in the pages of a widely read and widely respected magazine.

What bothers me the most is this constant sniveling from people who seem to think that if they can use magazines to convince the world they're "bad," they'll never have to back it up. I have always believed that the "cans" do and the "can'ts" talk.

I myself have been the victim of politics. I was the target of a nationwide smear campaign where someone wrote bogus letters to prominent martial artist and forged my name. I don't get bothered about it; I thought it was funny. The clown didn't even know how to spell "Vunak."

I have had my students challenged by other organizations for no reason at all (we're still battling 1000), and I've had my life threatened (I'm still waitin', Pal). I have had numerous rebuttal letters printed about things I have said in magazines; this is the risk of "going public." I have been made fun of in editorials and attacked in print. But I have never whined about it or found the need to blame everyone else for my problems.

Why? Because ability speaks for itself. Why explain things if you don't have to? People will know.

The root of the problem is martial artists placing image over training and knowledge. There's nothing wrong with becoming wealthy and famous, but it should come as the result of what you have done, not some skillful self-promotion strategy.

I hope that one of these days people like our letter writer will wake up and smell the coffee, and realize that when you badmouth your betters, you're only showing the rest of us you've still got a long way to go. It is not recognition that makes you a good martial artist, it's the process of reaching the point where you're worthy of recognition.

Having the gift of gab doesn't make you a good martial artist. You're not good because you go and chit-chat with an old master, and you're not good because you can impress some rube who is totally unfamiliar with your style.

You're good when you're confident enough to let world judge you by your deeds, not your words.

THE DREADED COMPLACENCY SYNDROME

A question that I'm often asked, regardless of what state I'm in, or which style I'm teaching . . . . is how to further improve one's skills. Many martial artists intuit that they've reached a stage where improvement is no longer happening. In most cases, their intuition is correct. In 99 percent of all endeavors in life, after a certain point, complacency and a cessation of growth begins.

截拳道

Martial arts are no different . . . in fact they're WORSE. How many instructors have you heard brag that they've been studying their art for twenty y ears? I say that they have been studying it for four years and repeating if for sixteen. In the average school that I see during a seminar. I find the brown belts to be better fighters than the black belts. This is simply because the brown belts are still "hungry". Once one loses the lust that originally attracted them to the field they have chosen, diminished capacity sets in.

One reason for Bruce Lee's incredible ability was simply due to the fact that he NEVER lost that lust to improve. To further complement that mentally . . . he despised the concept of having "belts." A black belt gives one a subconscious excuse to quit improving. One believes that they have finally "arrived." The way they have arrived is through that infamous black belt. This is why Bruce expounded using the philosophy of using "no way as way."

In closing, I would like to share some ideas that just might prevent one from feeling like he or she has "arrived."

1 - Go to your local boxing gym and find a pro. Get in and go a few rounds. (Get your shoulder chips knocked off.)

2 - Go to a college and find a wrestler. Go a few rounds on the mat.

3 - Investigate other schools or styles (combative schools) and exchange ideas.

4 - Look into weight training to complement your fighting.

5 - Experiment in other sports that require similar attributes.

6 - Expound on this list yourself, and come up with five more fresh ideas.

IF YOU'RE SUCH HOT STUFF, WHY DON'T YOU ENTER TOURNAMENTS?

Once again, our topic this month either runs the risk of being extremely controversial, or extremely cliché. The purpose of this column is not to discuss the merits and faults of ring and/or tournament fighting. For too many years, people have been surmising that the only thing that "really" constitutes a world-class fighter is his/her success or failure in the ring or tournament circuit.

I will once again say what has been reiterated for so long. FIGHTING IS NOT A SPORT, AND SPORTS HAVE NOTHING TO DO WITH STREETFIGHTING! Have people excelled in their chosen fields by training in totally unrelated topics? To measure the trues professional level or say, a Michael Jordan, requires one, and only one criterion . . . how he plays PING PONG!

If that statement seems to somehow clash with your gut sense of logic (as well it should), then perhaps readers can imagine how the tournament/ring issue sounds from my vantage point. Let us once again examine and compare sports with street-fighting. To further clarify our comparison, indulge me for a moment, and us rehash through the myriad questions I am often asked, regardless of what state I'm in, or what style I am teaching.

They all relate to either. Bruce Lee, or jeet kune do.

1 - If Bruce Lee was so great, why didn't he compete?

2 - In full contact, Bruce Lee was too small (in stature and neck size) and therefore could not take a punch . . .

3 - Why don't JKD people compete in the ring?

4 - Real karate is based on control . . . but if they "Real McCoy" ever came along, my "chi" would prevail.

截拳道

5 - Who would win in a fight, Bruce Lee or _____?

6 - I've heard all your excuses before... you say that your art is just too deadly to fight...

Well, here are my answers to those questions, in black and white:
First, for Bruce Lee to compete in a karate tournament would be akin to asking Albert Einstein to enter a high school spelling bee. Must we all work in restaurants to become chefs, or can't a woman be a stone fox unless she wins a beauty contest? Do you see my point?
Now, in a 16' x 20' ring with gloves on, a fight is turned into a pillow fight especially in terms of Bruce Lee. Then, and only then, does trading punches have relevance. Along with punches and kicks, today's JKD incorporates arm wrenches, eye jabs, groin and knee shots, nerve destructions, take-downs, pinching, biting, sweeps, tai chi "energy," the "straight blast," traps from wing chun, head butts, locks, savate, ground fighting, hair pulling, Western and Filipino wrestling, pontjak slat, Thai boxing, chokes and a profusion of other elements. Each of these elements had an inconceivable amount of training drills associated with each technique. Removing these elements. THEN it would be perfectly fair to speculate on the outcome of a "pillow fight."
Why don't JKD people compete? They were competing full contact before there was full contact, Bruce trained an aide corps of intense streetfighters full contact before the sport was ever invented. Included in that group is Daniel Lee (welter-weight boxing champion of Asia), Larry Hartsell (6'2", 240 lbs. two terms in Vietnam, a sheriff and worker in a mental hospital. Those are his gentle points!), Dan Inosanto (world--class martial artist with several different black belts, and super athlete, football player with a 100-yard dash at 9.4, leading ground-gainer for his college team). Consequently, Bruce met up with a guy by the name of Joe Lewis, who was enjoying no-contact tournament sparring at that time. Bruce then introduced certain of his basic training concepts which Joe later used to begin to popularize full contact. The ONLY common

denominator between Bruce's students is that none of them remember ever hitting him! The only guy in the group who could hold an air shield for Bruce, and remain standing, was Larry . . . and he simply recalls the migraines he had after just a short session. So much for Bruce's stature! Now, there are NO secrets about street-fighting. "Chi" certainly is a bodily function (chin-lo . . . the meridians), but so are other bodily functions such as blood flow, spinal fluid, kidney excretion, etc. I'm not saying that there are no people who can fight with chi (though I've never yet met one). I AM saying that instead of a lifelong quest of chi, I would strongly recommend learning how to stop a good, fast jab.

As to who would win in a fight, Bruce Lee or some other self-crowned martial arts miracle, or current (or old) star of the silver screen, I'll just say this: When Bruce was alive, NO ONE QUESTIONED HIM.

Finally, JKD is not an art. It's a harmonic, yet deadly, blend of many things, most of which are not applicable in the ring. To strip a JKD man of his tools (95 percent of which would not be allowed in formal tournament competition) would be like asking a brain surgeon to perform a delicate operation with a toothpick and a butter knife. . . and then get SCORED on his performance.

HIDDEN AGENDAS

The martial arts are a form of self-expression. Like any other art form, they require constant practice and years of introspection. Like any other art form, if practiced intelligently and with diligence, their benefits will be integrated into everyday life. By "intelligently", I mean practiced for the right reasons.

By "the right reasons," I'm not trying to make this a moral issue. I'm just speaking of the process. And in this case, the process has to be evaluated by the question: "What are your motivations for training in the martial arts?"

For example, if a person's primary motivation is to get a piece of paper, or become a particular instructor's top student, or secure a film contract, that person is missing the boat. As a matter of fact, he or she isn't even in the water!

I see a growing trend to place certification over ability. There are people walking around right now with heavy-duty ranks and impressive certifications, signed by impressive names. These people couldn't defend themselves against a 15-year-old mugger if their lives depended on it.

One of the reasons I formed my own organization was to further propagate my beliefs in terms of martial arts and how they should be taught and practiced. In the beginning, I was familiar with my material, but I had no idea ow to run an organization. As a result, I made a few mistakes in judging the caliber and motivations of certain students.

One thing I noticed early on was a tendency for people to enroll in my organization with the hidden agenda of "getting close" to my instructor, Dan Inosanto. Now I don't have a problem with this, and if someone were to come to me up front and ask for an introduction to Dan, I'd be happy to do it. But people who aren't up front (i.e., sneaky) aren't the type I want in Progressive Fighting Systems. All too often, a student wouldn't meet our standards of ethics and I would kick him out, only to have him run down to my instructor's school and sign up.

Ordinarily, this wouldn't bother me. I believe I provide the highest level of training in what I teach – I wouldn't have a right to be teaching if I didn't. I also believe that Dan provides the highest level of training in what he teaches – I wouldn't study from him if he didn't. But in these cases in point, the student's motivation wasn't to receive the highest level of training; it was to be associated with a "big name" martial artist. The interest in ability was zero – the main focus was on image.

Because of his association with Bruce Lee, there were (and are) many who saw an association with Dan as a short-cut to big bucks as an instructor, an inroad to a film career, or a "quick-fix" for an inferiority complex. To this day I am of the belief that there are a few who believe that Bruce conferred some sort of magic on Dan, and that if they can just be in his proximity this magic will rub off on them without them putting in any effort.

The only motivation for studying from me or from Dan or from Bill Wallace or from Gene LeBell or any other instructor is to learn the material. Politics are diametrically opposed to self-growth. I've said for many years that nothing speaks louder than ability, and ability speaks for itself, One should let the body do the talking and worry less about the pecking order in the studio or a piece of paper on the wall. The moment we become more concerned with ornamentation, certification, the hierarchy, who went out to lunch with the instructor, etc., we have compromised our original thirst for knowledge.

WHO THE HELL IS DEL POLLARD?

Anyone who has followed my column pretty much knows that I try to be as direct and honest as possible. Inside Karate has given me the latitude to pick and choose my subject matter, and license to use this space as I see fit. Since I've seen far too many people use this privilege or, should I say, abuse it, to further personal agendas (an entire magazine now exists which is blatantly self-serving). I've tried to refrain from abusing it. It is very easy to use the "power of the pen" to politically increase or decrease the public's opinions about certain people, styles, ideas, etc. However, once in a while, there comes a time when exceptions can and should be made. This is one of those times.

I come from an organization where political fallout is a fact of life. I was once told that half of the calls my instructor, Dan Inosanto, receives are from people calling to "rat on" instructors and other students. The problem is a direct result of our organization's connection with Bruce Lee, and the money making potential some feel that a sanction from such an organization can generate.

I have also spoken frequently in this column about the "zero sum" mentality. For those of you not familiar with this term, it is the childish notion that there I s only so much room for qualified instructors of a certain style, and that the way to become a success is to prevent anyone else's star from rising. Although this concept is diametrically opposed to the JKD philosophy, I am seeing more and more of it.

This brings us to the subject of this month's column – a man named Del Pollard. I first met Del in 1977, during a period where I had been training with Dan for one year. Del, on the other hand, had been training in Charlotte, North Carolina, for three years. Del and Larry Hartsell hit it off from the first day they met. They were training partners, friends, and, of course, situ student. In 1977, Del uprooted himself and his family form a lucrative job for the sole purpose of moving to Los Angeles and studying from Dan Inosanto. What Dan enjoyed most about Del was that he was not an opportunist. There were no plans for the Del Pollard Academy of Bruce Lee's Jeet Kune Do or the world premiere of The Flashing Fists of Del. He just wanted to learn art for art's sake. There was never any B.S., no gray areas, and never any lies.

At the old Kali Academy, when a formal jeet kune do class still existed, you had your "technicians," your "hobbyists," your "movie stars in waiting," your "classroom warriors," your "asters(?!)," etc. Then you had a few people who actually listened to what Dan was trying to convey to us. These people were the "fighters", the few who represented where JKD's roots really began. Del was, without a doubt, one of the foremost "fighters." Del began teaching for Dan at the academy, and was officially voted into the "closed door" JKD class in 1978.

Del and I had a difference of opinion on how best to perpetuate the art. In the beginning, there was an unwritten law that one did not profiteer off of JKD and the Bruce Lee name. Over the years, as more and more people began teaching the art, some qualified and some not, I saw the wisdom of getting with the program. As a professional martial arts instructor, I didn't see anything particularly alluring about sitting back and seeing far less qualified people, with far fewer years of training, reap the harvest. I also felt, and still feel, that the best way to propagate JKD is to expose myself to public scrutiny. Del's approach was always more low-key. When the certification program first began, he was very much against it. Though outvoted and overmuted, he did not want to be a hypocrite and ask to be certified, even though his understanding of JKD and his abilities to teach and pass on that knowledge is on one of the highest levels I personally have ever seen.

Del would often confront people he didn't feel were qualified with questions life, "Explain progressive indirect attack or broken rhythm." When they failed to respond, instead of inviting them to back up their claims physically or telling them they had no business teaching, he would implore them to train, do their homework, and get up to speed before they went out into the world, armed only with a piece of paper, and taught people. This approach never won him any friends, but it did win him a lot of respect.

Still, he preferred to shun public contact. And, as his juniors started giving seminar tours and opening their own schools, Del kept his group of students small and tight knit. In keeping with his low-profile mentality, he never sought certification. He just taught, taught and taught. And he kept getting better, as he does to this day.

In 1988, Del, weary of the California lifestyle, relocated to New England. Away from the political score of Southern California and the movie star/JKD "master" wannabe's, he was able to let the smoke clear and got an overview. When word slowly leaked out that he had trained in JKD for so many years, he was swamped with requests from enthusiastic, would be students. Finally, after seeing a groundswell of his juniors actively teaching and appearing in magazines, Del made the wisest decision – to share his vast experience with the public and open and academy in Boston, Massachusetts.

Immediately, word reached my ears that there were a few disgruntled clowns in the Midwest and on the East Coast saying he shouldn't be teaching because he didn't have a certificate. One of these people is an individual I personally discharged from Progressive Fighting Systems. All of the people speaking have certification to teach in a broad sense; i.e. they have been certified to teach what they know as an extension of the overall curricula because there aren't any other teachers in their geographical areas. I will go out on a limb and state that none, I repeat none, of the speakers remotely approaches Del Pollard's level. And, surprisingly, none have voiced any objections to his face!

Although, as a general rule, a certificate is evidence of one's qualification to teach, once again I will state that there are exceptions to every rule. I want the public to be aware of Del's abilities as an instructor, and his quality as an individual.

TIPS FOR SPOTTING FRAUDS

A recent column dealt with seminars, specifically how to spot competent instructors "worthy" of conducting seminars. Response to this topic deserves further comment. I have been asked to expound on how to spot "unworthy" instructors, the frauds of the martial arts. This subject could fill an entire book, let alone a monthly column. To keep it as simple as possible, I am going to use what I call the red flag technique. It's a sort of built-in "B.S" alarm.

Red Flag #1 - A "poker" mentality. A person with this mentality builds him/herself up by putting others down. To win in a poker game, someone else must lose. Conversely, a person with a "worthy" mentality acts as a springboard, helping other people by training and educating them. This latter approach generates a positive energy that will be directed back to the source, benefiting the whole. "What goes around, comes around."

Red Flag #2 - A person who is a legitimate instructor and /or fighter does not need to go out of his way to prove he/she has some omnipotent energy (chi/lo). If he/she does have "chi" and can only use it to do "tricks" (breaking bricks with the head, breaking chop-sticks on the throat, stepping on eggs without breaking them, etc.....) the point then becomes moot. If they can use this "chi" to actually spar or fight with, then why don't they do it? When you go to a Bill Wallace seminar, you never hear the work "chi" brought up. But he does make a point out of sparring with each one of his students. After lightly hitting them 10 to 1, he could talk about "chi" if he chose to do so.

Red Flag #3 - It has been said that a good instructor does not always have to be a good fighter. This is only a half-truth! If your potential instructor is in his 80's and holds a wealth of knowledge, it is not necessary to glove-up and start wailing on him. However, if I personally saw someone in their 30's bragging about how good he or she is, rather than pointing out the good points of their art for the purpose of educating, I would recommend sparring with this person to see if his/her actions back up his/her words.

Red Flag #4 - Any instructor who offers "instructorship" seminars or the "one-week" courses to make someone an "accredited" instructor is taking you for a fool. Or if he/she received such a certificate and is now "teaching" that art based on such a course that is absolute crap. I assure you these people are out in left field and the game is over! Nothing bothers me more than to take something as great as the martial arts and exploit it for financial gain. This bastardizes all of us. Common sense shows us that these "one-week" instructorship" courses are blatantly attempts to sell certificates.

Red Flag #5 - It a flyer or poster deals more with the person teaching the seminar than the material being taught, be careful. Although some "hype" is necessary so you know the instructor is qualified, as a general rule the "worthy" try to sell what they teach; frauds try to sell themselves.
Red Flag #6 - Water seeks its own level. If you see someone closely aligned with someone you know is a fraud, it's a safe bet that they are equally, if not more, fraudulent. Dishonest people have a way of finding each other.

Red Flag #7 - Lately, we are seeing a lot of sensationalistic buzzwords culled from today's headlines, such as "anti-gang tactics," "counterterrorism," "hostage retrieval," etc. Aside from the obvious fact that these things have no practical value for the civilian martial artist, they are taught by and for experts only. Very few martial artists teach police and military, and they guard their identities carefully because there have been reprisals against a fire bomb, and when crack teams like the Israeli Mossad can only engage in hostage retrieval under ideal circumstances, anyone who claims to teach these things to the public should be forced to wear two scarlet letters, one being "B" the other "S".

There are many other red flags that one should look for, but it is up to your own judgment to ask questions, make inquiries, spar, and know more in general about your prospective instructor. It is an important decision and one should weigh the choices carefully. I hope that these tips help to plant the seed or further develop the growth of your "B.S. alarm," because you deserve it, the martial arts deserves it, and most certainly, the frauds deserve it. Good luck!

GETTTING THE MOST OUT OF SEMINARS

Martial arts seminars are becoming more popular as time goes on. I don't believe it's a fad, but rather a natural evolution in martial arts brought about by modern technology.

Seminars are a welcome supplement to any student's martial arts training. They can act as a vehicle for personal growth if approached properly. On the other hand, if approached as an end rather than a means to an end, a two-day martial arts seminar holds about as much weight as a two-day spelling bee.

Seminars are not a substitute for the thousands of hours of flight time necessary to internalize anything. However, seeds can be planted, principles can be introduced, and mentalities can be adjusted. With these concepts in mind, seminars can now serve as an elevator to reach one's desired level, as opposed to a much longer walk up the stairs.

This column is dedicated to the concept of the seminar and I decided to compile this list of "Dos", and Don'ts" to help the student and seminar sponsor get the most out of a seminar.

DO –   Ask the instructor as many questions as necessary. You are being given a limited amount of time with this instructor, and you may never see him again.

DO -   (as a sponsor) take advantage of free advertising opportunities. Most major martial arts publications have listings of coming events, and will be happy to run your announcement free of charge, as long as you get the listing in three months ahead of time. I am amazed at how few promoters are aware of this.

DO -   Be aware that there are a lot of people of questionable background giving seminars. Just because a person is known to you doesn't mean they are competent or qualified seminar instructors.

DO -   Bring necessary materials. If you're going to a seminar in Filipino martial arts, for example, bring some sticks. Bring decent shoes and attire you can move in. Bring a notebook and a pen.

DO -   (as a sponsor) be prepared to entertain a large number of people, have refreshments. Have some extra pens and paper available for people who forget their own. You may also wish to get a supply of sticks if it is to be a stick-fighting seminar, and most people want them.

DON'T - Be shy or embarrassed or in awe of the seminar instructor. Most people on the circuit are very down-to-earth and are not to be considered celebrities.

DON'T - Be intimidated by the seminar instructor or the other participants. It's your money; you have as much right to the instructor's time as anyone else.

DON'T- Be afraid to ask questions about anything, even if it sounds dumb. Asking dumb questions is better than learning it wrong.

DON'T – (as a sponsor) Flood the area with too many seminars too soon. If you are constantly bringing people in to give seminars, realize that the students only have so much money, and you will dilute the attendance for the good instructors.

DON'T – Ever allow yourself to be lured into an "instructorship seminar" as there is no such thing!

ENOUGH IS ENOUGH

I would like to start out by thanking the readers of Inside Karate for such a warm show of support for this column. I don't want anybody to think I'm not grateful, and that I'm not deeply appreciative of the readers and their viewpoints.
That said, it's time to get down to some serious scolding. There has been far too much said about an issue that most people know far too little about – that is, jeet kune do concepts. Emulation of Bruce Lee is the opposite of what he wanted. The principles he left behind were at his own level, not ours! Therefore, only a handful of people understand their true meaning. This leaves a multitude of opportunities for people to either misconstrue concepts that were originally simple, i.e., "Using no way as way," or take advantage of the fact that these principles are not fully understood by the public and pretentiously misrepresent an understanding of them.
We are being bombarded by attempts to speak intelligently about jeet kune do concepts by people with absolutely no qualification or background in the field, and it only serves to increase the confusion. We are seeing articles interpreting what Bruce Lee said, when he said everything in plain and simple English without "hidden meanings" or subtle innuendos. He was a very direct man, and did not leave his statements open to interpretation.
In short, the latest trend in martial arts is to take jeet kune do and prac-

tice "Having no ambiguity as ambiguity."
The added problem faced by JKD practitioners is that many seek to become attached to the legacy of Bruce Lee not out of love of the art or the desire to improve one's skills, but out of the desire to be linked on a third-generation basis to a major film star. The problems created by this situation have given rise to other problems, and made modifications in the structure and hierarchy of the JKD "family" necessary.
Therefore, let me take this opportunity to spell things out, and clear up some points once and for all.

1 - Jeet kune do cannot be taught. Only jeet kune do concepts can be taught.

2 - Dan Inosanto is the only person certified by Bruce Lee to teach jeet kune do. As the closest living tie to Bruce Lee, it reached a point where everyone who took two or three classes from him, attended a seminar or passed him in the hallway was adding "jeet kune do" to their teaching curriculum. This made it necessary to "certify" legitimate instructors. Originally there was no certification because each individual developed at his or her own level.

3 - It is physically impossible for Dan and the rest of the legitimate JKD concepts instructors to travel around the world closing down all "fraud" JKD instructors, schools, seminars and Bruce Lee puppet manufacturers.

4 - Jeet kune do is not taught, it is acquired. It is confusing to everyone in the beginning. It was confusing to me too. Like anything, if pursued faithfully, it will become less confusing, until understanding is reached.

5 - Are there politics in JKD? Of course! The organization is made up of human beings. What organization doesn't have politics? JKD just happens to be in the limelight. And, as Bruce Lee said, "They only tackle the guy with the ball."

STREETFIGHT? WHAT IT IS?

We must first begin this column by defining just exactly what we mean by streetlight. A JKD man's definition of a streetlight consists of but one rule . . . there are no rules! The linear logic of the Western mind loves to compare. Therefore to define "which art is better," instead of first defining and clarifying the word "better," we pit style A against style B, or fighter A against fighter B. the problem with this is that a street fight is TOO multi-dimensional. For example, there aren't many street-fighters, boxers, or martial artists to whom I would give much of a chance in a fight against Mike Tyson. There also aren't many street-fighters, etc. whom I would give much of a chance fighting against Gene LeBell. Now, if we pit Tyson against LeBell – on whom would you put your money? (I'd put mine on the promoter.)
I could very easily see both fighters entering the room. Tyson opening up with a jab followed by an overhand, and the fight lasting just a few seconds. On the other hand, I could just as easily see Tyson opening up with a jab, LeBell rushing him, closing the gap, and either choking him out, or body-slamming him into the next zip code. You see my point.
With one fight, the question of who is best becomes academic, now let's insert one more person to the question . . . Larry Hartsell. Larry doesn't quite have the size of LeBell or the punching power of Tyson, but he has been trained extensively in trapping in which knees, elbows, and head--butts are very prevalent. Basically to beat Larry, you'd have to kill him! Now oblige me for just one minute.

Mike Tyson vs. Larry Hartsell. Tyson opens up with his jab, Hartsell follows with a various high kick, followed by a straight-blast to with a succession of elbows and knees. The winner . . . Hartsell.

Hartsell vs. LeBell. Hartsell opens up with a kick, LeBell grabs the leg and takes Larry to the ground. Now, in this game, he easily chokes Larry out. Winner. . Gene LeBell!

LeBell vs. Tyson. LeBell opens up with a double-leg take-down. Tyson stop-hits with a jab, followed up by a flurry of punches. The winner... Tyson.

Well, now we have a problem. Fighter A beats fighter B, fighter B beats fighter C, and fighter C beats fighter A. There goes our linear logic. It now becomes quite obvious that one cannot say with authority that one person can beat another person in a fight. Like in professional football, any given team can be victorious on any given day. That's why most professional sports have series of games. Perhaps we could be more accurate in evaluating a street-fighter if we had a series of fights . . . say best out of 10.

The purpose of this short column is to show the readers that street-fighting is a bit more complex than would first appear. Before we compare fighter A to fighter B, remember that there is always fighter C around the block!

WHAT'S MISSING IN MARTIAL ARTS TODAY

My seminars have taken me all over the world. Because of this, I have had a great opportunity to work with students from all different areas and geographical "attitude" regions. Based on this experience, if I had to pick the one factor missing from American students, it would be "passion".

In training, we try to simulate as closely as possible the physical and emotional realities of a street-fight. The physical aspect has proven to be relatively easy to simulate. The emotional aspect is much more difficult. Most people just don't realize how truly intense and fast a real street-fight is. It certainly doesn't help if you've never been in one. If you haven't (and good for you if you've managed to avoid them), you have to at least realize that your mentality must be one of total emotional commitment.

If a bear is fighting a wolf or a rabbit, does it fight the rabbit with less intensity because it is smaller and less threatening? A true street-fighter has the same attitude as the bear. When I work with students in the "lab," the average student's intensity, on a scale of 1-10, never exceeds a 3.

I hate to say it, but most of you reading this article fall into this category. I don't mean to offend, I mean to possibly save your life someday. You could be headed for a situation analogues to playing flag football for years, and suddenly finding yourself on the NFL gridiron. Good luck.

You've heard me and read me saying this many, many times: the average black belt against a three-time guest at San Quentin isn't a good bet. Why? Because, as I constantly remind everyone, it's not the techniques, it's the attributes with which they're executed. To train for the street, you have to train realistically.

Perhaps the biggest mistake students make is to try to recreate what Bruce Lee did by Thai boxing, doing a little Wing Chun here and there, and so on. Though their hearts are in the right places, the focus is all wrong. One must experience boxing to learn boxing, not just put on the gloves and go a few rounds.

I'm not advising people to go out there and try to hurt each other in the dojo. I'm simply saying that there has to be a lot more psychodrama taking place here. You have to picture your opponent as someone intent on taking your life, not your buddy or your rideshare.

If you ever are in a fight, it could be the most important 30 seconds of your life. It's just not the time to call up the same intensity you'd use in a checkers match.

CLOSING THE GAP

Every strike or technique, to be effective, must be used at the correct time and range. Many of the trapping and grappling arts need to be in close to apply their special brand of expertise. This is fact. You cannot judo throw someone three feet away. You must be in a range where you can grab to be able to throw.

The same holds true for trapping. Our body's most efficient and effective weapons all come into play in these ranges. Head-butting, kneeing and elbowing somebody is more likely to put that person out of commission than a sidekick or jab. Throwing somebody on his head and then landing on him and choking him out is more likely to create a favorable response than a reverse punch or crane's beak. This all is pretty obvious. Any thinking person will reason that it makes more sense to develop weapons that have the capacity to end an altercation.

However, a key aspect consistently overlooked is the ability and savvy to get into the deadly trapping/grappling range. Most practitioners assume they can just enter safely and apply their technique of choice. Against a good boxer or savateur, this is simply not the case. That essential ability to close the gap gets significantly more important if your opponent is a skilled fighter in the kicking/punching range. To trap or throw an uncooperative subject while he is moving and sticking you with a jab is quite difficult. Try to picture doing a pak sao on Muhammad Ali or a tai otoshi on Mike Tyson. Not very realistic. Unless you add one important element – pain.

Not chi, not harmonizing with the universe, but plain old pain. If you inflict pain on your opponent, the chances of getting into the trapping/grappling range in a condition where you can effectively apply your techniques has greatly increased. The manner in which you inflict pain is up to you, but two very efficient methods are the stop-hit and the destruction.

The stop-hit is a concept Bruce Lee borrowed form fencing. It's really quite simple to understand; all that is involved is picking up any telegraphic moment on the part of your opponent and negating the attack with a strike of your own. It definitely calls for a high level of awareness and razor-sharp tools, but it is probably the most efficient way to inflict pain prior to an entry.

Picture a person winding up with the barroom haymaker, instead of waiting for the blow to come to you and then blocking it, simply intercept during the windup with a jab of your own. It's pretty obvious he's not going to give you a friendly hug so why wait for the last moment to react? The jab, though not enough to end the fight, will definitely get his attention long enough to enter safely and apply your technique. A person who has just been intercepted will not be thinking about how to counter your entry (hook-double-leg takedown), but will be momentarily disoriented by pain which he didn't expect.

The next way is from kali and it I s the concept of destructions. This concept involves looking at any strike your opponent throws at you not as a weapon that can do you harm but as a target for you to hit. This may be even more unexpected because very few people who throw a punch expect to have their hand broken or bicep stunned. This requires a different sort of savvy from the stop-hit pull off.

Let's say that your opponent has a very fast jab. Instead of trying to intercept it, stick your elbow up in front of your face and let him break his hand on your extended elbow. This is not as difficult as it may seem. Your opponent is aiming at your face so you already have a pretty good idea of where his fist is going to be. With a little practice, you will find that you have a virtually air-tight defense. And as an added bonus, this is not a passive defense system such as armor, but an active one more akin to the Patriot antiballistic missile system.

It does takes quite a bit of "flight time" to functionalize these concepts. Plus, the weapons must be sharp to be effectively brought into play. Both concepts are based in the principle of inflicting pain to enter safety. In training jeet kune do, we practice these things daily as well as our big guns in trapping/grappling range. If your particular style does not address the entering process, assuming it to be given, I suggest you work with these two concepts to increase the combativeness of your art.

Once you have a person in a compromising position, what you do with him is not really the issue. If your opponent is retreating and off balance, does it really make that much difference what you do to him now, be it a head-butt or a throw? The real trick is getting him into the compromising position. Once you can consistently and effectively do that, applying your specialty becomes much easier.

"If people say Jeet Kune Do is different from 'this' or from 'that,' then let the name of Jeet Kune Do be wiped out, for that is what it is, just a name. Please don't fuss over it."

- Bruce Lee

JEET KUNE DO: GUIDE TO EQUIPMENT TRAINING
By Chris Kent

"MAXIMIZE YOUR FIGHTING SKILLS"
Regardless of what styles or methods of martial arts you train in, "Jeet Kune Do: Guide to Equipment Training" offers comprehensive and cohesive training information that will help you maximize your combat skills and achieve your full potential as a martial artist and fighter. Detailed and progressive instruction on how to use the heavy bag, focus mitts, forearm pad, kicking shield, etc... makes this book the main source of information about the proper use of equipment training. This book will take you to a new level of integration and mastery of your art, regardless of the style, if what you are interested in is real contact power!

US $45.00 – 7 x 10 – 350 pages approx.

**FOR PURCHASE VISIT:
WWW. MARTIALARTSDIGITAL.COM**

**ESSENTIAL JEET KUNE DO
The Way of Intercepting Fist
By Tim Tackett**

This book will serve way to decide what will work the best for you and what aspects of JKD you need to keep, as well as throw away. I feel that it would be impossible to learn this from your instructor, as he will mainly focus on what works best for him. I have been fortunate to have learned from many of the senior students of Bruce Lee and have noticed that they all focus on certain things and not on what some the others are doing. For some it may be the boxing aspects. For some it may be footwork. For others it was trapping energy and the Wing Chun elements. It was only when we started focusing on the Western fencing aspects of JKD that I was able to understand and focus on what has become my essence of JKD. Of course, an instructor cannot just hand you what will become your essence or foundation of your own JKD. This is something that you must discover for yourself as you work to become more a more efficient JKD practitioner. The purpose of this book is too show you most of what we teach in my garage and the basic principles behind each. Once you have worked on these you will come to realize what will work for you and what will not. Some of you will want to focus on distance and footwork. Others will feel comfortable crashing the line. Whatever works for you is the main thing. Just use the book as guideline to discover your own essential JKD.

US $45.00 – 7 x 10 – 350 pages approx.

**FOR PURCHASE VISIT:
WWW. MARTIALARTSDIGITAL.COM**

JEET KUNE DO PRINCIPLES
For All Martial Artist
By Tim Tackett

The title of this book is "Jeet Kune Do Principles". Principles and concepts that ALL Martial Artists – regardless of style - can use in their daily training. In fact, most of these principles are used everyday by all martial artists around the world, and most like speed and timing, are not unique to the art of Jeet Kune Do. The purpose of this book is to explain some of these principles and share some ideas on how to train for them. Some are principles like the use of distance and broken rhythm in combat, while others are sayings on combat by the founder of JKD Bruce Lee that perfectly illustrate a principle or a fighting idea. To understand the root, you need to understand the principles.

The principles of Jeet Kune Do are universal, but unfortunately these principles are no longer stressed as much anymore, because there is too much focus on "technique" alone, and seeing how many techniques you can "add" to your toolbox.

The purpose of this work is to discuss some of the principles that the art of JKD focuses on, and to give you some examples to put those principles in action. The hope of this book is that you do the same with the main techniques you either are studying or teaching – regardless of your style.

US $45.00 – 7 x 10 – 350 pages approx.

FOR PURCHASE VISIT:
WWW. MARTIALARTSDIGITAL.COM

JEET KUNE DO WISDOM
By Jose M. Fraguas

There are many pleasures to be derived from a book on quotations. There is the relief of finding something that has been buzzing in our minds, there is also the pleasure of finding some thought of which we approve but which we have not managed to express clearly and there is a purely retrospective delight. Of course, wisdom is meaningless until our own experience has given it meaning. While words are not substitutes for the difficult physical and mental training required to master the martial arts, they are a relevant aspect of the transmission and the learning process of every student. 'Jeet Kune Do Wisdom" is an anthology of the best words said by the great teachers of the art developed by Bruce Lee. It examines different elements of the art, including its tradition, philosophy, general training, self- defense, et cetera. If you, the reader, find this work useful as both a guide and a reference work and discover some unexpected sayings, the book will have served its purpose.

US $45.00 – 7 x 10 – 350 pages approx.

FOR PURCHASE VISIT:
WWW. MARTIALARTSDIGITAL.COM

FOR MORE INFORMATION ON
BRUCE LEE * JUN FAN GUNG FU *JEET KUNE DO

- BRUCE LEE
https://brucelee.com/

- BRUCE LEE FOUNDATION
https://bruceleefoundation.org/

- RICHARD BUSTILLO
https://www.imbacademy.com/our-founder

- DAN INOSANTO
https://inosanto.com/

- FRAN JOSEPH
https://www.jpjkd.com/fran-poteet-joseph/

- CHRIS KENT
https://www.ckjkd.com/

- TAKY KIMURA
https://www.junfangungfuseattle.com/
https://www.junfangungfuacademy.com/

- DAN LEE
https://www.jpjkd.com/2015/12/18/in-honor-of-sifu-daniel-lee/

- CASS MAGDA
https://mijkd.com/

- JERRY POTEET
https://www.jpjkd.com/

- TIM TACKETT
https://jkdwednite.com/

- PAUL VUNAK
https://teamvunak.com/

- TED WONG
https://jeetkunedoinstitute.com/about-us/ted-wong/

THE JEET KUNE DO ARCHIVES

www.ingramcontent.com/pod-product-compliance
Lightning Source LLC
Chambersburg PA
CBHW081439070526
44586CB00019B/2174